The Way to Work

The Way to Work

How to Facilitate Work Experiences for Youth in Transition

by

Richard G. Luecking, Ed.D.
TransCen, Inc.
Rockville, Maryland

with invited contributors

·P A U L·H·
BROOKES
PUBLISHING C⁰ ®

Baltimore • London • Sydney

Paul H. Brookes Publishing Co.
Post Office Box 10624
Baltimore, Maryland 21285-0624
USA

www.brookespublishing.com

Typeset by Broad Books, Baltimore, Maryland.
Manufactured in the United States of America by
Sheridan Books, Inc., Chelsea, Michigan.

The individuals described in this book are composites or real people whose situations
are masked and are based on the author's experiences. In all instances, names and
identifying details have been changed to protect confidentiality.

Library of Congress Cataloging-in-Publication Data
Luecking, Richard G.
  The way to work : how to facilitate work experiences for youth in transition / by
  Richard G. Luecking.—1st ed.
     p.   cm.
  Includes bibliographical references and index.
  ISBN-13: 978-1-55766-898-1 (pbk.)
  ISBN-10: 1-55766-898-1 (pbk.)
  1. Youth with disabilities—Employment—United States.   2. School-to-work
  transition—United States.   I. Title.
  HD7256.U5L842 2009
  362.4'0484—dc22   2008053604

British Library Cataloguing in Publication data are available from the British Library.

Contents

About the Author

Richard G. Luecking, Ed.D., President, TransCen, Inc., 451 Hungerford Drive, Suite 700, Rockville, Maryland 20850

Dr. Luecking is the President of TransCen, Inc., a non-profit organization based in Rockville, Maryland, that is dedicated to improving education and employment outcomes for people with disabilities. He has held this position since 1987, when he was charged by the Board of Directors as the organization's first employee to create improved linkages between schools, employment service providers, government, business, and families so that youth with disabilities experience improved postschool employment outcomes. During his tenure with the organization, he and his TransCen colleagues have been responsible for the design and implementation of numerous model demonstration and research projects related to school-to-work transition and employment of people with disabilities. He was a consultant in the original development of the "Bridges . . . from school to work" program of the Marriott Foundation for People with Disabilities, which has been replicated and established in several national locations with the help of TransCen.

Dr. Luecking has maintained active participation and held leadership positions in various local, state, and national initiatives, including school-to-career systems, workforce development boards, business/education associations, professional organizations, and national training and technical assistance centers on transition and employment. He regularly contributes to publications targeting practitioners in employment service programs and education. He is the author or coauthor of numerous publications on topics related to employment of people with disabilities, business partnerships, school-to-work transition, and career development, including the book *Working Relationships: Creating Career Opportunities for Job Seekers with Disabilities Through Employer Partnerships* (with Ellen S. Fabian and George P. Tilson; Paul H. Brookes Publishing Co., 2004).

Contributors

LaVerne A. Buchanan, Ed.D., is a senior research associate at TransCen, Inc. Dr. Buchanan has been affiliated with TransCen since 1991, when she joined the staff to serve as director of the Washington, D.C., office of the Marriott Foundation's "Bridges . . . from school to work" program. During her tenure with the organization she has also provided training, technical assistance, and program evaluation to a number of Maryland and District of Columbia school systems, as well as serving as a member of the Maryland State Department of Education Career Development Council and as a consultant to the D.C. Public Schools High School Improvement Institute. Currently, she works on projects addressing youth connectedness to schools and the community, drop-out prevention for middle and secondary students, and teacher implementation of authentic transition and career development. In addition, Dr. Buchanan is an adjunct faculty member at area colleges' and universities' graduate special education transition programs. She has maintained active leadership roles in national professional organizations, including serving on the Boards of the Council for Exceptional Children and its Division on Career Development and Transition.

Meredith Gramlich, M.A., has worked with TransCen, Inc., since 1992 in a variety of capacities helping youth and adults with disabilities find successful career opportunities. She has worked throughout Maryland to facilitate business education partnerships and collaboration among disability service providers in their business partnering efforts. Ms. Gramlich has contributed to expanded customized employment opportunities for people with disabilities who access MontgomeryWorks, Montgomery County's One Stop Career Center. She has also written and contributed to a number of publications about business–education partnerships, customized work opportunities for people with disabilities, and workplace mentoring.

Karen Leggett is a writer/journalist in Washington, D.C. As an advocate for improved special education services, Ms. Leggett chaired PTA special education committees throughout her daughter's school years, edited newsletters, and wrote newspaper articles. Currently, Ms. Leggett serves on the Montgomery County Special Education Continuous Improvement Team and chairs the Transition Work Group, an organization of parents and service providers working to improve the transition to adulthood for young people with disabilities in Montgomery County, Maryland. In 2006, Leggett wrote *The Parent Mentor Partnership: A Toolkit* (Southeast Regional Resource Center, 2006) about a groundbreaking mentoring program in Georgia public schools.

Christy Stuart, Ed.D., is a senior research associate at TransCen, Inc. Dr. Stuart has more than 18 years of experience in the fields of special education, school-to-work transition, and employment of individuals with disabilities, especially those considered to have severe disabilities. She began her career as a teacher assisting transition-age youth with disabilities and their families to coordinate and acquire services and supports as they make the transition from school to postschool environments. She has applied this experience to consulting with various school districts in Maryland and Florida as they strive to improve transition services. Currently, she is the technical assistance coordinator for the Maryland Seamless Transition Collaborative, a statewide initiative to improve postschool outcomes of students with disabilities requiring postsecondary support services. She has published professional journal articles as well as developed numerous products on topics that include disability disclosure and entrepreneurial activities for youth with disabilities, as well as various web-based training materials focusing on accommodations, inclusion, disability legislation, and job development.

George P. Tilson, Ed.D., is Senior Vice President of TransCen, Inc. He assisted the Marriott Foundation for People with Disabilities in creating its youth career program, "Bridges . . . from school to work," and subsequently became the national director. He has co-developed and directed numerous innovative demonstration and research projects and written numerous articles and book chapters on such topics as career counseling, job development, and accommodation strategies. He is the coauthor of *Working Relationships: Creating Career Opportunities for Job Seekers with Disabilities Through Employer Partnerships* (with Richard G. Luecking and Ellen S. Fabian; Paul H. Brookes Publishing Co., 2004). Dr. Tilson has conducted training nationally and internationally to corporations, employment service agencies, school systems, student and parent groups, and government agencies. He serves as an adjunct professor of education and human development at The George Washington University. Prior to joining TransCen in 1989, Dr. Tilson was a high school English and special education teacher, career counselor, and program evaluator.

Foreword

Policy makers and local youth advocates alike will relish this book being available to support what they have long held to be true: young people need work-based learning experiences to reinforce academics and to build their aspirations for the future. Too often these experiences, viewed as common for young people of privilege, are not built into the educational plans for all youth.

Rich Luecking and I first met and had the opportunity to work together in 1995 within the National School to Work Opportunities Office. I was opening the new federal office and pulling together talent to launch an incentive-based strategy, jointly funded with U.S. Department of Labor and Department of Education resources. Central to the design was leveraging work-based experiences as fundamental and core to young people acquiring the necessary skills and knowledge for college and careers. Rich joined the School to Work effort with a great deal of experience and knowledge on how best to assure that youth with disabilities were included in our design and advocacy work.

More and more literature and research is pointing out the importance of including work-based learning experiences in the educational plans for all students. To take this design to scale, strategies and tools are necessary that will assist educators, youth service providers, employers, and the young people involved with quality controls that maintain the fidelity of this important feature of career and life preparation. This book presents both strategies and case examples to assist with that effort.

Rich and his team are uniquely qualified to translate large policy ideas into actionable strategies for local implementation. It is my hope that this book pushes us further and enables us to bring learning to life by bridging the gap between school place and workplace for more young people in their pursuit of excellence.

JD Hoye, President
National Academy Foundation

Foreword

This text represents an important and timely contribution to the fields of special education and employment services, with a specific focus on the transition of youth with disabilities from school to gainful employment. Richard Luecking and his colleagues at TransCen, Inc., have identified and fully described the essential steps, strategies, and evidence-based practices that support youth in accessing and successfully participating in work experiences. The book conveys a critical message, "Work is good!" and the author argues that employment is the most important outcome of the transition process for youth with disabilities and families. Few of us can doubt the centrality of work in our lives, as a means of encompassing our destinies, realizing our aspirations, and, in many ways, defining our identity as citizens. Enhanced self-worth, pride, dignity, and social and economic independence are also powerful concepts that underscore the importance of work for us all.

For more than two decades, one of the principal goals of disability policy in the United States, as it has influenced special education, vocational rehabilitation, and employment services nationwide, has been to improve employment opportunities for young people with disabilities as they exit secondary education programs. These policies have strongly advocated for the goals of equal opportunity, nondiscrimination, inclusion, and economic self-sufficiency and independence. Specific strategies related to these policy goals have been those of removing structural and attitudinal barriers to employment, developing and testing new employment training strategies and support systems, creating connections to and partnerships with employers, and using interagency collaboration as a process for coordinating and financing services and achieving results. The promise of these policy goals in achieving increased employment opportunities for youth with disabilities, however, has been challenging to realize for many individuals. While it is important to acknowledge these employment challenges and difficulties, we must move forward with a sense of urgency to do better as professionals and community members. This book lays a foundation for this aim and offers important information and insights as to what must be done and strategies used to increase employment opportunities for youth with disabilities in transition.

Since the mid-1980s, federal school-to-work transition policies have evolved, along with other federal legislation intended to improve the labor force participation of working-age youth and adults with disabilities and increase the participation of individuals with disabilities in all aspects of community life. By the mid-1980s, for example, transition, as well as new opportunities for advancing employment opportunities for individuals with significant disabilities through supported employment, became federal policy priorities. Since this time, the federal government has continued to assume a key role in enacting legislation that has guided state and local efforts to improve transition and employment services through a variety of policy, interagency, systems change, demonstration, and research efforts.

These federal policy priorities, along with research and demonstration, and state and local initiatives, have all focused on improving school and postschool results for youth with disabilities and their families. This results-based ideology, focused on an array of transition outcomes, is an important contribution to public policy and has intensified the focus on employment as a critical outcome. This will no doubt continue to be a major influence on both transition and employment policies and practices throughout the current decade and beyond. Dr. Luecking and his colleagues devote considerable attention to the promise of these policies in supporting improved employment outcomes for youth with disabilities. They should know—they have been at the leading edge of transition practice for over 20 years!

Beyond the role of federal policy are the actions and strategies that must be applied by professionals at the state and local levels in addressing the transition and employment needs of youth with disabilities. Research, demonstration, and training initiatives, sponsored largely through federal and state agency funding, have resulted in a knowledge base of promising transition and employment approaches and strategies. These have included innovations and advances in interagency cooperation, improved strategies for accessing postsecondary education and training for employment, supported employment, transition planning, self-determination and self-advocacy, and others. Recently, the National Center on Secondary Education and Transition (NCSET), located at the Institute on Community Integration, University of Minnesota; the Center for Disability Studies at the University of Hawaii–Manoa; and the National Collaborative on Workforce and Disabilities for Youth (NCWD/Y) at the Institute for Educational Leadership in Washington, D.C., in partnership with TransCen, Inc., have been actively engaged in identifying and documenting program models, strategies, and research-based interventions focused on transition and employment services. Four levels of intervention, that parallel the chapters of this text, in part, include the following:

- *The transition planning process and content of preparation received by youth with disabilities in high school under the Individuals with Disabilities Education Act (IDEA) of 1990 (PL 101-476) and Section 504 of the Rehabilitation Act of 1973 (PL 93-112).* We know that the transition planning process itself is the primary mechanism by which school and postschool employment goals are determined and planned for, and, in addition, that important connections must be made between work experiences in high school, with other curricular requirements. We also recognize that students need to acquire the skills necessary to self-advocate and disclose their disability within the work environment and that we need to involve families in supporting their child's work experiences during and following high school.

- *Making transition and employment services and supports available, including transportation and the use of technology for students with disabilities in employment programs.* Advancing new models of support services that are personally responsive, flexible, and individualized, as well as coordinated with the student's needs for support within home and community, is highly interrelated with positive work experiences.

- *Coordination and management of school and community services and supports.* Coordination and management are also important strategies through which youth with disabilities achieve positive postschool employment outcomes.

Students with disabilities have a range of health, social, community-living, transportation, and other needs that must be addressed as employment goals and services are planned. Interagency collaboration is essential in achieving students' employment goals.

- *The transition or transfer of educational services and supports the student has received in high school or from the postsecondary education setting to subsequent employment settings.* Transferring supports to subsequent employment settings must also be taken fully into consideration and planned for. Lack of access to these supports in employment limits the individual's potential for success and far too often results in failure in the workplace.

The Way to Work: How to Facilitate Work Experiences for Youth in Transition addresses each of these levels of intervention, with the addition of other important strategies that support youth in transition to employment. This book will have broad appeal to professionals, support staff, university students, and families, as well as youth with disabilities as they prepare for and engage in productive, gainful employment. I am excited about the potential influence this book will have on the field of transition and employment services, and it ultimately will increase opportunities for all youth with disabilities to expand their sense of self-worth, pride, dignity, and independence through employment. Work is, indeed, good!

David R. Johnson, Ph.D., Professor and Director
Institute on Community Integration
College of Education and Human Development
University of Minnesota

Preface

This book incorporates lessons learned from more than 20 years of developing, implementing, and evaluating approaches to helping youth with disabilities pursue work experiences and jobs. These lessons were taken from major national initiatives such as the Marriott Foundation's "Bridges . . . from school to work" program, from local transition employment programs in several states, from various demonstration projects, and from partnerships with a range of transition professionals and a range of school districts and employment service organizations all over the United States. It is gratifying to say that well over 10,000 youth and young adults have gained employment as a result of the work of TransCen and its partners in these various programs and demonstration projects.

The net effect of this work is overwhelming anecdotal and empirical evidence that work experience during secondary and postsecondary school years is one of the most important factors that predicts long-term adult employment success, regardless of a youth's disability label or the nature of his or her educational services. Just as importantly, the evidence is clear that a path to a self-determined career can and should be paved throughout publicly supported education for youth with disabilities.

Transition from school to work has been a national policy priority since 1984. It remains so at all levels of policy and government. Although there has been definite headway in terms of postschool employment outcomes for youth, so much more needs to be done. We need to assist more youth to have more work experience, and we need to support more professionals to become more adept at helping youth get to work.

Unlike many other books on school-to-work transition for youth with disabilities, *The Way to Work* is strictly dedicated to one aspect of the school-to-work transition process: assisting youth to plan for and succeed in work. This is not to say that other aspects of this process, especially well-conceived academic preparation, are not vitally important. However, if our goal as professionals in the field is to help youth with disabilities benefit from special education and other youth services so that they become self-sufficient adults and contributing citizens, then the ultimate measure of the success of these services should be whether or not they have achieved meaningful employment. To that end, throughout the book, the text is complemented by numerous case examples of youth involvement in work experience. These examples are gleaned from actual situations with actual youth with whom TransCen and its various collaborators have worked. Some examples are composites to make a clearer point. All names are pseudonyms to protect youth privacy.

TransCen continues to identify better ways to assist youth to find their career path and to further examine the value of work for youth in transition. Representative of this endeavor is our involvement in the National Youth Transition Demonstration (YTD) sponsored by the Social Security Administration.

To date, YTD represents one of the few large-scale undertakings that applies strong research rigor to the issue of what influences the postschool employment success of youth with disabilities. Significant to this project is its focus on youth who are receiving, or at risk of receiving, Supplemental Security Income (SSI). To be eligible for SSI, youth must have a significant disability and meet financial eligibility standards. That is, by definition these youth are wrestling with both poverty and disability as they try to make their way to work.

TransCen is pleased to be working with the Social Security Administration, Mathematica Policy Research, Inc., and MDRC, Inc., in the implementation of this monumental research study. We are especially pleased to be working in the field with the various YTD sites throughout the nation to help YTD participants experience work as part of this demonstration. These efforts will yield much more information about the efficacy of work interventions, effective ways to implement them, and the development of transition personnel adept at assisting youth to achieve work outcomes.

In fact, the need for transition professionals to gain skills and the capacity to help youth make their way to work has not only inspired the idea for this book, but it has also prodded TransCen to create a convenient, just-in-time online learning venue called Transition Online. Designed for the in-the-field professional, the content of Transition Online coincides with and complements this book's topics. Readers who want to learn about these offerings and to stay current with contemporary transition practice are invited to visit the web site http://www.transcen.org for details.

Acknowledgments

A great deal of the credit for this book, and the methodology represented throughout, goes to the many dedicated and effective professionals who have helped youth learn the way to work. Foremost among these professionals are my colleagues at TransCen who made important contributions of ideas, examples, design, or all three, including LaVerne A. Buchanan, Kelli Crane, Jose Diaz, Amy Dwyre, Meredith Gramlich, Meg Grigal, Maggie Leedy, Hyun Masiello, Sara Murphy and the WorkLink staff, Marie Parker, Lisa Cuozzo Stern, Christy Stuart, and Marian Vessels. My long-time TransCen colleague, George Tilson, deserves special mention for not only coauthoring selected chapters in the book but also for the creative and dedicated work he continues to contribute to the field.

I would also like to extend acknowledgment to a number of other professionals who worked with us in various transition projects and who offered many of the fitting examples of youth at work that were included in this book. These helpful colleagues include Larry Abramson and Kathy Bridgeman of St. Luke's House Career Transition Program (Maryland); Mark Chamberlain of Delaware State Department of Education; Haydee dePaula of Montgomery County Arc (Maryland); Mark Donovan of the Marriott Foundation for People with Disabilities; Lisa Ladner and Kathy Williams of the Mississippi Model Youth Transition Innovation (MYTI) project; Shawn Lattanzio of Montgomery County Department of Health and Human Services (Maryland); Roberta Menn of Saddleback Valley Unified School District, Mission Viejo, California; Annette Miles of Fairfax County Public Schools (Virginia); Karla Nabors of Montgomery College (Maryland); Beth Shepherd of Montgomery County Public Schools (Maryland); Katie Shockro of Sussex Technical School District (Delaware); Tony Silva and Donna Depamphilis of Charles County Public Schools (Maryland); Ann White of Caroline County Public Schools (Maryland); and Mary Young of Loudoun County Public Schools (Virginia). A special thanks to Karen Leggett, who assisted in gathering the numerous work experience examples included throughout the book.

I am indebted to JD Hoye and David Johnson, two giants in the school-to-work arena, for graciously agreeing to provide forewords for the book.

Acknowledgments also are in order for many youth and their families who wish to remain anonymous but who graciously allowed their work experience stories to be told. Finally, a special thanks to my colleague, friend, and wife, Debra Martin Luecking, whose ideas, support, encouragement, and patience with the author made the completion of this book possible.

*To the founding members of the TransCen, Inc., Board of Directors,
who had the vision and commitment to pursue the ideal that
public education for youth with disabilities should culminate
in productive and meaningful employment and careers*

Introduction

Work is good! Every effective transition professional knows this. In fact, anyone who has watched youth blossom in self-confidence and skill as they perform in an authentic workplace can attest to this phenomenon. Not surprising, a large body of research also agrees with this premise. Ever since school-to-work transition became a federal policy priority (Will, 1984) and transition planning became a legal requirement (Individuals with Disabilities Education Act [IDEA] of 1990, PL 101-476; Individuals with Disabilities Education Improvement Act [IDEA] of 2004, PL 108-446), we have become increasingly aware of the value of work experience and work for youth with disabilities as they prepare to exit publicly mandated education. We have known for a long time that it is critically important for youth with disabilities to experience learning in work-based environments, that is, situations in which they spend concentrated and structured time in actual work settings provided by cooperating companies and employers. Work experiences, of course, are not the only factors that contribute to postschool success, but it can be argued that they are among the most important.

There have been an abundance of studies on youth with disabilities making the transition from school to work and adult life. In spite of the fact that few of those studies represent classic research rigor and empirical validation of specific interventions, they nevertheless have produced general agreement among researchers and practitioners on key interventions that promise positive impact on transition outcomes. Consistently, the most prominent factors shown to be associated with successful postschool employment outcomes are paid and unpaid work experiences during the last years of secondary school and the completion of a high school diploma (Colley & Jamison, 1998; Johnson & Thurlow, 2003; Luecking & Fabian, 2001; Wagner, Newman, Cameto, & Levine, 2005). Other factors suggested by the literature include training in specific vocational skills, transition planning and coordination, self-determination training, and family support (Johnson et al., 2002; Newman, 2005; Wehmeyer & Palmer, 2003).

Recent attempts to synthesize what works so that the features of effective interventions can be applied and refined in practice have emphasized these findings. The National Alliance for Secondary Education and Transition (NASET), consisting of more than 30 national advocacy groups, professional organizations, and education associations, conducted a thorough review of extant research on what youth need to succeed as they make the transition from secondary education. Using this research synthesis, NASET (2005) produced a set of standards and quality indicators as a useful structure for identifying the critical needs for all youth, including those with disabilities. These standards consist of five general areas of intervention:

- *Schooling*, that is, academic instruction and targeted curriculum
- *Career preparatory experiences*, including vocational training and work experiences

1

- *Youth development and youth leadership*, especially as it relates to self-determined transition planning
- *Family involvement*
- *Connecting activities*, that is, those activities that enable youth to be linked with organizations and services that complement their transition services and/or enable necessary postsecondary supports.

Drawing from the NASET framework, the National Collaborative on Workforce and Disability for Youth (NCWD/Y) conducted its own extensive review of research, demonstration projects, and acknowledged effective practices. From this review, NCWD/Y (2005) developed a practical tool, called *The Guideposts for Success,* for practitioners and policy makers alike to conceptualize optimum service delivery for youth with disabilities. The guideposts include more or less the same areas highlighted by NASET but slightly reconstituted:

- School-based preparatory experiences
- Career preparation and work-based experiences
- Youth development and leadership
- Connecting activities
- Family involvement and supports

Both the NASET standards and the NCWD/Y guideposts represent attempts to identify practices that are universally accepted by education, transition, and youth service professionals as useful and effective in helping youth achieve better education and employment outcomes. This book touches on all of these factors, but the obvious thrust of this book is on work. The other features of the NASET standards and the NCWD/Y guideposts are discussed intermittently as they relate to making work experiences and work successful. Many publications are available that highlight aspects of all of these factors, but few exist that exclusively address how to help youth learn how to work and how to build their employment portfolios so that they begin their adult careers *before* they exit school. This book is intended to begin filling that void.

NEED FOR A RENEWED EMPHASIS ON WORK

Since the mid 1980s, research has shown that youth with disabilities who participate in work experiences, especially paid work, while in secondary school are significantly more likely to hold jobs after they exit school than those who do not have these experiences (see, e.g., Colley & Jamison, 1998; Hazazi, Gordon, & Roe, 1985; Luecking & Fabian, 2001; National Longitudinal Transition Study 2, 2006; Wagner, 1991). Simply stated, youth benefit from frequent and continuous exposure to real work environments throughout the secondary school years and beyond.

This same body of research has also demonstrated that work experiences during secondary school years are valuable for *any youth with a disability,* regardless of his or her primary disability label, race, gender, relative need for accommodation and support, or any other descriptive characteristic. This is also the case regardless of the intensity, location, or nature of the special education services youth may receive. In other words, it could be argued that work experience and work during the secondary school years are among the most, if not *the most,* important predictors of adult employment success for all youth who receive special education services. Predictors of success need not, nor should not, be determined by a label or demographic descriptor. A case could be made that the nation's educational system can only be deemed to have achieved its aims when the climax of students' educational experience is the beginning of a productive adult life. For most people this means a job or, even better, a career.

There is every reason to expect, therefore, that youth with disabilities and their families can look forward to the day when these youth enter the workforce for what ideally will be the start of a long career. The statistics, however, suggest that this expectation is still not the norm and that employment is still an elusive postschool outcome for many youth with disabilities. In fact, it is clear that we can certainly improve the way in which special education transition creates and offers to students important work experience opportunities and how work experiences are integrated into curricula requirements so that public education culminates in productive postschool employment. Here's what we know:

- The latest national survey of youth with disabilities making the transition from public education to adult life indicates that these youth continue to experience employment rates that do not approximate that of their peers without disabilities (Wagner et al., 2005).

- Postschool employment support services are not sufficient to meet the demand from transitioning youth, and the quality of these services is widely variable (Mank, Cioffi, & Yovanoff, 2003; Wehman, 2006).

- Youth with disabilities are much more likely than their same-age peers to drop out of school and to be unemployed and experience poverty as adults (National Organization on Disability, 2004).

The news is particularly disappointing for some categories of youth. Consider these findings pertaining to youth with intellectual disabilities:

- Community employment service agencies struggle to provide quality supported employment to youth and adults with intellectual disabilities (Boeltzig, Gilmore, & Butterworth, 2006; Braddock, Rizzolo, & Hemp, 2004; Connelly, 2003).

- One study found that 75% of adult vocational services participants, most of whom have an intellectual disability, receive services in some type of segregated, congregate setting (Braddock et al., 2004).

- Subminimum wage and sheltered employment is the fate of thousands of people with intellectual disabilities (U.S. General Accounting Office, 2001).

For other categories of youth, the news is not much better. For example, as a group, youth with serious emotional disabilities

- Have a school completion rate of only 56% (Kaufman, Alt, & Chapman, 2000)
- Tend to experience poor postschool employment rates, and when they do work, their standards of job performance tend to vary noticeably from those expected by employers (Carter & Wehby, 2003; Clark & Davis, 2000)
- Experience higher rates of criminal activity and substance abuse than any other group of youth (Bullis & Fredericks, 2002)

Less than optimal postschool employment outcomes could be cited for all categories of youth with disabilities including mobility disabilities, sensory disabilities, learning disabilities, and multiple disabilities. We may be moving in the right direction, but we are not there yet.

EMPLOYMENT FOR ALL?

Many of the studies cited previously suggest that all of these circumstances could be addressed, at least in part, by focused work experiences throughout secondary as well as postsecondary education. Carefully organized and supervised work experiences, where opportunities are provided to receive guidance and feedback on work performance, would go a long way to mitigate the continuingly disappointing postschool outcomes. Furthermore, these experiences serve as career building blocks as adolescents exit school, especially when adolescents require supports that will help them continue to pursue the work and career opportunities to which they were exposed during secondary education. Thus, this book's purpose is to offer strategies essential for creating opportunities for successful work experience, for integrating these experiences into curricula requirements, and for bolstering the likelihood that publicly supported education leads to productive postschool employment.

The good news is that youth and their families do not have to be satisfied with historically disappointing postschool outcomes. It has been repeatedly shown that work-based experiences such as job shadowing, internships, cooperative work placements, service learning, and unpaid work sampling experiences are effective and important prerequisites to successful postschool employment success. Moreover, when *paid work*, the "gold standard," so to speak, of youth in the workplace, is paired with education, either as an ancillary activity or as an integral aspect of curriculum, youth are considerably more likely to obtain and retain employment as adults (Wagner et al., 2005).

This book is thus framed by the belief that the culmination of publicly supported education for youth with disabilities can and should be real adult employment. This book shows readers how to help youth choose and pursue work experiences and also provides approaches for identifying, developing, organizing, and monitoring work-based learning opportunities in authentic workplaces.

The experience of my work at TransCen and that of committed colleagues around the country has led to the driving philosophy of this book, the belief that every youth who wants to can achieve an adult life of productive and successful employment, regardless of disability label, need for support and accommodation, intensity of special education services, or even the economic vitality of his or her community. The approaches described in this book can be applied to help all youth achieve this goal. This book shows how work experiences can be more than mere adjunctive afterthoughts to curriculum, but rather essential features of contextual learning so that postschool employment becomes the rule rather than the exception for youth with disabilities.

HOW THIS BOOK IS ORGANIZED

The chapters are arranged so that ideas and strategies presented in each chapter are logical precursors to the ideas and strategies presented in the subsequent chapter. The chapter order builds a continually reinforcing knowledge base. Although the chapters follow a logical sequence, each chapter has stand-alone strategies that can be extracted for application in direct practice related to the chapter topic.

The first two chapters set the stage for the practical strategies that will be presented later throughout the book. Chapter 1 illustrates the need for work experiences and how they foster the development of a career pathway for youth. Chapter

2 goes into some detail about the types of work experiences and their respective uses and importance in job and career pursuits. It also provides the framework for making sure that quality is built into youth work experiences and that the roles of youth, educators, families, employers, co-workers, and other interested parties are carefully considered and well defined. These chapters are intended to provide a basis for proceeding with the strategies found in subsequent chapters.

The process of and strategies for organizing and supporting quality work experiences begin in Chapter 3 and continue through Chapter 9. In these chapters, the practitioner will be able to garner specific and directly applicable strategies for planning, developing, and supporting successful work experiences. Again, although these chapters are ordered in a sequence that suggests a practical progression, readers can read them out of order if their experience and learning needs are more in one area or another. Because these chapters represent the heart of work experience practice, they will include specific Learning Labs designed to help the reader practice and implement the strategies each chapter presents.

Every chapter contains specific case examples of youth and/or case examples of how strategies have been applied to good effect. These are meant to illustrate real world application of these ideas and strategies. They are all actual examples taken from field experiences, or composites of actual examples, using pseudonyms to protect confidentiality. Many chapters also contain sample forms and guidelines that the reader is free to reproduce or adapt for direct use in transition practice.

Chapters 10 and 11 discuss important issues that are related to strengthening the impact of work experiences. Chapter 10 presents important considerations for maximizing workplace success by involving partners that can contribute to supporting work experience, as well as partners that can help youth sustain the learning and the promise of work experiences beyond the school years. It discusses how to identify and involve community services and nonschool partners to assist with planning, implementing, and supporting work experiences so that gains in skills and workplace success are maintained after school exit.

Finally, Chapter 11 presents challenges as well as distinct notable trends that may affect the future of work-based learning, work experience, and employment for youth with disabilities. It presents a context for thinking about how transition practice might be affected by these trends and how transition professionals and advocates might work to ensure that the "way to work" might be constantly improved, rather than hindered, by these developments.

IMPORTANT NOTE ON CHARACTERIZING YOUTH

There are admitted distinct biases of the book's presentation, and these biases drive editorial prerogative taken here. First, too often assumptions are made about youth circumstances that are either stereotypical or limiting when a disability label is the major descriptor of the youth. Therefore, throughout the book the use of specific disability labels when referring to youth in the case studies is done sparingly. Unless there is a compelling reason to identify a disability for case study clarity, there are few references to specific disabilities. It is important, of course, to factor in accommodations that individual youth may need in order to succeed in the workplace. However, it is important also to know that even within particular disability categories, the range and type of accommodations are broad and depend entirely on each individual's circumstances. Thus, in general discussion, the book almost always refers to youth with disabilities simply as youth. The reader, with noted exceptions, will be able to apply the concepts discussed here to any youth seeking or participating in a work-based experience, regardless of the nature of the disability, need for support, or disability label.

Second, employers are absolutely essential partners in creating work experiences for youth. In Chapters 6 and 7, more will be made about the importance of their cooperation and about the importance of viewing them as another ultimate customer of transition programs that promote work experiences and jobs for youth. Employers are as heterogeneous as the youth with whom they may come in contact. They come in all sizes and descriptions: private sector, for profit entities; local, state, and federal government entities; and nonprofit and civic entities. Some have a handful of employees; others hire thousands. As well, a host of industry sectors exist under which various employer entities could be classified. To simplify matters, the book uses in general discussion the terms *employer, business*, and *company* interchangeably to refer to any entity—public or private, large or small—that could potentially offer work experiences and jobs to youth. Again, the issues and strategies that help create successful linkages with individual employers on behalf of and with individual youth ultimately frame the success of our work, no matter the labels that we use to describe it.

As the reader considers the ideas and strategies that the book offers, I sincerely hope that more and more people will adopt the belief that "Work is good!" It is good to learn in work environments, to learn how to work, to learn where to work, to find the best ways to be supported and accommodated at work, and to produce at work to the satisfaction of current and future employers. The intent is that through these activities the ultimate good is that youth can find life satisfaction as contributing citizens and as self-supporting adults.

REFERENCES

Boeltzig, H., Gilmore, D., & Butterworth, J. (2006, July). *The national survey of community rehabilitation providers, FY 2004–2005: Employment outcomes of people with developmental disabilities in integrated employment.* Boston: University of Massachusetts Boston, Institute for Community Inclusion.

Braddock, D., Rizzolo, M., & Hemp, R. (2004). Most employment services growth in developmental disabilities during 1988–2002 was in segregated settings. *Mental Retardation, 42,* 317–320.

Bullis, M., & Fredericks, H.D. (2002). *Vocational and transition services for adolescents with emotional and behavioral disorders: Strategies and best practices.* Champaign, IL: Research Press.

Carter, E.W., & Wehby, J.H. (2003). Job performance of transition age youth with emotional and behavioral disorders. *Exceptional Children, 69,* 449–465.

Clark, H.B., & Davis, M. (Vol. Eds.). (2000). *Systems of care for children's mental health series: Transition to adulthood: A resource for assisting young people with emotional or behavioral difficulties.* Baltimore: Paul H. Brookes Publishing Co.

Colley, D.A., & Jamison, D. (1998). Post school results for youth with disabilities: Key indicators and policy implications. *Career Development for Exceptional Individuals, 21,* 145–160.

Connelly, R. (2003). Supported employment in Maryland: Successes and issues. *Mental Retardation, 41,* 237–249.

Hazazi, S., Gordon, L., & Roe, C. (1985). Employment of youth with and without handicaps following high school: Outcomes and correlates. *Journal of Special Education, 23,* 243–255.

Individuals with Disabilities Education Act of 1990, PL 101-476, 20 U.S.C., 1400 *et seq.*

Individuals with Disabilities Education Improvement Act of 2004, PL 108-446, 20 U.S.C., 1400 *et seq.*

Johnson, D., Stodden, R., Emanuel, E., Luecking, R., & Mack, M. (2002). Current challenges facing secondary education and transition services: What research tells us. *Exceptional Children, 68,* 519–531.

Johnson, D.R., & Thurlow, M.L. (2003). *A national study on graduation requirements and diploma options* (Technical Report 36). Minneapolis: University of Minnesota, Institute on Community Integration, National Center on Secondary Education and Transition, and National Center on Educational Outcomes. Retrieved February 4, 2007, from http://education.umn.edu/NCEO/OnlinePubs/Technical36.htm

Kaufman, D., Alt, M., & Chapman, D. (2000). *Drop out rates in the United States: 2000. Educational Statistics Quarterly, 3.* Retrieved February 2007, from http://nces.ed.gov/programs/quarterly/vol_3/3_4/q3-3.asp

Luecking, R., & Fabian, E. (2001). Paid internships and employment success for youth in transition. *Career Development for Exceptional Individuals, 23,* 205–221.

Mank, D., Cioffi, A., & Yovanoff, P. (2003). Supported employment outcomes across a decade: Is there evidence of improvement in the quality of implementation? *Mental Retardation, 41,* 188–197.

National Alliance for Secondary Education and Transition. (NASET). (2005). *National standards and quality indicators: Transition toolkit for systems improvement.* Minneapolis: University of Minnesota, National Center on Secondary Education and Transition.

National Collaborative on Workforce and Disability for Youth (NCWD/Y). (2005). *Guideposts for success.* Washington, DC: Institute on Educational Leadership.

National Longitudinal Transition Study 2. (2006). *NTLS2 data brief: Youth employment, a report from the national longitudinal transition study-2.* Retrieved April 2007, from http://www.ncset.org/publications/default.asp#nlts2

National Organization on Disability. (2004). *N.O.D./Harris survey of Americans with disabilities.* Washington, DC: Author.

Newman, L. (2005). *Family expectations and involvement for youth with disabilities.* Menlo Park, CA: SRI International.

U.S. General Accounting Office. (2001). *Special minimum wage program: Characteristics of workers with disabilities, their employers, and labor's management, which needs to be improved.* Washington, DC: Author.

Wagner, M. (1991). *Young people with disabilities: How are they doing?* Menlo Park, CA: SRI International.

Wagner, M., Newman, L., Cameto, R., & Levine, P. (2005). *Changes over time in the early postschool outcomes of youth with disabilities: A report of findings from the National Longitudinal Transition Study (NLTS) and the National Longitudinal Transition Study-2 (NLTS2).* Menlo Park, CA: SRI International. Available at www.nlts2.org/reports/2005_06/nlts2_report_2005_06_complete.pdf

Wehman, P. (2006). *Life beyond the classroom: Transition strategies for young people with disabilities* (4th ed.). Baltimore: Paul H. Brookes Publishing Co.

Wehmeyer, M.L., & Palmer, S.B. (2003). Adult outcomes for students with cognitive disabilities three years after high school: The impact of self-determination. *Education and Training in Developmental Disabilities, 38,* 131–144.

Will, M. (1984). *OSERS programming for the transition of youth with disabilities: Bridges from school to working life.* Washington, DC: U.S. Department of Education, Office of Special Education and Rehabilitative Services.

1

• • •

Work-Based Learning and Work Experiences as Indispensable Educational Tools

This chapter introduces the reader to

- The primary benefits to students who participate in work experiences
- The types and purposes of work experiences
- What constitutes a quality work experience
- The primary responsibilities of students, teachers, and employers during work experiences
- Examples of established transition models that feature work experiences and that provide evidence of their value

Rosa has always wanted to be a journalist. She is a diligent student and writes well. Her need for accommodation, however, is extensive. She uses a motorized wheelchair and an electronic communication board. She and her transition teacher worked to find a place where she could perform a volunteer internship with a reporter for a weekly community newspaper. This experience helped Rosa identify how she might ask for and use accommodations during her future career. It also solidified her resolve to be a journalist. She is now attending a state university, where she is pursuing a degree in journalism.

Before James began his internship as an information technology assistant with a large research company, he was on the verge of dropping out of school. He had been in and out of alternative high school programs due to persistent disruptive behavior. His successful internship gave purpose to his schoolwork and direction to a fledgling career. James graduated from high school and is now enrolled in a community college, where he is pursuing a career in electronics.

Jamal has several traits that most employers value: He is very organized, can attend to his work for long stretches of time, and rarely makes a mistake once he masters a task. He also loves sports. With help from his transition teacher, Jamal found a job that emphasized these skills. In his last year of secondary school, he began working at a local sporting goods store's shoe department, where he was taught by his teacher to organize mismatched shoes and incoming shipments of new merchandise. Three years later, Jamal is still working at this store where he thoroughly enjoys his work.

Alex is very precise in his work when it is organized carefully and he is supported by a job coach. During the last 3 years of secondary school, Alex's transition plan included several work experiences as a volunteer that progressively led to a paid job at a real estate office, where he assembled open house packets and performed other office tasks. Each of these experiences helped Alex and his teachers to better understand the types of tasks at which Alex excels, the kinds of work environments that are best suited for his accommodation needs, and what he likes to do. Alex worked at the real estate office for 2 years after he exited school. With the help of an employment specialist from his supporting agency, he was later able to find a job that he enjoyed even more as an administrative aide at an accounting firm using the skills he learned during his previous work experiences.

Rosa, James, Jamal, and Alex demonstrate the success that youth with disabilities can achieve in today's world. The literature shows a rising employment rate among youth with disabilities as they exit publicly supported education compared with 20 years ago (Wagner, Newman, Cameto, Garza, & Levine, 2005). Youth with all categories of disabilities are faring better in terms of postschool employment rates. For students with disabilities who finished secondary school in the late 1980s, employment rates at 2–5 years postschool ranged from less than 15% (for youth with significant and/or multiple disabilities) to 50% (for youth with learning disabilities) (Blackorby & Wagner, 1996). In recent years, the number of youth working after high school has increased by 9 percentage points across disability groups, including significant increases for youth with learning disabilities (Cameto, Marder, Wagner, & Cardoso, 2003).

Knowledge has increased considerably on how to prepare youth with disabilities for the world of work. This is good news for the youth, their families, disability advocates, professionals, and policy makers. School-to-work transition outcomes are starting to catch up to the ongoing legislative intent, which was clearly the goal when transition planning was required to be included in students' individualized education programs (IEPs) by the Individuals with Disabilities Education Act (IDEA) of 1990 (PL 101-476). These requirements were included in all subsequent reauthorizations of IDEA, which indicates the continuing importance of transition planning and its expected effects.

Reasons for this positive development include the fact that secondary education and transition professionals have identified better ways to prepare youth with disabilities for transition to employment and adult life. Special education law now also requires transition planning. In addition, professionals in the field have improved on ways to structure resources and services so that youth are better supported through this transition. Perhaps most importantly, professionals in the field have learned that connecting youth with disabilities to workplaces early and often throughout the secondary school years is a valuable way to help youth get started on productive postschool careers.

Unfortunately, many students with disabilities continue to struggle to successfully make the transition from school to adult employment. For every Rosa, James, Jamal, and Alex, there are one or two other youth with disabilities who will not have their education lead directly to a job or career path. However, this does not have to be the case. The field of transition is ever evolving, and its methodology is constantly improving. Carefully organized and monitored work experiences are part of this evolution. This chapter elaborates on why work experiences are so important, illustrates the potential benefits it has for youth with disabilities, introduces components of quality work-based learning, and briefly discusses transition models that feature work experiences as a centerpiece intervention.

BENEFITS OF WORK-BASED LEARNING

Work-based learning refers to a planned program of training and work experiences that occurs in authentic workplaces (Hamilton & Hamilton, 1997). Essentially any activity that puts youth in the workplaces of employers and that offers an opportunity to learn about careers and work behaviors can be considered work-based learning. Throughout this book, we refer to this type of purposeful educational activity as *work experience*. Work experiences can include such sporadic and brief activities as job shadowing, informational interviews, and workplace tours; more intensive activities of various durations such as workplace mentoring; and other more protracted experiences including volunteer work, service learning, on-the-job training, internships, apprenticeships, and paid employment. Each of these activities contributes to the career development, career choice, and career success of individuals with disabilities.

Student Benefits

Table 1.1 summarizes research-supported benefits associated with work experiences as an educational tool. For all students, with and without disabilities, work-based learning has long been shown to improve students' self-esteem, to teach and reinforce basic academic and technical skills, to promote an understanding of workplace culture and expectations, and to develop a network for future job searches (Haimson & Bellotti, 2001; Hoerner & Wehrley, 1995; Olson, 1997;

Table 1.1. Benefits of work-based learning

Students who participate in work-based learning benefit by having the opportunity to

- Identify career interests, skills, and abilities
- Explore career goals
- Identify on-the-job support needs
- Develop employability skills and good work habits
- Gain an understanding of employer expectations
- Link specific classroom instruction with related work expectations and knowledge requirements
- Develop an understanding of the workplace and the connection between learning and earning
- Gain general work experience, as well as experience connected to a specific job function, that can be added to a work portfolio or résumé

Wehman, 2006). Such experiences also expose students to work and career options that would otherwise be unknown to them. Work experiences are especially critical to youth with disabilities, for whom the exposure to the range of career options is often very limited. Furthermore, these experiences serve as opportunities to identify the particular workplace supports that youth with disabilities may require as they pursue later employment and career prospects (Hughes & Carter, 2000; Sitlington & Clark, 2006).

Meeting Special Education Legal Requirements

Although not specifically cited in current special education law, work experiences can be valuable tools for education systems to meet *indicators*—requirements for monitoring the transition components of the law. For example, states are required to measure the "percent of youth aged 16 and above with transition planning that includes coordinated annual goals and transition services that will reasonably enable the student to meet his/her post-secondary goals in the identified areas" (Indicator 13, Individuals with Disabilities Education Improvement Act [IDEA] of 2004, PL 108-446). Obviously, if those goals include employment and/or postsecondary education, then work experiences are critical to help students meet postsecondary goals.

States are also required to monitor the "percent of youth who had IEPs, are no longer in secondary school and who have been competitively employed, enrolled in some type of postsecondary school, or both, within one year of leaving high school" (Indicator 14, IDEA 2004). If this percentage is high, then it can be inferred that youth were adequately prepared for postschool life. Research indicates that work experiences contribute to successful postschool employment outcomes (e.g., Luecking & Fabian, 2000; Wagner et al., 2005). The incentive exists, therefore, for states to require that local school systems adopt curricula and teaching methodology that address these indicators. The clear intent is for local school districts to receive the help they need to deliver the best possible transition services for their students. The specific directives of the laws requiring transition planning are important to meeting the intent of IDEA 2004 and preceding special education laws (e.g., IDEA 1990, IDEA Amendments of 1997, PL 105-17) to help students make an effective transition from school to work and adult life. Youth with disabilities are showing gains (however modest) in postschool employment rates, which illustrates the value of these requirements.

Thousands of youth, particularly those like James who are labeled as having serious emotional disturbances, would drop out of school and be lost to the education system without appropriate incentives and relevant curricula (Bartick-Ericson, 2006). Again, special education laws address this issue by requiring the reporting of the percent of youth with IEPs who drop out of high school compared with the percent of all youth in the state who drop out of high school (Indicator 2, IDEA 2004). Although it would be naïve to suggest that work experience is the only intervention that addresses this issue, it certainly is an important one. It is crucial for schools to find ways to mitigate an alarmingly high dropout rate among special education students.

Compliance with special education laws is obviously important to schools; federal and state funding support depends on it. However, the laws exist to ensure that students benefit from their education and ultimately realize the benefits of transition planning, especially when that planning includes work experiences. These experiences have direct, tangible benefits for youth, as the examples of Rosa, James, Jamal, and Alex illustrate. Each of these youth had opportunities to identify career interests, explore the need for on-the-job support requirements, learn work skills, become aware of employer expectations, and connect school-based education with the world of work. Most importantly, these experiences resulted in either direct adult employment or the path to obtain it. The following sections examine the various types of work experiences.

DIVERSE TYPES AND USES OF WORK EXPERIENCES

Work experiences may include any combination of the following: career explorations, job shadowing, work sampling, service learning, internships (paid and unpaid), apprenticeships, and paid employment. These experiences offer opportunities for youth to learn both the "soft skills" (e.g., following instructions, getting along with co-workers) needed to succeed in the workplace and specific occupational skills. These experiences also help youth to identify employment and career preferences, as well as supports and accommodations that may be essential to long-term workplace success. The types of work experiences are presented and defined in Table 1.2.

Table 1.2. Types of work experiences

Career exploration	Career exploration involves visits by youth to workplaces to learn about jobs and the skills required to perform them. Visits and meetings with employers and people in identified occupations outside of the workplace are also types of career exploration activities from which youth can learn about jobs and careers. Typically, such visits are accompanied by discussions with youth about what they saw, heard, and learned.
Job shadowing	Job shadowing is extended time, often a full workday or several workdays, spent by a youth in a workplace accompanying an employee in the performance of his or her daily duties. Many companies have "take your child to work" or "job shadow" days, during which youth are invited to spend time at the company.
Work sampling	Work sampling is work by a youth that does not materially benefit the employer but allows the youth to spend meaningful time in a work environment to learn aspects of potential job tasks and "soft skills" required in the workplace. It is important for transition specialists to be familiar with the Fair Labor Standards Act (PL 75-718) requirements for volunteer activity.
Service learning	Service learning is hands-on volunteer service to the community that integrates with course objectives. It is a structured process that provides time for reflection on the service experience and demonstration of the skills and knowledge acquired.
Internships	Internships are formal arrangements whereby a youth is assigned specific tasks in a workplace over a predetermined period of time. Internships may be paid or unpaid, depending on the nature of the agreement with the company and the nature of the tasks. Many postsecondary institutions help to organize these experiences with local companies as adjuncts to specific degree programs and are alternatively called *cooperative education experiences, cooperative work,* or simply *co-ops.*
Apprenticeships	Apprenticeships are formal, sanctioned work experiences of extended duration in which an apprentice learns specific occupational skills related to a standardized trade, such as carpentry, plumbing, or drafting. Many apprenticeships also include paid work components.
Paid employment	Paid employment may include existing standard jobs in a company or customized work assignments that are negotiated with an employer, but these jobs always feature a wage paid directly to the youth. Such work may be scheduled during or after the school day. It may be integral to a course of study or simply a separate adjunctive experience.

Work experiences during the secondary school years can be organized in many different ways. They may be

- Structured as essential elements of educational instruction, such as when they are a primary element of the transition plan and most of the educational instruction happens in relation to the work experience
- Complements to classroom instruction, such as when a youth is on a work assignment related to the course content
- Adjuncts to classroom instruction, such as when a youth has a full complement of mandated coursework related to achieving a diploma but has a work experience assignment that counts as class credit
- Unrelated to any specific classroom or educational instruction, such as a part-time after-school job, but nevertheless useful and important to career development

Career Explorations

Career explorations are an opportunity for youth to be briefly exposed to a specific kind of work environment or job type. For example, one middle school teacher organized half-day trips to three different local companies every semester for youth to learn about available jobs in those companies and the skills required for performing them. After each visit, the class discussed the different types of jobs they saw, what skills the workers needed, and whether these jobs were of interest to them.

Another teacher assigned students in her learning disabilities resource class to arrange and conduct company visits and informational interviews. During the visits, students asked a key employee what the company was most known for, what skills and traits they looked for in new employees, and what they saw as future workforce needs. After these visits, the class discussed how these job requirements might relate to their current classroom curriculum, as well as how the visits helped them learn about what kinds of jobs and careers they might want to pursue.

Job Shadowing

One way to understand the requirements of a job is to spend a day with someone who is performing that job. One high school required all ninth-grade students—general curriculum students and students receiving special education services—to spend a day shadowing someone on the job. Throughout the day, each youth accompanied an employee of a company, which was either chosen by the student or facilitated by the school, as the employee performed daily duties. Students then prepared a report and/or participated in a discussion on what the student learned about the job and the company during the shadowing experience. In this way, students were introduced to jobs, their requirements, and potential career options. This introduction to the workplace provided a foundation on which the students could begin identifying other work experience options for the rest of their high school years, as well as the beginning considerations for career options after high school.

Other job shadow experiences can be less formal but no less valuable, such as when students participate in "take your child to work" days sponsored by many schools and communities. These types of episodic experiences are ways to introduce students to workplace circumstances and provide them with initial knowledge about work and careers.

Work Sampling

Many teachers expose students to work by organizing opportunities for them to spend time in a workplace as an unpaid worker. For example, many schools will provide rotations through several workplaces during a school year so that students can "sample" different types of job tasks and different work environments. These experiences also help students to learn the soft skills that are required in the workplace. These work experiences take many forms and can be conducted in the workplace of almost any employer. They are especially useful for youth who have difficulty generalizing their education from simulated environments to authentic work environments. Sampling work experiences is another way for students to be exposed to a variety of workplace environments, discover work preferences and interests, and identify accommodation needs.

Although these are common and valuable work experience options for many youth, educators need to be aware of Fair Labor Standards Act (FLSA) of 1938 (PL 75-718) requirements, which exist so that employers do not take advantage of workers or benefit from free labor. Essentially, as long as the student in the work sampling experience does not perform work that materially benefits the employer's operation, FLSA has not been violated (see Chapter 2).

Service Learning

Another common type of work experience is when students provide purposeful volunteer service, such as assisting with delivering Meals on Wheels or helping at a homeless center. When these types of volunteer experiences are formalized into a structured process that contributes to community improvement or addresses a charitable or community need in some way while integrating course objectives, they are often called *service learning*. When participating in service learning, students learn work behaviors that reinforce classroom learning such as being on time, completing assigned tasks, working as a team, and dealing with distractions —all while serving the community.

In some states, a certain number of service learning hours are required to receive a diploma. One teacher helped students participate in an oral history project in which they recorded the stories of military veterans for consideration for inclusion in a Library of Congress archive on veteran history. For the community, this activity helped to capture and maintain the contributions that veterans made to their country. For the students, this activity helped them to learn valuable lessons on planning, organizing, and completing purposeful tasks. Of course, they also earned service hours that counted toward their graduation requirements. For some students, service learning can also suggest a career path. For example, one student decided to pursue a postsecondary education program in media communications as a result of learning about audio and video recording during this service learning project.

Internships

Internships are extremely valuable to students, either as stand-alone experiences or when paired with a particular curriculum requirement, such as when a vocational preparation program requires cooperative work or *co-ops*. They can be paid or unpaid, depending on the arrangement with the employer and the nature of the internship. One example of a stand-alone internship that is adjunctive to the high school experience is the Bridges program of the Marriott Foundation for People with Disabilities (MFPD; Fabian, 2007). Students referred to this program participate in a semester-long paid internship experience with a local company. The youth learn job skills in a real workplace, but they and the employer are under no obligation to continue the relationship at the conclusion of the internship. Participating youth learn both job-specific and soft work skills, become aware of employer expectations for performance, build a résumé, and earn extra spending money.

Apprenticeships

Apprenticeships are less common than other work experiences because they are primarily associated with a particular trade, such as construction, electrical contracting, or auto mechanics. Not many schools offer this type of vocational education, but when available, apprenticeships offer not only skill development under a set of predetermined requirements but also a direct path to postschool employment. One manufacturing company in Wisconsin partners with a local school district so that at-risk students, including those with disabilities, participate in a formal, sanctioned work experience of extended duration in which student apprentices learn specific occupational skills related to advanced manufacturing processes. These apprenticeships offer paid employment along with classroom work, which leads to both a high school diploma and an apprentice certificate issued under guidelines established by the state of Wisconsin. Many of the program's graduates are offered full-time positions at the company immediately after graduation; all of the students report good postschool employment outcomes (Hurd, 2004).

Paid Employment

Paid employment may be full-time or part-time work in a regular or customized position; the job may be scheduled during or after school. The common denominator, however, is that students are paid a wage. Usually and preferably, the wage is paid directly by the employer, although wage stipends or contract work arrangements are occasionally used in paid work experiences. Paid employment may occur because a student's IEP specifies a work objective; other times, it is simply an after-school job. For reasons that will become more obvious to the reader by the end of this book, paid work in an authentic community setting is ultimately one of the strongest contributors to a youth's postschool employment success.

Chapter 2 discusses when and how to incorporate each of these types of work experiences. Subsequent chapters explain how to use various strategies for planning, developing, organizing, and monitoring work experiences, regardless of the type of experience. So how can we ensure that youth receive the maximum benefit from their work experiences?

QUALITY WORK EXPERIENCES

Several factors require consideration when organizing work experiences. Among these are connections between workplace and school-based learning, clear expectations of student activity at the workplace, clearly defined roles of teachers and worksite supervisors, and well-structured feedback on student performance. It is also important for students with disabilities to have appropriate supports and accommodations in place. Training and guidance for workplace personnel is also an important feature of creating a welcoming and supportive environment in which students can thrive. Table 1.3 summarizes the characteristics of quality work-based programs that are supported by research (Benz & Lindstrom, 1997; Haimson & Bellotti, 2001; Hamilton & Hamilton, 1997; Hoerner & Wehrley, 1995). These characteristics and how to achieve them will be discussed in detail in subsequent chapters, particularly Chapter 3.

Quality work experiences are especially dependent on all participants' knowledge and fulfillment of their roles in the arrangement. Students must know what is expected of them, how they are expected to behave on the job, and general and specific workplace guidelines. Transition specialists must carefully and thoroughly orient the student to the workplace, communicate and coordinate procedures with the hosting employer, ensure that everyone is clear about their respective responsibilities, and link the work experience to the student's course of instruction.

For their part, employers are often viewed as "donating" their facilities to be used as the learning environment. More will be said about minimizing this perception and about ensuring that cooperating employers receive reciprocal benefits from work experiences in Chapters 6 and 7. For now, it is important to know that employers will have critical basic responsibilities to fulfill if the work experience is to be productive for both them and the students. These responsibilities include, among a host of other possible roles, communicating behavior and performance expectations, informing the student and teacher about workplace

Table 1.3. Quality work-based learning characteristics

Clear program goals

Clear expectations and feedback to assess progress toward achieving goals

Clear roles and responsibilities for worksite supervisors, mentors, teachers, support personnel, and other partners

Training plans that specify learning goals tailored to individual students with specific outcomes connected to student learning

Convenient links between students, schools, and employers

On-the-job learning

Range of work-based learning opportunities, especially those outside traditional youth-employing industries (e.g., hospitality and retail)

Mentor(s) at the worksite

Assessments to identify skills, interests, and support needs at the worksite

Reinforcement of work-based learning outside of work

Appropriate academic, social, and administrative support for students, employers, and all involved partners

Table 1.4. Shared responsibility for work experience success

Student responsibility in work-based learning

Perform job responsibilities

Communicate needs and suggest support strategies

Adhere to workplace guidelines and procedures

Comply with expectations for job performance, behavior, and social interactions

Show respect, be responsible, and follow through on commitments

Learn as much as possible about the work environment and the job

Transition specialist responsibility in work-based learning

Orient students to the workplace, their roles, and their responsibilities

Communicate expectations for job performance, behavior, and social interactions

Explain consequences for inappropriate behavior

Orient employers to their roles as mentors and supervisors

Help students communicate their support needs and strategies

Help employers to capitalize on students' learning styles and identify support strategies

Communicate with students and employers on a regular basis

Link work-based learning experiences to classroom learning and academic curriculum

Employer responsibility in work-based learning

Model expectations

Provide clear, detailed, and repeated directions

Communicate expectations for job performance, behavior, and social interactions

Explain consequences for inappropriate behavior

Identify the best methods of communication for each student

Capitalize on each student's learning style and identify support strategies

Discuss progress and improvements in performance

Teach skills needed for successful job performance

Communicate with students and school liaisons on a regular basis

---

requirements, and training students on necessary job skills. Table 1.4 lists the basic responsibilities of students, transition specialists, and employers that contribute to the effectiveness of work-based learning experiences, which is discussed in considerable detail in Chapter 3.

MODELS THAT WORK

Schools and transition programs can help students to obtain and benefit from work experiences in many different ways. Most educators and transition professionals organize work experiences with students through a locally designed—and usually school-specific—approach in which students regularly have access to a community's workplaces for various work experiences. A host of models throughout the country feature successful implementation of work experiences as essential transition components, for which there is considerable evidence of resultant student gains. A few models are summarized here to further illustrate the various ways in which work can improve the transition experience for youth with disabilities.

Although these programs are often highly standardized and applied in only select school systems, they represent what is possible for any student: learning in real work environments. Schools and communities do not need formal and highly visible models like those described next to incorporate work experiences into a student's educational program. In fact, most often individual professionals working in school systems or youth employment programs make work experiences successful for youth with disabilities.

Bridges . . . from School to Work

"Bridges . . . from school to work" (or simply Bridges), developed by the Marriott Foundation for People with Disabilities (MFPD), has served some 15,000 youth since its inception in 1989. It operates in seven major metropolitan areas: Atlanta, Chicago, Dallas, Los Angeles, Philadelphia, San Francisco, and Washington, DC. Bridges was originally designed to create paid internships in local companies for youth with disabilities who were in their last year in high school (Tilson, Luecking, & Donovan, 1994). It has since made several adaptations: to serve out-of-school as well as in-school youth, to focus on vocational development in addition to initial placement, and to provide a more extended follow-up to help cement initial job success. However, the core elements of Bridges have remained: 1) initial career counseling and job search, 2) placement in a paid position with training and support available from program staff to ensure job success, and 3) postplacement follow-up support and tracking of participants to enable and measure vocational growth. Local employers in each program site, whose needs are prioritized in the job development and employment process, provide the competitive placements for the youth (MFPD, 2007).

The participating youth are typically referred to the program by program partners, primarily local teachers and transition personnel for in-school youth. Serving the entire spectrum of special education students, the program has boasted a typical placement rate of 68%–90%, regardless of the primary disability, gender, and race of the participants (Fabian, 2007). Follow-up studies of participants also demonstrate a high rate of postschool employment among the participants, with more than 75% of the youth completing 90 days on the job and being retained beyond that benchmark (Luecking & Fabian, 2000).

The success of Bridges suggests two things about the practice of pairing paid work experiences with other educational activities. First, the youth obviously benefit because, as an aggregate group, they are achieving an employment rate that notably exceeds typical employment rates of transitioning youth with disabilities. Second, employers seem to be benefiting as well. With a high percentage of long-term employment, it is apparent that exposure to youth with disabilities—along with the competent support of Bridges professionals—enables employers to gain access to contributing workers.

Start on Success

Start on Success (SOS) was developed and is sponsored by the National Organization on Disability (NOD). SOS operates in several cities and serves a primarily urban population. The program introduces young people with disabilities to workplace realities before they leave high school through paid internship experiences with large employers such as universities, hospitals, and corporations—thus offering exposure to a broad sampling of career pathways. Participating students work 10–15 hours per week for 8–32 weeks. In special cases, students are allowed to participate for 2 years. There is no expectation that interns will become candidates for regular employment at their job sites, but these experiences are important building blocks for later jobs and careers.

The focus of SOS is on students whom NOD calls "gap kids"—students who, if they cannot find their place in the working world or in continuing education by the time they graduate, will be prime candidates for isolation, welfare, or incarceration. The SOS program philosophy is that, given early opportunity and close individual support, young people with disabilities from low-income, mostly urban families can be successfully prepared for competitive employment and lives of independence. SOS participation includes

- Student-centered planning for the internship
- Strong individual support system on the job during the internship
- Family involvement and support
- Objective evaluations of youth performance on the job
- Fair compensation by the employer during the internship

   SOS reports that approximately 225 youth with physical, learning, emotional, and/or intellectual disabilities participate in its programs each year (NOD, 2007). NOD does not maintain aggregate data on participant outcomes, but the participating school systems consistently report both high rates of internship completion and higher rates of subsequent school completion than same-age peers receiving special education who do not participate (Charles Dey, personal communication, November 27, 2007). The value of SOS is the same as any other transition initiative that exposes youth to real work: It is an opportunity to learn work behaviors and employer expectations, identify job and career preferences, discover the most effective job accommodations and supports specific to each student's circumstance, and participate in important experiences to include on work résumés. Receiving pay makes the experience all the more authentic (and the extra spending money is almost always welcomed by the youth).

Transition Services Integration Model

The Transition Services Integration Model (TSIM) develops integrated career and employment options for individuals with significant disabilities who will be enrolled in public school through age 21, as allowed by special education law (Luecking & Certo, 2003). TSIM is designed to combine the resources of school and postschool systems during the last year of a student's enrollment in public education, thus sharing the costs of a student-driven approach to transition planning and resulting in long-term employment placement before school exit. Most of the youth participating in TSIM are not likely candidates for standard or advertised jobs because of a lack of requisite work experience and skills and/or because of extensive or unique accommodation and support needs. However, successful employment can be achieved through job development, which identifies employers who can benefit from the youth's particular attributes in alternative, customized ways. TSIM features these components:

- Person-centered planning, which occurs in the spring or the summer before the final year of school
- Job development, which begins in the spring or summer before the final year of school
- Customized jobs with support shared by school and adult employment agency personnel
- Pre-exit planning so that the youth exit school with both the job and the supports to maintain it

With TSIM, the last day of school is no different than the day after: same job, same supports. During participating students' last year in school, their school system enters into a formal service contract with a local private non-profit community rehabilitation program that serves adults with significant support needs and that agrees to work with pending graduates *before* and *after* school exit through a combination of school district resources, state vocational rehabilitation agency funding, and state developmental disabilities agency funding. Because the intended result is fully integrated direct-hire employment and community activities, there is no need to assign students to a fixed classroom or school site during their last year of school. The instruction that students receive during this last year in school is provided entirely in job and community settings. The postschool employment rate of more than 65% for TSIM students, compared with the low rate (less than 15%) for youth in this disability category who do not participate in TSIM, speaks to the value of real work as part of the education experience for these youth (Certo & Luecking, 2006).

High School/High Tech

The High School/High Tech (HS/HT) program was originally developed by the former President's Committee for Employment of People with Disabilities as a way of encouraging careers in technology fields in which people with disabilities are underrepresented (Office of Disability Employment Policy, 2008). It features opportunities for youth with disabilities to spend time (through visits, job shadowing, internships, and/or paid employment) at participating high-tech companies and workplaces. Collaborating employers include those with a preponderance of technology-related jobs, such as the National Aeronautics and Space Administration and Microsoft. HS/HT programs, however, also recruit a variety of large and small companies in their areas to provide work experiences that expose students to high-tech fields, including the following:

- Connections with mentors who work in high-tech fields
- Field trips to representative companies where students can see the types of jobs and career opportunities that exist in the field
- Job shadowing
- Paid and unpaid summer internships in participating companies where students can experience the activity, demands, and rewards of working in high-tech jobs

Typical eligibility requirements for HS/HT participation include the following:

- A physical, sensory, or learning disability
- Enrollment in the regular diploma program in Grades 9–12
- An interest in the sciences, math, engineering, or technology
- An interest in pursuing postsecondary education and/or training

HS/HT encourages students with disabilities to explore the fields of science, math, engineering, and technology by motivating and encouraging students to explore their own interests and potential in science, math, engineering, and technology; encouraging students to aim for technology-related education and careers; and assisting professionals in science, math, engineering, and technology fields to better understand assistive technology, accommodation, and facility-access needs of individuals with disabilities. Reports from companies that have participated and from professionals who have facilitated these experiences demonstrate the postschool career success of many youth who have participated (e.g., Black, 2004).

Career Transition Program

As a group, youth with serious emotional disabilities or mental illnesses have low school completion rates and low postschool employment rates that are exacerbated by higher rates of criminal activity and substance abuse (Bazelon Center for Mental Health Law, 2004). The Career Transition Program is designed to address these issues and is an example of pairing work experience (specifically, paid jobs) with other complementary educational and social service interventions to prevent youth from dropping out of school and to encourage postschool employment (Martinez et al., 2008). The Career Transition Program has been operating in Montgomery County, Maryland, since 1993 and has been replicated in school districts in three other states. The following components form the Career Transition Program intervention:

- Individualized, person-centered planning
- Flexible case management and support
- Paid work experience
- Family support activities

Youth are referred to Career Transition Program case managers by teachers during the junior year of high school. The case managers often link the youth with necessary ancillary mental health services. However, their main function is to help youth find and maintain paid employment. This has consistently proven to be the "hook" that keeps youth in school and prevents many of the social problems endemic to this population.

One follow-up study (Tilson, Luecking, & Schmid, 2007) of youth participating in the Career Transition Program found that 94% of the participants complete high school compared with the reported national average of 56% for youth with serious emotional disabilities (Wagner et al., 2005). Just as significantly, 84% of participants were employed upon school exit, with another 15% either in postsecondary education or actively looking for employment. These findings illustrate the value of work experience as a primary intervention that, when purposefully paired with educational and social service interventions, has the potential to significantly boost positive postschool outcomes.

IMPROVING THE QUALITY AND AVAILABILITY OF WORK EXPERIENCES

The value of work experiences may be supported by the research and models described in this chapter, but there are still hurdles to implementing them on a broader scale so as to benefit all youth with disabilities in secondary school, now numbering more than 2 million in the United States (U.S. Department of Education, 2006). The three general challenges to making work experiences a bigger priority in secondary and postsecondary education are described next.

First, there is concern that time spent away from classroom learning at the workplace will negatively affect academic success, particularly since the passage of the No Child Left Behind Act of 2001 (PL 107-110), which emphasizes school system accountability for student academic achievement. Thus, work-based learning will need to be seen as academically rigorous to be more widely supported by parents, educators, and policy makers (Haimson & Bellotti, 2001). Chapter 11 will focus on strategies to address this need.

Second, school personnel often struggle to find time to establish and maintain relationships with participating employers. Employers, for their part, require convenient ways to connect with students. Thus, easy and effective mechanisms for linking students with employers need to be created and/or expanded in most school systems (see Chapters 6 and 7). In addition to resources within the typical school system, youth employment programs funded by the Workforce Investment Act of 1998 (PL 105-220) can help to facilitate this process. In many communities, these programs create work experiences for a range of youth, including those with disabilities. Also, disability-specific resources, such as those funded by state vocational rehabilitation agencies, are important pregraduation links to jobs and work experiences that lead to eventual successful adult employment (see Chapter 10).

Finally, work-based learning and academic coursework need to be integrated to allow students to understand the value and application of their education and experience, regardless of whether students are on track to receive a regular high school diploma or a certificate of completion (Bailey & Hughes, 1999; Benz & Lindstrom, 1997; Hamilton & Hamilton, 1997). Work experiences can contribute to a student's overall academic development through journal writing, formalized training plans, participation in internship seminars or classes for debriefing, final reports or presentations on the experience, or planned learning experiences at work.

Positive public perceptions of work-based learning, better connections to employers, and integration with school learning are necessary for wider adoption and implementation of quality work experiences for students receiving special education services. Subsequent chapters will provide strategies for addressing each of these concerns while ensuring that youth with disabilities are provided with opportunities to receive this important exposure to work during their formative education years—helping youth to achieve productive and meaningful employment in their adult lives.

SUMMARY

Research has consistently demonstrated that education and employment outcomes for youth with disabilities can be significantly improved by frequent and systematic exposure to a variety of real work experiences. Compared with their peers without disabilities, the persistently low employment rates of young adults with disabilities suggest that these types of experiences should be integral to secondary education for students with disabilities, regardless of the nature of the disability or the need for special education services. This chapter provided a rationale for work experiences, described the type and function of different types of work experiences, examined models that embody the best features of work as integral aspects of transition planning and service, described indicators of quality for such experiences, and provided examples of work-based learning models that

have proven effective in boosting the career development of youth with disabilities. Chapter 2 discusses in detail the types of work experiences introduced here,
when and how to use them, and ways to ensure their inclusion in transition
planning.

REFERENCES

Bailey, T., & Hughes, K. (1999). *Employer involvement in work-based learning programs.*
Berkeley, CA: National Center for Research in Vocational Education.
Bartick-Ericson, C. (2006). Attachment security and the school experience for emotionally
disturbed adolescents in special education. *Emotional and Behavioral Difficulties, 11,* 49–60.
Bazelon Center for Mental Health Law. (2004, August 8). *Facts on transitional services for
youth with mental illness.* Retrieved November 29, 2006, from http://bazelon
.org/issues/children/factsheets/transition.htm
Benz, M., & Lindstrom, L. (1997). *Building school-to work programs: Strategies for youth with
special needs.* Austin, TX: PRO-ED.
Black, C. (2004). Boosting the high-tech workforce. In R. Luecking (Ed.), *In their own
words: Employer perspectives on youth with disabilities in the workplace.* Minneapolis:
University of Minnesota, Institute on Community Integration, National Center on
Secondary Education and Transition.
Blackorby, J., & Wagner, M. (1996). Longitudinal postschool outcomes of youth with dis-
abilities: Findings from the national longitudinal transition study. *Exceptional Children,
62*(5), 399–413.
Cameto, R., Marder, C., Wagner, M., & Cardoso, D. (2003). *Youth employment.* Retrieved
July 10, 2008, from http://www.ncset.org/publications/viewdesc.asp?id=1310
Certo, N., & Luecking, R. (2006). Service integration and school to work transition:
Customized employment as an outcome for youth with significant disabilities. *Journal of
Applied Rehabilitation Counseling, 37,* 29–35.
Fabian, E. (2007). Urban youth with disabilities: Factors affecting transition employment.
Rehabilitation Counseling Bulletin, 50(3), 130–138.
Fair Labor Standards Act (FLSA) of 1938, PL 75-718, 29 U.S.C. 201 *et seq.*
Haimson, J., & Bellotti, J. (2001). *Schooling in the workplace: Increasing the scale and quality of
work-based learning, final report.* Princeton, NJ: Mathematica Policy Research.
Hamilton, M., & Hamilton, S. (1997). *Learning well at work: Choices for quality.* New York:
Cornell University Press.
Hoerner, J., & Wehrley, J. (1995). *Work-based learning: The key to school-to-work transition.*
New York: Glencoe/McGraw-Hill.
Hughes, C., & Carter, E.W. (2000). *The transition handbook: Strategies that high school teachers
use that work.* Baltimore: Paul H. Brookes Publishing Co.
Hurd, B. (2004). Manufacturing and production technician youth apprentices. In R.
Luecking (Ed.), *In their own words: Employer perspectives on youth with disabilities in the work-
place.* Minneapolis: University of Minnesota, Institute on Community Integration,
National Center on Secondary Education and Transition.
Individuals with Disabilities Education Act Amendments of 1997, PL 105-17, 20 U.S.C.
§§ 1400 *et seq.*
Individuals with Disabilities Education Act of 1990, PL 101-476, 20 U.S.C. §§ 1400, *et seq.*
Individuals with Disabilities Education Improvement Act of 2004, PL 108-446, 20 U.S.C.
§§ 1400 *et seq.*
Luecking, R., & Certo, N. (2003). Service integration at the point of transition for youth
with significant disabilities: A model that works. *American Rehabilitation, 27,* 2–9.
Luecking, R., & Fabian, E. (2000). Paid internships and employment success for youth in
transition. *Career Development for Exceptional Individuals, 23,* 205–221.
Marriott Foundation for People with Disabilities (MFPD). (2007). *Bridges employer representative training manual.* Washington, DC: Author.
Martinez, J., Scott, M., Baird, P., Fraker, T., Honeycutt, T., Mamun, A., et al. (2008). *The
youth transition demonstration project: Profiles of the demonstration projects.* Washington, DC:
Mathematica Policy Research.
National Organization on Disability. (2007). *Start on Success.* Retrieved August 28, 2008,
from http://www.startonsuccess.org/

No Child Left Behind Act of 2001, PL 107-110, 115 Stat.1425, 20 U.S.C. §§ 6301 *et seq.*

Office of Disability Employment Policy. (2008). *High School/High Tech.* Retrieved June 8, 2008, from http://www.dol.gov/odep/programs/high.htm

Olson, L. (1997). *The school to work revolution: How employers and educators are joining forces to prepare tomorrow's skilled workforce.* Reading, MA: Addison-Wesley.

Sitlington, P., & Clark, G. (2006). *Transition education and services for students with disabilities* (4th ed.). Boston: Allyn & Bacon.

Tilson, G., Luecking, R., & Donovan, M. (1994). Involving employers in transition: The Bridges model. *Career Development for Exceptional individuals, 17*(1), 77–89.

Tilson, G., Luecking, R., & Schmid, P. (2007). *Effective transition for youth with serious emotional disabilities: An evaluation of the Career Transition Project.* Unpublished manuscript.

U.S. Department of Education. (2006). *Children and students served under IDEA, Part B, in the U.S. and outlying areas by age group, year and disability category: Fall 1996 through fall 2005.* Retrieved January 2, 2008, from https://www.ideadata.org/tables29th/ar_1-9.htm

Wagner, M., Newman, L., Cameto, R., Garza, N., & Levine, P. (2005). *After high school: A first look at the postschool experiences of youth with disabilities. A report from the National Longitudinal Transition Study 2 (NLTS2).* Menlo Park, CA: SRI International.

Wehman, P. (2006). *Life beyond the classroom: Transition strategies for young people with disabilities* (4th ed.). Baltimore: Paul H. Brookes Publishing Co.

Workforce Investment Act of 1998, PL 105-220, 29 U.S.C., §§ 2801 *et seq.*

2

...

Setting the Stage for
Quality Work Experiences

This chapter provides the reader with

- A review of work experience functions
- An overview of when work experiences can be incorporated into student and youth career development
- A conceptual model for the work experience process
- Legal considerations when developing work experiences

Several of Eddie's high school work experiences helped him to assess his career interests and skills: job shadowing at two nonprofit organizations during 10th grade, an unpaid internship in an accounting office where he stocked deliveries of office supplies in 11th grade, and a paid part-time job as a copy clerk in a government agency during his final year of high school. Through each of these work experiences, Eddie learned something new about what he wanted to do (office work), what he was good at (organizing), and what accommodations he would need (a secluded work area free of distractions). When Eddie exited his public school program, he was able to convert his part-time job in the government office into a full-time permanent job—a seamless transition facilitated by sequential, well-organized work experiences in high school.

Cindy's work experiences were all problematic because of her social behavior. Cindy was always in inclusive settings in high school, where she received attention from her peers for inappropriate social behavior (e.g., singing, speaking out, unacceptable language). She was fired from one part-time job because of this inappropriate behavior and noncompliance: When she didn't want to do something, Cindy would just cross her arms and not move.

Fortunately, Cindy's school district offered a transition-year program that provided Cindy with additional work experiences—and ultimately a job—before she was scheduled to exit the school system at age 21. After 3 months of training and preparation, during which she had the opportunity to practice and be reinforced for appropriate work behaviors, Cindy got a job as a hotel housekeeper. Cindy began by working 1 day per week, during which her teacher coached her by ignoring inappropriate behavior and praising appropriate behavior. Within 4 months, right before she exited school, Cindy was working 5 days per week with no personal job coach. Now she wears a uniform willingly and exceeds the inspection standards of the housekeeping staff. Cindy has held this job for 3 years, during which time she has learned more difficult skills and trained a new member of the housekeeping team.

Eddie and Cindy demonstrate the value of work experiences that are spread out over the secondary school years. In Eddie's case, the progression of work experiences beginning in 10th grade led him to find a good vocational fit for his postschool career. For Cindy, the progression of work experiences enabled her to develop more mature and acceptable behaviors so that by the end of her educational experience, she was on her way to productive adult employment.

The primary assumption of this book is that all youth—no matter the disability label or need for support—can ultimately experience self-determined and meaningful employment. Of course, as Eddie and Cindy demonstrate, the path to that desired outcome is not always simple or straightforward, nor does it occur without continuous exposure to workplace options and experiences. This chapter discusses the functions of different types of work experiences, when to consider introducing them in youth career development, a conceptual model for the process of establishing and supporting quality work experiences, and legal considerations that may affect how work experiences are developed and monitored.

WORK EXPERIENCES AND CAREER PROGRESSION

Few people chart a clear and linear path to their career; most will experience fits and starts, multiple changes of directions, and more than a few pitfalls as they pursue adult employment and careers. Therefore, career and transition experts have identified typical stages in career progression that enable all youth, including those with disabilities, to eventually craft a career direction. Many models of career development identify typical stages that are widely accepted as leading to a satisfying and productive career (Brolin, 1995; Flexer, Baer, Luft, & Simmons, 2008). These stages include

1. *Career awareness,* when individuals begin to develop self-awareness and learn about work values and roles in work, usually in elementary school

2. *Career exploration,* when individuals gather information to explore work interests, skills, abilities, and the requirements of various employment options, usually starting in middle school or early high school

3. *Career decision making,* when individuals begin to select job and career areas that match interests and aptitudes, usually beginning in high school, but often continuing well into adulthood

4. *Career preparation,* when youth begin to understand their strengths and challenges, and make informed choices about preparation activities that will

lead them to a chosen career area, usually throughout high school and post-secondary school

5. *Career placement,* when youth begin to responsibly and productively participate in a job and a career area

These stages may not look the same for everyone or follow the typical order; however, one thing is constant: The more exposure youth have to work experiences, the easier it is for them to decide what they like, what they are good at, and what help they might need to establish their eventual career.

As discussed in the previous chapter, the importance of work experiences is ingrained in the *National Standards and Quality Indicators for Secondary Education and Transition* (National Alliance for Secondary Education and Transition, 2005) for all students. The National Standards and Quality Indicators are organized into five content areas, the second of which is called *Career Preparatory Experience.* To set the stage for quality work experiences, it is useful to look at the standards and indicators for Career Preparatory Experiences reproduced in Table 2.1. These clearly represent a foundation on which to help youth to arrive at chosen and productive careers. Note the emphasis on meaningful work experiences in Standard 2.3.

To ensure that a work experience is meaningful, the reader should consider the following questions:

- Is the youth pursuing work experiences for the most fitting purpose?
- Are work experiences being used at the right times in the youth's career development?
- Is there a process for identifying and implementing good work experiences?
- Do the work experiences reflect quality? How?

The following sections will generate some answers to these questions.

Functions of Work Experiences

Chapter 1 provided descriptions of common types of work experiences. These work experiences range from cursory exposure to intensive on-the-job learning and training. They are not always linear but generally are introduced at particular points in youth education and career development; each serves a distinct purpose in preparing youth for eventual employment choices and employment success.

Table 2.2 outlines the types of work experiences, representative examples of each, when these experiences might be considered, and their typical functions. Although the progression is logical, many youth with disabilities may start later than described or may not experience them in any particular order. Ideally, however, the work experiences will occur sequentially and build on the preceding experiences, ultimately resulting in postschool employment and careers.

The approximate grade level for each type of work experience should also be considered, so as to build a progressively expanding repertoire leading to postschool careers. Again, the sequence and availability of work experiences will vary considerably among school systems and youth employment systems, as well as for individuals within these systems. A typical progression is outlined in Table 2.3.

Diploma-bound students may experience work as a cooperative learning aspect of a particular career emphasis in the curriculum or as an unrelated adjunct to their curriculum (i.e., after-school and summer work programs). Students who are not seeking a diploma and/or who continue in school through

Table 2.1. Standards and indicators for career preparatory experiences

2.1	**Youth participate in career awareness, exploration, and preparatory activities in school- and community-based settings.**
2.1.1	Schools and community partners offer courses, programs, and activities that broaden and deepen youths' knowledge of careers and allow for more informed postsecondary education and career choices.
2.1.2	Career preparatory courses, programs, and activities incorporate contextual teaching and learning.
2.1.3	Schools, employers, and community partners collaboratively plan and design career preparatory courses, programs, and activities that support quality standards, practices, and experiences.
2.1.4	Youth and families understand the relationship between postsecondary and career choices, and financial and benefits planning.
2.1.5	Youth understand how community resources, experiences, and family members can assist them in their role as workers.
2.2	**Academic and nonacademic courses and programs include integrated career development activities.**
2.2.1	Schools offer broad career curricula that allow youth to organize and select academic, career, or technical courses based on their career interests and goals.
2.2.2	With the guidance of school and/or community professionals, youth use a career planning process (e.g., assessments, career portfolio, etc.) based on career goals, interests, and abilities.
2.2.3	Career preparatory courses, programs, and activities align with labor market trends and specific job requirements.
2.2.4	Career preparatory courses, programs, and activities provide the basic skills crucial to success in a career field, further training, and professional growth.
2.3	**Schools and community partners provide youth with opportunities to participate in meaningful school- and community-based work experiences.**
2.3.1	Youth participate in quality work experiences that are offered to them prior to exiting school (e.g., apprenticeships, mentoring, paid and unpaid work, service learning, school-based enterprises, on-the-job training, internships, etc.).
2.3.2	Work experiences are relevant and aligned with each youth's career interests, postsecondary education plans, goals, skills, abilities, and strengths.
2.3.3	Youth participate in various on-the-job training experiences, including community service (paid or unpaid) specifically linked to school credit or program content.
2.3.4	Youth are able to access, accept, and use individually needed supports and accommodations for work experiences.
2.4	**Schools and community partners provide career preparatory activities that lead to youths' acquisition of employability and technical skills, knowledge, and behaviors.**
2.4.1	Youth have multiple opportunities to develop traditional job preparation skills through job-readiness curricula and training.
2.4.2	Youth complete career assessments to identify school and postschool preferences, interests, skills, and abilities.
2.4.3	Youth exhibit understanding of career expectations, workplace culture, and the changing nature of work and educational requirements.
2.4.4	Youth demonstrate that they understand how personal skill development (e.g., positive attitude, self-discipline, honesty, time management, etc.) affects their employability.
2.4.5	Youth demonstrate appropriate job-seeking behaviors.

From National Alliance for Secondary Education and Transition (NASET). (2005). *National standards and quality indicators: Transition toolkit for systems improvement* (pp. 6–7). Minneapolis: University of Minnesota, National Center on Secondary Education and Transition; reprinted by permission.

age 21 will often experience work in a slightly different chronology. These students may participate in work sampling and paid work throughout their final 3 years in school, ideally experiencing paid work as one of the culminating features of their education. Similarly, youth who pursue postsecondary education may also have work experiences integrated into their curricula, depending on the type of program in which they are enrolled. As these youth progress in school, more advanced and intensive work experiences may be introduced.

Table 2.2. Work experience occurrences and functions

Type	Examples	When to consider	Function
Career exploration	Company tours/field trips Talks with employers	As youth begin awareness of adult occupational opportunities	Initial exposure to jobs and careers
Job shadowing	"Take your child to work" day Job shadow day Disability mentoring day Teacher-arranged shadowing	When youth begin to sample work and workplace interests	Observation of work environment Exposure to jobs and careers
Work sampling	Rotation through various community worksta-tions Job task sampling Career assessments Any unpaid workplace experience	When youth begin exposure to workplace environments and expectations and as a prelude to more intensive work experiences	Job task sampling Exposure to work environments Identification of poten-tial supports and accommodations
Service learning	Volunteer for community and social programs Formal volunteer service in a structured commu-nity service program	As adjuncts or alterna-tives to other work experiences	Learning the responsi-bility of following through Taking directions Community involvement
Internships	Paid or unpaid student co-op Formal time-limited work experience paired with course of instruction Formal arrangement with an employer to learn identified work skills	As adjuncts to a specific course of study, most commonly during late high school or in post-secondary education and training	Intensive career/job preparation Prelude to a career choice In-depth exposure to a job and work-place
Apprenticeships	Trade-related paid or unpaid work with a cer-tified skilled journeyman	As an integrated component of specific occupational training	Building occupational skills related to trade certification
Paid employment	Part-time jobs Full-time jobs Jobs related to course of study and/or transition plan Adjunctive or unrelated experiences to school and course work, such as after-school, week-end, and summer jobs	Latter secondary school years and postsec-ondary education	Building a résumé Earning money Continuing to build work skills Identifying workplace and vocational pref-erences

Certain opportunities may not be available to youth at the various stages of their education. For example, transition specialists may be tasked with helping youth find paid work, even though those youth may have had limited or no exposure to career exploration, job shadowing, or career assessments that often include volunteer and work sampling experiences. This lack of exposure makes it difficult for both the youth and the transition specialist to decide where and under what circumstances the youth wants to work. It is not a disadvantage that is insurmountable, but it is a challenging one nevertheless. To avoid this challenge, the full array of work experiences should be available to youth as they move through their education experience. When this is not possible, strategies exist to

Table 2.3. Typical work experience progression

Year in school	Typical work experience pursued
Middle school	Career exploration Job shadowing
9th grade	Career exploration Job shadowing
10th grade	Work sampling Service learning Paid employment
11th grade	Work sampling Service learning Paid employment
12th grade	Service learning Internships Apprenticeships Paid employment
Beyond 12th grade (ages 18-21)	Work sampling Paid employment
Postsecondary education (any age)	Internships Apprenticeships Paid employment

help youth take advantage of available work experiences. To help the reader conceptualize this process, the next section presents a model to organize the steps toward the most individualized, effective, and quality work experience.

Conceptual Model for Establishing and Monitoring Work Experience

To establish work experiences of any kind, there are recommended steps to be followed. Figure 2.1 represents the process, from the first identification of work experience goals to providing the necessary support for youth to succeed in the work experience.

Planning for the work experience begins with identifying the goals of the work experience and the opportunities it offers. Is the work experience meant to expose youth to a type of work environment, a type of occupation, or merely to sample work? Will it be paid or unpaid? What should the youth learn during the experience? Once the purpose and goals of the work experience are identified, the youth's skills, interests, and support needs should be considered. These will be the basis for finding an employer and a workplace where these characteristics are welcomed and accommodated. The ideal work experience occurs in a workplace where the employer's expectations and requirements overlap with the youth's goals, strengths, and support needs.

If the considerations of both the youth and the employer mesh—or at least appear to be compatible—then negotiating begins with the employer. Items to consider in these negotiations include

- *Purpose of the work experience*—Is it to sample new tasks, shadow a particular employee, learn through an internship of specified duration, earn money, or another reason? Each of these reasons suggests unique considerations in terms

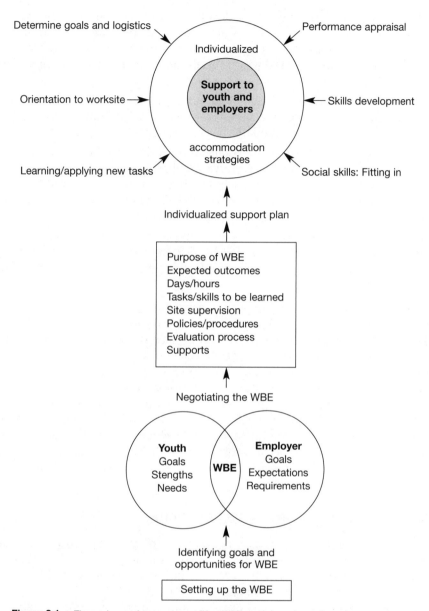

Figure 2.1. The work experience process. (*Key:* WBE, work-based experience.)

of youth performance, the extent of co-workers' involvement, and how the employer should prepare the work environment for the youth's presence.

- *Expected outcomes*—How long will the work experience last? What is the level of mastery expected for task performance? What happens when the experience ends? The answers to these questions will be different for each type of work experience and for each youth.

- *Conditions of work*—How many hours and/or days per week is the youth expected to be at the worksite? Is the experience paid or unpaid? Both educational and legal implications exist for these conditions, as discussed later in this chapter.

- *Site supervision*—How involved and available will the transition specialist be? Will a co-worker or mentor have supervisory responsibilities? A critical feature of a quality work experience is clear role clarification of all involved parties; no role is more important to youth success at the workplace than that of overseeing performance.

- *Workplace policies and procedures*—What are they? Who will make sure that the youth knows them? Creating an opportunity for orientation when youth start at the workplace is critical to later performance and workplace assimilation.

- *Evaluation process*—What will it entail? Who will contribute to evaluating the youth's performance? At what intervals will performance be reviewed and by whom? Almost all work experiences will have a way for the youth's performance to be reviewed; this maximizes the experience's contribution to the youth's learning, future work, and career direction.

- *Supports and accommodations*—What supports are necessary, and who will ensure they are in place? As will be discussed in Chapter 8, success in a work experience often hinges on effective, individually tailored supports and accommodations.

Once the conditions and expectations of the work experience have been clarified to all concerned, a plan for supporting the work experience should be implemented to maximize the youth's workplace success. Many programs and school systems have found that a written learning "contract" ensures that youth, families, worksite supervisors, and transition specialists are clear about their respective responsibilities (e.g., Kansas City Kansas Public Schools, 2007). Also, most youth will need some help in certain areas, such as worksite orientation or social adjustment. Some youth will need very carefully planned and intensive support. As Chapter 8 will outline in detail, developing an individualized support plan is a helpful strategy, especially for those youth who have limited or no exposure to work environments and/or who need considerable support and accommodations to succeed at work.

LEGAL ASPECTS OF WORK EXPERIENCE

When planning for work experiences begins, it is important for transition specialists to be aware of certain legal considerations. Two of the most relevant laws that might affect the pursuit of work experience are the Fair Labor Standards Act (FLSA; PL 75-718) and the Americans with Disabilities Act (ADA; PL 101-336). When work experiences are unpaid, such as in career explorations and volunteer job sampling, provisions of the FLSA describe when and under what conditions a youth can be in the workplace and not receive remuneration. When work experiences involve pay and wages, the FLSA also provides guidance about conditions that must be met regarding the employee's age, job hazards, and wage levels. Finally, discrimination and accommodation provisions of the ADA often apply to youth with disabilities in transition work experiences. These situations are discussed in the following sections.

Fair Labor Standards Act
Provisions for Nonpaid Work Experience

Federal policy makers and federal agencies have long recognized the importance of work-based learning and work experiences in preparing youth with disabilities for employment (Simon, Cobb, Halloran, Norman, & Bourexis, 1994; Simon

& Halloran, 1994). When youth are in the workplace for planned instruction and work experience, unique circumstances may affect certain protections afforded to workers under federal law. As a result, the U.S. Departments of Labor and Education adopted a joint statement of principle as follows.

> The U.S. Departments of Labor and Education are committed to the continued development and implementation of individual education programs, in accordance with the Individuals with Disabilities Education Act (IDEA), that will facilitate the transition of students with disabilities from school to employment within their communities. This transition must take place under conditions that will not jeopardize the protections afforded by the Fair Labor Standards Act to Program participants, employees, employers, or programs providing rehabilitation services to individuals with disabilities. (Johnson, Sword, & Habhegger, 2005, p. 8)

The FLSA established the guidelines for minimum wage regulations, child labor provisions, and distinguishing unpaid vocational and instructional training that may occur in the workplace from conditions that require employers to pay employees. To clarify how these guidelines affect students with disabilities in the workplace, Johnson et al. (2005) updated the guidelines that govern the participation of youth with disabilities in unpaid work-based experiences. Students with disabilities are not considered employees of the businesses in which they engage in work experiences if they can demonstrate compliance with all of the following guidelines provided by Johnson et al. (2005).

- Participants are youth with physical and/or intellectual disabilities for whom competitive employment at or above the minimum wage level is not immediately obtainable and who, because of their disability, will need intensive ongoing support to perform in a work setting.

- Participation is for career exploration, career assessment, or work-related training at a worksite placement under the general supervision of public school personnel.

- Worksite placements are clearly defined components of individualized education programs (IEPs) developed and designed for the benefit of each student. The statement of needed transition services established for the exploration, assessment, training, or cooperative work experience components will be included in the student's IEP.

- Information contained in a student's IEP does not have to be made available; however, documentation as to the student's enrollment in the work-based learning program must be made available to the U.S. Departments of Labor and Education if requested. The student and his or her parent(s) or guardian(s) must be fully informed of the IEP and the career exploration, career assessment, or work-related training components and have indicated voluntary participation with the understanding that participation in these components does not entitle the student-participant to wages or other compensation for duties performed at the worksite placement.

- The activities of the student at the worksite do not result in an immediate advantage to the business. The U.S. Department of Labor looks at the following factors to determine if this guideline is being met:

  There has been no displacement of employees, vacant positions have not been filled, employees have not been relieved of assigned duties, and the students are not performing services that, although not ordinarily performed by employees, clearly are of benefit to the business.

The students are under continued and direct supervision by either representatives of the school or by employees of the business. The student receives ongoing instruction and close supervision at the worksite during the entire experience, resulting in any tasks the student performs being offset by the burden to the employer of providing ongoing training and supervision. Such placements are made according to the requirements of the student's IEP and not to meet the labor needs of the business.

The periods of time spent by the students at any one site or in any clearly distinguishable job classification are specifically limited by the IEP.

- Students are not automatically entitled to employment at the business at the conclusion of their IEP; however, once a student has become an employee, all laws pertaining to employer–employee relationships apply.

Schools and participating businesses are responsible for ensuring that all of these guidelines are met. If any of these guidelines are not met, an employment relationship exists, and participating businesses can be held responsible for full compliance with the FLSA, meaning that they must pay youth according to applicable wage laws.

When youth are no longer in school, there may still be legitimate purpose to unpaid work experiences and workplace training. The same considerations apply as listed previously, with the exception of guidelines regarding IEPs. Therefore, in this case

- The training is for an identified vocational preparation purpose
- The training is for the benefit of the youth, not the employer
- The youth does not displace regular employees but works under close supervision of either a transition professional or supervisor/co-worker
- The business derives no immediate advantage from the activities of the youth and the placement may involve extra effort on the part of the employer
- The youth is not entitled to a job at the conclusion of the work experience
- The youth understands that he or she is not entitled to wages for the period of training

The FLSA, of course, ensures that youth are protected from unfair labor practices of employers. However, the value of unpaid work experience for youth is such that under the conditions outlined, youth have the opportunity to enjoy the advantages these experiences offer. It is important, therefore, to plan work experiences according to the career objectives, preferences, and interests of the youth, which will be discussed in Chapter 3, and according to the recommended practices of the employers who will host the youth, as will be discussed in Chapters 6 and 7.

Paid Work Experiences and Fair Labor Standards Act

When an employment relationship exists, youth must be paid the same as any employee who performs the same tasks—overtime pay, minimum wage provisions, and child labor provisions apply. The FLSA contains several provisions addressing younger employees who are age 14 and 15, employees who are age 16 and older, and workers with disabilities, as summarized by Johnson et al. (2005).

- *Youth age 14 and 15*—These youth can work outside of school hours if they work no more than 3 hours on a school day with a limit of 18 hours in a school week. They may not work in jobs declared hazardous by the Secretary of Labor. (Hazardous jobs are defined as any occupation that may be detrimental to the health and well-being of children younger than 18 years of age or an occupation that may jeopardize their educational opportunities.) They may work in retail stores, food service establishments, and gasoline service stations with some restrictions. A 14- or 15-year-old may not perform certain tasks in the retail and service industries such as baking, cooking, and operating certain equipment. They can, however, perform such tasks as bagging and carrying customer's orders; cashiering; clean-up work; grounds maintenance (the young worker may use vacuums and floor waxers, but he or she cannot use power-driven mowers, cutters, and trimmers); and delivery work by foot, bicycle, or public transportation.

- *Youth age 16 and 17*—Except in states that have laws limiting work hours, these youth may work any time for unlimited hours in all jobs not declared hazardous by the Secretary of Labor.

- *Youth age 18 and older*—These workers may perform any task, whether defined as hazardous or not.

The FLSA contains provisions for circumstances when employers can pay less than the federal minimum wage to students enrolled in specific full-time student programs. These programs are rare, and employers must obtain a special certificate from the U.S. Department of Labor. The FLSA also allows workers with disabilities in supported employment programs to be employed at wage rates that may be below the statutory minimum, but wages paid must always be commensurate with the workers' productivity as compared with the productivity of workers without disabilities performing the same tasks. To pay a wage rate below the statutory minimum, an employer must obtain a special minimum wage certificate from the U.S. Department of Labor.

Useful summary resources on the FLSA as it applies to work-based experiences are available from the National Center on Secondary Education and Transition (2008). Johnson et al. (2005) advised transition specialists to consult with the U.S. Department of Labor, Employment Standards Administration, Wage and Hour Division Regional Office, for additional guidance, as well as state and local government agencies in cases where clarification of an employment relationship may be necessary. It is important to know, however, that the U.S. Department of Labor, with the guidelines summarized previously, has made it clear that it agrees that there is a valuable educational purpose to work experiences of all kinds. The guidelines for how the FLSA applies to transition programs strikes an important balance between protecting workers' rights for fair compensation and allowing employers to make their workplaces available for youth to learn about work and to acquire work skills.

Nondiscrimination and Reasonable Accommodations

The ADA is considered a landmark civil rights law that, among other things, prohibits discrimination by employers against job candidates and employees with disabilities. Title I of the ADA requires private employers with 15 or more employees, as well as state and local governments (regardless of how many employees they have), to make reasonable accommodations for qualified job applicants and employees with disabilities. Under the law, *reasonable accommodations* are adjustments and modifications that range from making the physical work environment accessible to providing assistive technology to offering flexible work scheduling for qualified individuals. *Qualified individuals* are those who can perform the essential functions of the job, with or without reasonable accommodations.

Reasonable accommodations are designed to enable individuals to perform essential functions of a job (i.e., those fundamental tasks required of a position, often represented in a job description). Reasonable accommodations also pertain to enabling individuals to enjoy equal benefits and privileges of employment, such as fringe benefits, office social functions, and staff meetings. An employer is not required to provide any accommodation that would constitute an undue hardship (i.e., something that imposes significant difficulty or expense or that fundamentally alters the operation of the business). This is distinctly different from education settings governed by the Individuals with Disabilities Education Improvement Act (IDEA) of 2004 (PL 108-446), under which schools must provide learning and physical accommodations if they are identified as necessary in the IEP.

Legally required reasonable accommodations in the context of youth work experiences only apply to paid employment, when the youth can reasonably be expected to perform the essential functions of a job *and* when the cost and difficulty of providing the accommodations are not excessive. For work experiences in which there is no legal employer–employee relationship (e.g., many volunteer positions, unpaid internships, career explorations, job shadowing opportunities), employers are not required to provide accommodations, reasonable or not. It should be noted, however, that there are some unpaid work situations in which elements of the employment relationship exist, such as when volunteers are provided with benefits (e.g., insurance, worker's compensation) or when such work is required for or regularly leads to paid positions with the employer (e.g., some internships). In such situations, the reasonable accommodations provisions of the ADA apply.

Many youth will be able to perform jobs with standard job descriptions with or without accommodations. Even if the accommodations are extensive, such as wheelchair accessibility or modified keyboards, the employer must offer them if they are not an undue hardship on the company. Many individuals in transition programs, however, may only be able to perform some tasks within a standard job description. In these cases, the employer is under no obligation to provide accommodations or to hire the youth. As will be discussed throughout this book, however, it is important to note that necessary accommodations are most often accepted by employers as minimally intrusive and ultimately beneficial to a worker's performance on the job when presented in the context of how they will help make the work experience successful. Often, employers are quite willing to work with youth and transition specialists in implementing necessary accommodations, no matter the circumstance of the youth or the presence or absence of a legal obligation, as long as they receive competent help and service from transition specialists.

The ADA directly applies to many youth in transition who are seeking and will be hired into regular jobs as part of their transition experience. It will continue to apply to youth as they seek and enter employment as adults. It is therefore important for youth to be aware of their rights if they require an accommodation. They also will need to decide how and when to disclose their disability and to ask for accommodations. Chapter 4 discusses disclosure considerations in detail.

Furthermore, the need for and type of accommodations are often part of the negotiation with employers when the youth is establishing a relationship with an employer. Considerations in negotiations with employers about establishing workplace supports and accommodations will also be covered in later chapters. Ultimately, when accommodations are needed, it is important to prepare or assist youth to negotiate accommodations with the employers who host work experiences (see Chapter 3).

SUMMARY

This chapter reviewed the types of work experiences and their functions, as well as how and when they may be used to prepare youth in their career development. There are many junctures throughout a youth's educational program, and even well after school, when work experiences might be introduced. Although there is an ideal and logical order in which different work experiences might be introduced to youth, no hard-and-fast rule exists as to when or in what order youth should be exposed to work experiences. This often depends on the available educational services and a host of other circumstances, which may be out of the control of youth and the transition specialists who are assisting them. Nevertheless, the standard is that the earlier and more often youth are exposed to career and work options, the better the outcome.

This chapter also introduced a conceptual model for the process of establishing and supporting work-based learning opportunities. The mechanics of this process will be covered in subsequent chapters. This chapter also introduced aspects of quality that should be considered as youth move into and through work experiences. Ideally, work experiences are characterized by clear goals and expectations, clearly defined roles of various people involved with youth at the workplace, purposeful feedback on youth performance in the workplace, and linkages from what was learned in the workplace to what is learned in other aspects of the youth's education and transition programs. Legal aspects of work experience relating to compensation and conditions of work were also discussed.

Overall, this chapter presented considerations for organizing activity so the greatest positive impact can be pursued for youth work experience. The remainder of this book will discuss strategies to make that happen: how youth must participate in planning work experiences, considerations for disclosing disability and asking for accommodations, ways to involve families in work experience planning and implementation, strategies for recruiting and retaining employer partners, ways to support and mentor youth in the workplace, considerations for linking work experience with other curriculum requirements, and tips on connecting and partnering with other professionals and programs to foster and sustain work experience success. The stage has been set. Now use the remainder of this book to help make work happen for youth!

REFERENCES

Americans with Disabilities Act (ADA) of 1990, PL 101-336, 42 U.S.C. 12101 *et seq.*
Brolin, D. (1995). *Career education: A functional life skills approach* (3rd ed.). Upper Saddle River, NJ: Prentice Hall.

Fair Labor Standards Act (FLSA) of 1938, PL 75-718, 29 U.S.C. 201 *et seq.*

Flexer, R., Baer, R., Luft, P., & Simmons, T. (2008). *Transition planning for secondary students with disabilities* (2nd ed). Upper Saddle River, NJ: Pearson/ Merrill Prentice Hall.

Individuals with Disabilities Education Improvement Act of 2004, PL 108-446, 20 U.S.C. 1400 *et seq.*

Johnson, D., Sword, C., & Habhegger, B. (2005). *Handbook for implementing a comprehensive work-based learning program according to the Fair Labor Standards Act.* Minneapolis: University of Minnesota, Institute on Community Integration.

Kansas City Kansas Public Schools. (2007). *Quality work-based learning toolkit: Workplace partner guide to the work-based learning plan.* Retrieved November 10, 2007, from http://www.nww.org/qwbl/tools/kcktoolkit/guides/partners_guide_wbl.pdf

National Alliance for Secondary Education and Transition (NASET). (2005). *National standards and quality indicators: Transition toolkit for systems improvement.* Minneapolis: University of Minnesota, National Center on Secondary Education and Transition.

National Center on Secondary Education and Transition. (2008). *Essential tools: Handbook for implementing a comprehensive work-based learning program according to the Fair Labor Standards Act.* Retrieved August 1, 2008, from http://www.ncset.org/publications/essentialtools/flsa/default.asp

Simon, M., Cobb, B., Halloran, W., Norman, M., & Bourexis, P. (1994). *Meeting the needs of youth with disabilities: Handbook for implementing community-based vocational education programs according to the Fair Labor Standards Act.* Fort Collins: Colorado State University.

Simon, M., & Halloran, W. (1994). Community-based vocational education: Guidelines for complying with the Fair Labor Standards Act. *Journal of the Association for Severely Handicapped, 19,* 52–60.

3

• • •

Planning for Work Experiences

Richard G. Luecking and George P. Tilson

This chapter provides the reader with

- Ways of gathering information for planning work experiences
- Guiding principles and considerations for planning work experiences
- The Positive Personal Profile as a useful tool in planning work experiences
- A Learning Lab on work experience planning

"My teacher always asked me what I liked to do. I liked that."

High school student who had several successful work experiences

Susi lived with a foster family for most of her life. During her last 2 years in school, she was placed in food service and cleaning work experiences at an eldercare facility. She was not placed there because she was interested in those jobs or because she had skills that might be further developed in these jobs. Rather, the school had a long-standing relationship with each of these employers. These employers allowed special education students from the school to rotate through 3-month trial work experiences. Susi was not involved in any of the decision making related to the work experiences, nor was she ever asked to contribute to the planning for the experience. She hated working at the eldercare facility and did poorly there. Also, her foster family changed twice during her secondary school years, leading to confusion about how she would get to work and with whom teachers should communicate about Susi's work experience schedule. Susi, her teacher, and her foster families struggled with managing her attendance throughout these experiences. By the time she was 21 and ready to exit school, Susi still had no prospects for adult employment. She is now on a waiting list for referral to an adult employment agency for help obtaining a job.

Chris loves baseball and knows everything about the players and the sport. He told anyone he met that his dream job would be connected to baseball. Chris

41

has a pleasant personality and is always excited about his work. His high school schedule combines classroom work in life skills with on-the-job training and experience. When planning for his initial work experience began, his love of baseball figured prominently in the discussions with his transition specialist. A profile was developed that listed his interests (baseball, of course!), skills (meeting new people and following directions), and accommodation needs (initial coaching on the job). When Chris's transition specialist learned that the local minor league baseball team was recruiting employees for the upcoming season, Chris applied and landed a job as a part-time usher and greeter. He was ecstatic! Chris's supervisors at the baseball stadium willingly learned from the transition specialist how to monitor his tasks and provide feedback. Chris's job worked out so well that, even before he exited high school, the team contacted him directly to ask him to return for the next season.

Charging headlong toward a goal without adequate planning is never a good idea, as Susi's case illustrates. However, careful, individualized planning that features informed choices by the youth can be a great springboard to success at the workplace, as was the case for Chris. Planning for work experiences is both a science and an art. It is a science in the sense that there are a number of well-validated assessment instruments that can help identify skills, interests, and aptitudes of youth. It is an art in that there are creative ways to augment information gathered from assessments with other useful information about youth characteristics. All available information about youth can then be used to identify and plan for potential work experiences.

This chapter discusses ways of gathering information in planning for work experiences, outlines guiding principles of planning for work experiences, and presents a useful tool to guide planning for work experiences.

GATHERING INFORMATION FOR WORK EXPERIENCE PLANNING

Since the advent of the Individuals with Disabilities Education Act of 1990 (PL 101-476), planning for transition from school to work and adult life has been a federal mandate. Transition assessment is a foundation of this planning (Sax & Thoma, 2002; Sitlington, Neubert, Begun, Lombard, & Leconte, 2007). Sitlington et al. (2007) defined *transition assessment* as "an ongoing process of collecting information on the student's strengths, needs, preferences, and interests as they relate to the demands of current and future living, learning, and working environments" (p. 2). This type of information gathering enables youth, families, special educators, transition specialists, and other people assisting youth to make decisions about educational goals, postschool work and community living goals, and ultimately career goals. Although transition assessment offers useful information to help plan activities for a host of important transition issues, this chapter focuses on how to use this information for a subset—albeit a very important subset—of transition activities. That is, what will this information tell us about helping youth plan for work experiences and jobs?

There are a host of formal assessments that gather various types of information about youth competencies and interests. Traditional and formal assessments include standardized tests, such as those available from commercial publishers.

Many of these tests must be administered by trained professionals, whereas others can be administered by classroom teachers or career specialists. The purposes of these tests include a range of targeted assessment areas including general aptitude, adaptive behavior, cognitive or learning aptitude, occupational interests, personality/social skills, and learning styles. These various assessments can have an important place in information gathering that precedes a work experience. It is therefore useful for transition specialists who are facilitating work experiences to be familiar with the range and uses of transition assessments so that they may periodically glean information to plan and support work experiences. For detailed summaries of these various assessments and how they apply in transition planning, see Sitlington et al. (2007) and Timmons, Podmosko, Bremer, Lavin, and Wills (2004).

Traditional paper-and-pencil assessments, however, may limit thinking about potential work experiences for individuals with disabilities, especially those with significant disabilities (Inge, Targett, & Armstrong, 2007). Not only are they often less than perfect predictors of youth performance, but they often lead to conclusions that youth are not ready or able to work in a chosen occupational area. Paper-and-pencil tests do not fairly evaluate an individual's aptitude or potential if the person has trouble taking tests due to learning disabilities, cognitive comprehension, language proficiency, or a test's cultural bias. Thus, information gleaned from such tests and assessments may be useful in the larger picture of the person's abilities and interests, but one should not solely rely on them as a determinant of work experience planning. More direct and immediately relevant ways exist to gather useful information about youth and inform the planning for work experiences.

Additional sources of information about youth that are useful in work experience planning include school and program records, interviews and questionnaires, observations in various school and natural environments, situational assessments, and portfolio assessments (Rogan, Grossi, & Gajewski, 2002). Table 3.1 summarizes various methods of gathering information for work experience planning.

Families are often key contributors to work experience planning. They know the youth best and can therefore contribute valuable information about youth traits and preferences. They often have unique insights into youth motivation, interpersonal behavior, self-esteem, and interests. For youth with significant disabilities who are not easily able to express their own preferences, families can be the foundation for planning and are often actively involved in the planning for work experiences.

Although the process of assessment is useful for a number of purposes, there is little value to the information unless there is an end goal associated with it. In the context of planning for work experiences, any assessment information should be used to determine

- What type of work experience environment is appropriate for the individual youth
- Considerations for matching individual traits of youth to potential work experience sites
- How specific barriers might need to be accommodated in a work experience
- How the work experience will pave the way for career and employment planning
- Where to look for a work experience for individual youth

Table 3.1.   Methods for gathering information for work experience planning

Method	Description and function in planning
Formal assessments	Includes standardized tests such as those available from commercial publishers, which can target a range of assessment areas including general aptitude, adaptive behavior, cognitive or learning aptitude, occupational interests, personality/social skills, and learning styles
School or program records	Courses taken, grades, test scores, attendance records, individualized education programs, and any documentation of youth participation and performance
Interviews	Interviews with youth, family members, teachers, social service professionals, counselors, or anyone who knows the youth well to determine unique interests, traits, skills, and needs for accommodations
Observations	Watching the youth in typical daily environments and activities to identify patterns of behavior, personal preferences, task performance skills, and so forth
Situational assessments	Observing youth in situations that resemble potential future work environments to determine task performance skill and potential future worksite support needs
Portfolio assessment	Samples of youth work behavior over time, such as performance reviews, functional résumé, sample supervisor recommendations, pictures of past work performed, or any other material chosen by the youth that represents their activities and accomplishments
Positive Personal Profile	An inventory of all the attributes of the youth that will be relevant to identifying potential work experiences and jobs; information obtained from multiple sources that becomes a compilation of the youth's dreams and goals, interests, talents, skills, knowledge, learning styles, values, positive personality traits, environmental preferences, dislikes, life and work experiences, support system, specific challenges, creative solutions and accommodations, and creative possibilities and ideas for pursuing work experiences

Planning for work experiences is always better served when it is driven by positive youth traits, as opposed to perceived deficits.

GUIDING PRINCIPLES OF PLANNING WORK EXPERIENCES

Two concepts should drive good work experience planning. First, planning should be individualized and person-centered, as one size does not fit all. Each youth has unique interests, talents, and needs for support, regardless of disability label or educational circumstance. Second, planning should feature self-determination and informed choice. Each individual has preferences and should be given an opportunity to express them. Accordingly, transition specialists should follow assessment and planning principles that incorporate these concepts and that have been espoused by many experts in transition (Rogan et al., 2002; Sitlington et al., 2007; Wehman, 2006; Wehmeyer, 2002). These principles apply to the context of work experience planning:

- All youth have unique talents and gifts.
- Assessment should focus on these talents and preferences, rather than on deficits. When challenges are identified, supports and accommodations to minimize the effects of the challenges should be considered.

Turning "Negatives" into "Positives"

Roy is a high school junior who has received special education services since junior high school because of identified learning and emotional disabilities. He and his transition specialist began talking about a work internship experience to complement his academic curriculum. When the transition specialist began reviewing Roy's file, however, she found a wealth of information summarizing his academic deficits and "problem" behaviors. Without another way of viewing Roy's traits, this information's only value was to eliminate various work environments. She needed another perspective.

She talked at length with Roy, his father, and other teachers who knew him. She soon came to a new view of Roy. Instead of seeing him as his files seemed to emphasize, she used other information to guide the planning for his work experience. According to the files, Roy has attention deficit-hyperactivity disorder, can't sit still, can't concentrate on tasks, and has limited academic skills, reading several grades below his level in school. What his father and others said was that he is an active guy, likes to be in environments where he can move around, likes variety in tasks, can follow oral directions well, and loves cars.

With this more useful information, it did not take long for Roy and his transition specialist to find an internship at an auto parts store, where he helped to retrieve parts from inventory, helped customers find parts, and kept shelves stocked. He became a favorite of one of the store's assistant managers, who later helped Roy convert the internship experience into a part-time paid job that he held throughout the rest of high school.

- Youth should be directly involved in planning and should be empowered to provide information that reflects their interests, talents, positive traits, and need for accommodations and supports.
- Families should be given opportunities to be involved in planning decisions and encouraged to contribute information and suggestions about the youth's history and experiences during the planning.
- Based on the type of information and the background of youth, various methods of collecting information should be used, including formal assessment information, school and employment records, interviews with youth and those who know them well, and observations of youth in a natural situation.
- As much information as possible should be collected in natural, rather than simulated, environments and situations.
- Youth should be given supports, modifications, and accommodations as necessary when engaging in assessment and planning activities.

Self-determination is just as valuable in work experience planning as it is in any aspect of transition assessment or planning activity. The following definition of *self-determination* has been supported by the Division on Career Development and Transition of the Council on Exceptional Children.

> Self-determination is a combination of skills, knowledge, and beliefs that enable a person to engage in goal directed, self-regulated, autonomous behavior. Self-determination is an understanding of one's strengths and limitations together

with a belief in oneself as capable and effective. Then acting on the basis of these skills and attitudes, individuals have a great ability to take control of their lives and assume the roles of adults in society. (Field, Martin, Miller, Ward, & Wehmeyer, 1998)

Youth should be encouraged to learn to be the final voice in work experience planning. Youth are self-determined during the planning for work experiences when they

- Are able to list tasks that they perform well
- Can list hobbies, favorite leisure opportunities, and areas of interest
- Know what accommodations they might need and can ask for them, both during the planning process and in the workplace
- Can ask reasonable questions about what is expected during the work experience
- Understand the purpose of the prospective work experience
- To the fullest extent possible, are able to express their preferences about aspects of the work experience (e.g., location, schedules, tasks, accommodation needs)
- Can list, discuss, and identify what they learned from previous work experiences

This is the information that will ultimately guide what type of work experiences youth have, what they learn from these experiences, and what the experiences do to prepare them for eventual jobs and careers. Many youth will not have been exposed to a wide range of options from which to make choices. Therefore, it will sometimes be difficult to determine clear preferences during work experience planning. When this is the case, given limited information available, often the planning for work experience is done from a perspective of "Let's see what we and the youth can learn from this experience." The youth, however, should be fully involved in the planning and implementation of the work experience and should be fully aware of what can be expected from it. Then, the work experiences themselves will often act as ways of gathering important experience from which to inform future work experience and employment planning. As articulated by Sax and Thoma (2002), we "have no right to plan for another without their participation or permission" (p. 14).

THE POSITIVE PERSONAL PROFILE

One approach that incorporates features of individualized, self-determined, and positive-oriented planning is the Positive Personal Profile (Tilson & Cuozzo, 2001). The use of the Positive Personal Profile in job development activities for individuals with disabilities is documented in detail elsewhere (e.g., Luecking, Fabian, & Tilson, 2004), but its features apply equally as well to planning for any type of work experience for youth. A Positive Personal Profile is a practical way to "take inventory" of an individual's attributes that will be relevant to identifying potential work experiences and jobs, as well as later job searches, job matches, job retention, and long-range career development. It is a mechanism for collecting information from a variety of sources, including traditional assessments, school records, observations, and interviews and discussions with youth and people who know them well, including family members, teachers, youth workers, and others.

The Positive Personal Profile is not a formal assessment but rather a way of gathering information about youth and their traits that will be helpful in planning for and finding work experiences and jobs. The components of the Positive Personal Profile include a compilation of basic information, including the youth's dreams and goals, interests, talents, skills, knowledge, learning styles, values, positive personality traits, environmental preferences, dislikes, life and work experiences, support system, specific challenges, creative solutions and accommodations, and creative possibilities and ideas for pursuing work experiences. The Positive Personal Profile can form the basis for developing goals on individualized education programs and transition plans, but in the context of this book it can be used as the basis for pursuing the right work experience. It is a means of ensuring that the transition specialist and others helping the youth have a clear picture of the youth's positive attributes, as well as areas where the youth may need support or accommodations. This information can then be used to identify and pursue work experience opportunities from which to build a "way to work."

The Positive Personal Profile has a number of other practical uses. It can be used as a worksheet to help in the development of résumés or assist the youth in preparing for interviews. It can be used to develop goals for an individualized work experience or job search plan. It is a natural and useful prelude to guide the search for the optimal work experience that is matched to youth characteristics and circumstances. At its most practical level, when a prospective employer asks the youth, "Tell me about yourself," the youth can recall highlights from the profile. A youth's positive attributes are always the basis for securing the work experience. Then, the necessary accommodations and supports can be negotiated based on what the youth has to offer.

See Appendix 3.1 for a sample Positive Personal Profile and Appendix 3.2 for a blank version. The reader can use the Positive Personal Profile Interview Sheet in Appendix 3.3 to gather useful information from the youth, family members, or others who know the youth well. This information, which positively profiles the youth, can be a useful basis for planning for work experiences and jobs. The components of the Positive Personal Profile are described in the following sections.

Dreams and Goals

The place to start any inventory of a youth's attributes is to identify the "big picture" of his or her aspirations. Almost everyone can say what they dream to be, however unrealistic it may seem to others: actor, basketball star, rap artist, doctor, homeowner, rich. These dreams suggest areas of interest and are places to start the discussion when planning for work experience. The teacher's job is not to diminish these goals but to acknowledge them and suggest that the path to these goals requires various stepping stones. Remember, a youth's goals will change with experience, not by adult judgments of what those dreams should be.

After a youth has identified a career dream, you can acknowledge the general field of interest and plan from that point. For example, when a youth says that he wants to be professional basketball player, he is stating a dream. You can use that as a starting point for connecting how a work experience contributes to that dream.

Youth with the seemingly loftiest dreams can obtain work experiences with some connection—however remote—to that dream occupation. Some quickly relinquish their dream occupation as a result of a work experience that did not turn out as expected. Even if unsuccessful, however, important learning takes place.

Talents, Skills, and Knowledge

Everyone has certain "natural gifts," talents, or things for which they simply have a knack. Often, youth's skills can be identified simply by asking them, "What do people compliment you about?" Of course, the formal and informal assessments discussed previously can be good sources of information about youth's talents and skills, as long as the focus is on aptitudes and skills rather than deficits. In all work experience planning, the objective is to help youth put their best foot forward. Thus, the youth's profile should list as many of these skills and talents as possible.

Skills fall under many categories: academic, artistic, manual, physical, social. These skill sets apply to everyone, but it is particularly useful to identify alternative skill areas when academic performance is low. Remember that skills can be gleaned from a youth's hobbies, interests, and leisure pursuits.

Learning Styles

The transition specialist should determine the youth's learning style. Does the youth learn best by hearing information, reading it, or being shown how to perform a task? Assessments will often reveal this information, but families, teachers, and the youth themselves can often say what type of instruction yields the best learning for the youth. When planning for work experiences, it is important to understand how learning styles affect the youth with regard to the organization of the work environment, who helps youth learn the work tasks, how youth are helped to learn the work tasks, and what types of follow-up support youth may need after they are on the jobsite.

Interests

Often, a youth's hobbies and leisure pursuits can provide ideas for potential work experiences. These interests often generalize not only to a work or jobsite choice, but also to later career pursuits. Youth, families, and transition specialists can use information about the youth's interests to craft a work experience plan. Sports, fashion, music, cars, cooking, and a host of other potential areas of interest may suggest types of work experiences to pursue.

Many youth with disabilities have a narrow set of interests simply because they have had limited opportunities to explore the world around them. Remember that experience precedes interests. One work experience will often spark interests that will help to refine the next work experience search. As experience broadens, so do interests. Thus, a youth should not be discouraged from trying a work experience outside of his or her current interests, as long as the youth is fully involved in the decision-making process.

Positive Personality Traits

What is it that people really like about the youth? Ability to stay focused on a detailed task? Friendly disposition? Nice smile? Honesty? Sense of humor?

Determination? Lots of energy? Although everyone has personality traits that are less than ideal, they are not the basis on which we try to sell ourselves to a prospective employer and not what we build our careers around. Find out what people see as the best features of each youth, and use that information to plan for work experiences that will take advantage of these traits.

Values

What we value in life is often closely related to our personality and temperament. In terms of work experience planning, values that youth hold may be useful in determining what kind of company they want to work for, what kind of work environment is desired, and what kinds of demands can be made of the youth. Values are individual; they often reflect family, cultural, and societal views. Work experience planning is thus often informed by the individual values held by youth. Does the youth value hard work or a more deliberate pace? Being alone or being around lots of people? Making money or making a difference? Lots of excitement or a quiet environment? Recognition or being in the background? Does the youth have faith-based values that may favor one type of workplace or the conditions of work? The list is endless, but the values that are uncovered can be of great help in directing youth to work experiences that fit them well.

Environmental Preferences

Everyone has a unique rhythm when responding to different situations and environments. Does the youth prefer routine or varied tasks? Is a youth's temperament suited to a fast-paced work environment where things change rapidly? Does the youth like to be outdoors? Does the youth favor work in a cubicle to avoid distraction or a noisy environment with lots of activity? Does the youth prefer music in the background or a totally quiet setting? These preferences should be considered when planning because they can make the work experience either successful or miserable for the youth.

Dislikes

Dislikes are not simply the opposite of environmental preferences; rather, they encompass a broader set of circumstances. Everyone has dislikes that would make a work experience miserable if they had to be endured on the job. A good question to ask youth is, "What is a job that you do *not* want to do?" Youth may not always know the answer to this question without a lot of previous experience. However, the youth or the family may have a good idea about what the youth really dislikes, such as getting dirty, being bored, loud noises, or sitting for long periods of time.

Life and Work Experiences

For youth who have had previous work experiences, it is beneficial to know what those experiences were and what tasks were performed. For youth who have had little or no work experience, it is helpful to know areas of life experience that could translate into a useful skill in a workplace. Have they sorted laundry, babysat, performed household chores, surfed the Internet, learned to use a motorized wheelchair, put together puzzles, or talked to a church group?

Planning for a successful work experience can benefit from all kinds of work and life experiences.

Support System

A youth's support system includes those people around the youth who can provide support, encouragement, and/or resources for planning, developing, and supporting the work experience. This system may include family, friends, neighbors, acquaintances, teachers, coaches, personal assistants, and social service agency personnel, among others. Any or all of these people may perform various roles such as advocacy, transporting the youth to the worksite, offering a service that makes the work experience possible, or simply standing on the sidelines offering encouragement to the youth.

The youth's support system may include family members and friends who simply have the youth's best interest at heart, as well as paid professionals who offer a service that the youth may need, such as those described Chapter 10. In some cases, the system of support will be extensive and offer a host of help to the youth. Other times, such support may be scarce in the youth's life. Planning for work experiences should therefore take into account how much or how little support exists for the youth as he or she pursues work-based opportunities.

Specific Challenges

When determining challenges in planning work experiences, the effects of a disability—not the disability itself—should be considered. For example, in pursuing work experiences, an intellectual disability is not a challenge, but the inability to read will be a challenge for some people with intellectual disabilities. Cerebral palsy is not a challenge, but unintelligible speech might be for some youth with cerebral palsy. Blindness is not a challenge, but lack of transportation access could be a challenge for a blind person who does not live close to public transit. Autism is not a challenge, but changes in familiar routine might be challenging for some youth with autism.

Specific life circumstances can also pose a challenge to work experiences, such as poverty, family problems, an abusive home environment, substance abuse, or any number of other situations or circumstances that might interfere with successful work experiences if not addressed in some way. Thus, a critical part of the Positive Personal Profile is to identify what might interfere with a youth's pursuit of his or her dreams or aspirations. Transition specialists then can help youth to find creative solutions or accommodations that may be necessary to pursue the work experience goal.

Solutions and Accommodations

As will be discussed in detail in Chapter 8, accommodations are creative solutions to specific challenges or barriers. They range from simple solutions, such as finding a co-worker to give the youth a ride to work, to technical ones, such as a communication board for a youth with no speech. Youth's Positive Personal Profiles will need to identify tentative solutions and accommodations so that challenges are not seen as insurmountable barriers to work, but rather as temporary obstructions that can be removed or minimized.

Possibilities and Ideas

This section of the Positive Personal Profile is simply a place to record any thoughts or brainstorms on work possibilities or any matter related to planning for the work experience—no matter how random or unrealistic they may seem. Thoughts can include ideas of employer leads, things to explore, actions to take, or simply reminders of what to consider. There will be plenty of opportunities to refine these ideas and thoughts as a work experience or job search plan is developed. In the meantime, consider these ideas as potential gems to be polished. They are included in the Positive Personal Profile so as not to lose those creative sparks of insight that might contribute direction to the pursuit of a work experience or job.

Taking the Next Step with the Positive Personal Profile

The ultimate purpose of the Positive Personal Profile is to provide information that will guide the youth's search for the right work experience or job. Information gleaned from the Positive Personal Profile can be used in the development of a résumé. It can be used to help prepare youth for interviews with prospective employers as they learn to present themselves and their skills in the best possible way. It can also be used to identify accommodation needs that will influence decisions about the need for disability disclosure (see Chapter 4). Most importantly, the Positive Personal Profile is the basis for finding the work experience that best fits the youth's characteristics.

The Work Experience/Job Search Plan in Appendix 3.4 is useful in framing the search for a well-matched work experience—a search that takes into account positive youth characteristics and the need for accommodation and support, which will help to bring out the best in the youth during the work experience. Of course, work experiences do not materialize out of thin air. It takes work to find employers who are willing to consider bringing youth into their workplaces. This work, however, will be made much easier and much more successful when youth and transition specialists are armed with the kind of positive and useful information that the Positive Personal Profile provides. This information, along with the strategies detailed in Chapters 6 and 7 about recruiting employers to provide work experiences and for keeping them happy when they agree to host youth, will yield the kinds of learning opportunities that show the "way to work."

SUMMARY

This chapter outlined important considerations in planning for youth work experiences and jobs. A host of ways of gathering information will assist in this planning, including formal assessments, observations, and interviews. This chapter also introduced principles that should guide the planning process. Among these principles is the concept of individualized and self-determined planning. Youth who are able to assume a greater responsibility for their actions related to work experience planning and behavior in the workplace will learn from the experience, will be able to use the experience to continue to build a career path, and will continue to achieve greater levels of independence in their life and careers.

A tool was also introduced, the Positive Personal Profile, which can help to organize information about youth. This information will help the youth to put their best foot forward when pursuing work and will help to identify considerations for personal preferences and needs for support and accommodations. This tool can be used for developing a résumé, preparing for interviews, and for organizing the actual work experience or job search. Sample forms are included to organize information for the profile.

The most important thing is for youth to experience work. Work experiences are ways of adding to the inventory of information available to the youth in making decisions about subsequent work experiences, future jobs, and ultimately careers. This chapter provided an outline of planning considerations, as well as a tool for gathering information useful in this planning. However, transition specialists should not get so bogged down in the process of planning that the next step of actually getting the work experience never happens. Planning is useful only to the extent that it leads to the goal. Not all work experiences will be ideal, but each work experience will be a chance for youth to learn more about work, how to work, and where to work.

LEARNING LAB: *Using the Positive Personal Profile*

---

1. Refer to the Positive Personal Profile Interview Sheet in Appendix 3.3, and answer the questions as if you were planning for yourself. After completing it, identify how closely the answers match up to the job that you now do and the working conditions associated with it. This will allow you to reflect on how well items in your own Positive Personal Profile might have influenced your choice of jobs and choice of career.

2. Use the Positive Personal Profile Interview Sheet in Appendix 3.3 to gather information about a youth you know. Chart out a work experience plan for that youth using the Work Experience/Job Search Plan in Appendix 3.4.

REFERENCES

Field, S., Martin, J., Miller, R., Ward, M., & Wehmeyer, M. (1998). Self-determination for persons with disabilities: A position statement of the Division on Career Development and Transition, Council for Exceptional Children. *Career Development for Exceptional Individuals, 21,* 113–128.

Individuals with Disabilities Education Act of 1990, PL 101-476, 20 U.S.C. 1400 *et seq.*

Inge, J.K., Targett, P.S., & Armstrong, A.J. (2007). Person-centered planning. In P. Wehman, K.J. Inge, & W.G. Revell, Jr. (Eds.), *Real work for real pay: Inclusive employment for people with disabilities* (pp. 57–73). Baltimore: Paul H. Brookes Publishing Co.

Luecking, R., Fabian, E., & Tilson, G. (2004). *Working relationships: Creating career opportunities for job seekers with disabilities through employer partnerships.* Baltimore: Paul H. Brookes Publishing Co.

Rogan, P., Grossi, T., & Gajewski, R. (2002). Vocational and career assessment. In C.L. Sax & C.A. Thoma, *Transition assessment: Wise practices for quality lives.* (pp. 103–117). Baltimore: Paul H. Brookes Publishing Co.

Sax, C.L., & Thoma, C.A. (2002). *Transition assessment: Wise practices for quality lives.* Baltimore: Paul H. Brookes Publishing Co.

Sitlington, P., Neubert, D., Begun, W., Lombard, R., & Leconte, P. (2007). *Assess for success: A practitioner's handbook on transition assessment* (2nd ed.). Thousand Oaks, CA: Corwin Press.

Tilson, G., & Cuozzo, L. (2001). *Positive Personal Profile.* Rockville, MD: TransCen.

Timmons, J., Podmosko, M., Bremer, C., Lavin, D., & Wills, J. (2004). *Career planning begins with assessment: A guide for professionals serving youth with educational and career development challenges.* Washington, DC: National Collaborative on Workforce and Disability for Youth.

Wehman, P. (2006). *Life beyond the classroom: Transition strategies for young people with disabilities* (4th ed.). Baltimore: Paul H. Brookes Publishing Co.

Wehmeyer, M. (2002). Self-determined assessment: Critical components for transition planning. In C.L. Sax & C.A. Thoma, *Transition assessment: Wise practices for quality lives* (pp. 25–38). Baltimore: Paul H. Brookes Publishing Co.

Appendix

- Sample Positive Personal Profile for Stacey
- Positive Personal Profile
- Positive Personal Profile Interview Sheet
- Work Experience/Job Search Plan

APPENDIX 3.1

Positive Personal Profile

Name: _Stacey_

Dreams and goals

To move her family out of the projects

To have a good job

To buy a house in a safe neighborhood

Talents

Working with young kids

Getting people and things organized

Being in control of a situation

Recognizing fashion

Quick learner

Skills and knowledge

Taking care of a household

Cooking

Getting around the neighborhood and beyond independently

Good survival skills—recognizing safe and unsafe situations

Learning styles

Show once, then use a checklist, sample, or reminder sheet

Likes to do hands-on things and likes to be able to move around

Likes listening to music—helps her to concentrate

Better working mainly on her own

Interests

Music (mainly R & B and some rap)

Window shopping

Fashion/decorating

Positive personality traits

Good perseverance

Quick learner

"Woman of few but wise words!"

Organized

Pleasant—never raises her voice

Giving

Nonjudgmental

Good caregiver

Good problem solver

Temperament

Calm

Focused

Committed

Tries not to stand out

Serious

Values

Family

Hard work

Safety and comfort

Taking care of others is important and a family duty

Clean and comfortable surroundings—making the environment you can control as pleasant as possible

APPENDIX 3.1 *(continued)*

Work experiences	Support system
School office as clerical support	*Very little—Mom has severe disabilities, including depression*
School cafeteria (didn't like so much—very, very noisy and the area was always dirty and smelly)	*Family at home consists of 12-year-old brother, 9-year-old sister, and 7-year-old cousin*
Household chores and child care (home, unpaid)	*Has a grandma and aunt on the South Side, but she doesn't see them often*
	Gets help from neighbor two apartments down on her floor and has a good friend who goes to another school

Specific challenges	Solutions and accommodations
Living situation and lack of solid support	*Finding her a mentor*
Difficulty with academics, particularly reading	*Helping her plan for a way out of the projects*
Has trouble asking for help	*Role-playing situations to practice asking for help*
Sometimes confused by money	

Work experience ideas and possibilities to explore

Clean office environment

Place where organizational skills are needed

Child care

Clothing store

Music store

APPENDIX 3.2

Positive Personal Profile

Name: _____

Dreams and goals	Talents
Skills and knowledge	**Learning styles**
Interests	**Positive personality traits**

Values	Environmental preferences
Dislikes	**Life and work experiences**
Support system	**Specific challenges**
Solutions and accommodations	**Possibilities and ideas**

APPENDIX 3.3

Positive Personal Profile Interview Sheet

Name: _____   Date: _____

Transition specialist: _____   Interviewee: _____

Relationship to youth	How long has the interviewee known the youth?
☐ Self ☐ Family member	☐ 0–3 years ☐ 3–5 years
☐ Friend/peer ☐ Service provider	☐ 5–10 years ☐ more than 10 years
☐ Other _____	☐ n/a (self)

Interests and preferences	
What are some activities the individual enjoys?	
What are preferred leisure time activities (e.g., sports, hobbies)?	
In what environmental conditions does he or she thrive (e.g., indoors/outdoors, noisy/quiet, many/few people, slow/quick pace, time of day)?	
What are some of his or her talents?	
How does he or she best learn a new task?	
Other comments	

APPENDIX 3.3 *(continued)*

Life and work experiences	
Please describe any paid or unpaid work experiences (including volunteer activities). Focus on the tasks completed rather than the place.	
What types of household chores are completed regularly (both assigned and voluntary)?	
In what community activities does he or she participate?	
Other comments	
Skills and knowledge	
Has the individual been involved in any specific vocational training?	
Can you describe his or her academic skills (reading, math, time, money)?	
Other comments	
Dislikes	
Are there particular activities he or she is known to dislike?	

APPENDIX 3.3 *(continued)*

Are there particular situations you recommend we avoid when searching for work experience or job opportunities?	
Other comments	

Accommodation and support needs	
What accommodations or supports are currently provided in school or other settings?	
What accommodations should be in place in the workplace for this individual (e.g., physical accessibility, technological, special schedule, personal care)?	
What supports might need to be maintained beyond the initial placement?	
Other comments	

Transportation resources	
How does the individual currently get around in the community?	
What transportation resources will be necessary in order for the individual to get to and from a worksite?	
Other comments	

APPENDIX 3.3 *(continued)*

Other general observations	
How would you describe his or her temperament?	
What characteristics do you most admire in the individual?	
Please explain a dream job for this youth.	
Can you describe any habits, routines, or idiosyncrasies the individual demonstrates?	
Is there any additional information you would like to share regarding this individual?	

Notes

APPENDIX 3.4

Work Experience/Job Search Plan

Date:_____ (initial)   _____ (subsequent)

Name:_____

Telephone number: _____

Transition specialist:_____

Information on file

☐ Résumé   ☐ Student information form

☐ Authorization/general release form   ☐ Photo release

Summary of Positive Personal Profile

Interests and preferences	Dislikes, issues, or concerns

Position desired

Geographical location preferred

Schedule preferred

☐ Part time   ☐ Full time

☐ Mornings   ☐ Afternoons   ☐ Evenings   ☐ Hours not available

Transportation resources

Potential accommodations needed

Potential support or resources

Additional training or assessment needed

Employers to contact	Date contacted	Outcome
1.		
2.		
3.		
4.		
5.		
6.		
7.		
8.		

Update contact with student	Quarterly review of plan
Employer	Position

4

• • •

Work Experience
and Disability Disclosure

Richard G. Luecking, Christy Stuart, and LaVerne A. Buchanan

This chapter provides the reader with

- Considerations for when to disclose disability
- Considerations for what to disclose about disability and accommodations
- Considerations for how to disclose disability and need for accommodations
- A Learning Lab on disability disclosure

"The expert on my disability is me."

Kirsten Davidson, self-advocate

In school, Nick is often defiant and oppositional with his teachers and argumentative with peers. As a result, he has been in and out of an alternative school program for students labeled as having serious emotional disabilities. Outside the classroom, Nick is usually friendly, converses easily, and makes good eye contact, but only with people he knows well. For his cooperative work experience, he wanted to work at a video game store. Because he often gets anxious around people he doesn't know, he invited his transition teacher to accompany him to a job interview that the teacher helped him arrange.

Nick came across well enough during the interview to convince the store manager about his knowledge and interest in video games. During the interview, the store manager, wondering why the teacher was with Nick, asked him if he had any trouble getting along with people. Nick responded truthfully that he sometimes gets nervous around people, which causes trouble for him at school. Asked by the manager what it would take for him to stay calm around the kids in the store, Nick replied, "I will ride my bike to work and wear off my stress before I get here." The manager agreed to hire him, and Nick went on to work successfully at the store. For Nick, disclosing manifestations of his disability did not cost him a shot at a work experience he wanted. It may have even helped him get the job because he was honest and impressed the manager with his idea of how he would calm himself.

Elaine works well with children and started a part-time volunteer work experience at a child care center. She has only moderate use of one arm, which is not immediately apparent to an onlooker. Because she is embarrassed about revealing or discussing her disability, she told no one at the child care center about it. Unfortunately, she was very slow to change diapers because of mobility restrictions caused by her disability. When her supervisor asked her why she was so slow, she was unwilling to discuss the problem and stopped coming to the worksite. When the supervisor later found out about Elaine's disability, she told Elaine's teacher that there were several ways she could have accommodated Elaine had she known about the disability. For Elaine, not disclosing her disability resulted in an opportunity lost.

Stephen is in a special education class for youth with intellectual disabilities. He cannot read but has good basic verbal communication skills and is very organized. He worked with his job coach to find potential work experiences that capitalize on his skills of organizing and sorting items. Because Stephen had no personal network to identify job opportunities, he agreed to have his job coach represent him to prospective employers. Also, because he needed several job accommodations, including a job coach to teach him new work tasks, Stephen agreed that his job coach could explain to prospective employers about his disabilities and his need for initial coaching on the job. After several interviews where he and his job coach met with prospective employers, he was hired by a bookstore to remove antitheft devices from music CDs and to remove covers from outdated and unsold magazines that the store sent back to the publisher for credit. Disclosing his disability was necessary in Stephen's case because of his need for representation in negotiating with the employer and his need for onsite coaching. Otherwise, he would likely never become employed.

The decision to disclose a disability is a very personal one. It is also one that has many ramifications—some useful, others problematic. It could mean succeeding in a workplace where accommodations and supports can be provided, as in Stephen's case, or failing because an effective accommodation for the disability was not made, as in Elaine's case. Disclosure could be the reason for getting a job, as in Nick's case. Alternatively, it could mean failing to get a job offer because an employer is uncomfortable with a stereotype associated with the disability, as could have happened with Nick. The latter is subtle discrimination, but it happens—and there is usually no way to prove it.

Youth, therefore, have many important questions to consider: Disclose or not? When? To whom? How? Such questions frequently arise for youth and their families, counselors, teachers, and other people in their lives who might help them pursue work experiences and jobs. This chapter addresses these questions and provides considerations for deciding how best to answer them.

WHETHER OR NOT TO DISCLOSE

For youth with visible disabilities, the decision to disclose is much easier. They most often will not need to disclose because it is clear that they have a disability.

However, they will often have to decide how and in what context to discuss with prospective and current employers and co-workers how their disabilities affect their work, which will be discussed later in the chapter. For youth with learning, intellectual, emotional, or some health-related disabilities, the decision becomes more complicated because their disabilities are not always readily apparent. These youth may understandably be reluctant to disclose information about the presence or the nature of their disability for fear of discrimination or negative perceptions.

Chapter 3 discussed ways to ensure that youth participate in and lead the planning for their work experiences. The concepts of self-determination and person-centered planning are equally as paramount in decisions about disability disclosure as they are in planning for work experiences. The choice about when and how to disclose personal information about a disability, as well as any need for accommodation and support, should always be made by the youth.

The youth's decision to disclose may change with circumstance. Disclosure may be necessary to ensure adequate accommodation in one situation, such as to a supervisor who can approve a flexed schedule. In another case, it may not be a good idea to disclose a disability to co-workers who do not need to know about it. Whatever the circumstance, the youth needs to make informed decisions about disclosure.

Guidance is often necessary to help youth decide whether or not to disclose a disability, as well as in their management of the decision. Nick's situation is a good example: He asked the teacher to help him, and it was his choice for the teacher to accompany him to the job interview. Although Nick did not name his disability, he was comfortable disclosing that he got anxious in certain situations. He was also ready to offer an accommodation that helped him to counter the manifestation of his anxiousness. It was an indirect disclosure, but it was enough to inform the employer of how Nick could work successfully in spite of past difficulties with people in other situations.

Many factors can influence the ultimate decision of whether or not disclosure is the best course of action in a given circumstance. Youth will often need guidance in making sound judgments regarding disclosure. Ultimately, youth who can articulate their needs and goals, and who have been coached on the selective sharing of personal information, enjoy greater control over disclosure decisions. To make these decisions, a youth needs to understand the advantages and disadvantages of disclosing personal information about his or her disability.

Advantages of Disclosure

Disability disclosure can create opportunities that may not otherwise be available without accommodations to minimize barriers to workplace participation. Proper accommodation and workplace support can make the difference between succeeding in the workplace and failing miserably. Here are some advantages to disclosing information about a disability.

- Disclosure makes it possible to receive reasonable accommodations under the Americans with Disabilities Act (PL 101-336). If an employer hires someone who is qualified to perform the essential functions of the job, the employer must provide reasonable accommodations—and employers obviously cannot provide accommodations if they are not aware of a disability. For example, Michael has attention-deficit/hyperactivity disorder and needs directions in written form because he will miss steps if they are presented verbally. When he was hired as a stock clerk at a warehouse, Michael told his boss that he would have no trouble keeping up with his assignments, but it would be important to have his daily instructions posted in the aisle where he primarily worked. His boss gladly complied.

• Disclosure ensures that youth get the help they need to perform well in the workplace. For example, Jared needed a job coach to help him learn tasks in every new work experience. He gave his job coach permission to tell prospective employers about this accommodation so that the coach could negotiate with employers about it.

• Disclosure gives youth the opportunity to fully present their abilities under conditions of effective accommodation. For example, in an interview to be an archivist intern with a local cable television station, Jason asserted that his encyclopedic knowledge of television shows would make his job easier and lead to high productivity and quality of work. Jason added that he would need to ask his supervisor to provide instructions in writing due to an oral processing disability. With this small accommodation, he informed the station manager, he thought he could do the job quickly and be available to help out with other tasks. Jason's articulate self-advocacy led to being accepted into what became a very successful internship experience.

• Disclosure provides the groundwork for advocating for additional accommodations and supports when task assignments change or when new co-workers or supervisors interact with the youth. For example, June's new boss wondered why she got an extra break in the afternoon but no one else did. June was able to explain that stamina was often an issue because of her neurological condition. An extra break enabled her to complete her assignments in the same time frame as the other staff members.

• Disclosure improves the youth's ability to advocate for him- or herself and to improve his or her self-image, as in Jason's experience at the television station.

• Disclosure can create a comfortable work environment in which the youth does not have to worry about keeping the disability a secret. For example, Liz has epilepsy. Her seizures are mostly under control, but in case she has one on the job, she wants her supervisors and co-workers to know how to respond.

Disadvantages to Disclosure

For various reasons, youth may decide that disclosure is not necessary or that it will create discomfort, stigma, or rejection. Here are some potential disadvantages to disclosing a disability.

• Disclosure can result in discrimination in consideration for a work experience or a job. For example, many youth with emotional disabilities may feel stigmatized by the label and choose not to tell anyone outside of school, especially employers who, because of misperceptions, might be reluctant to hire them if the employers knew about the disability.

• Disclosure can result in stereotyping or inaccurate perceptions of the youth's ability. For example, JaMarcus knows that his learning disability is accommodated well in school but doesn't want people to think he is "stupid," as he has occasionally been called as a child. Consequently, he does not want his work experience supervisor or his co-workers to know he has received special education services.

• Disclosure can lead to disparate treatment—either overly solicitous attention or exclusion. In either case, the youth is being treated differently than others. For example, Marcie told a co-worker that she has to take insulin shots every day for her diabetes. After that, her supervisor was reluctant to give her anything to do because he was afraid she would go into insulin shock. In another case, William feared that if any of his co-workers knew about his hospitalizations, he would never be accepted by them or included in any of their social activities.

• Disclosure can be difficult or embarrassing for the youth. For example, Jeannette is very sensitive about the fact that she has seizures and has opted to not tell anyone at her worksite.

• Disclosure can lead to ill treatment or suspicion from co-workers. For example, Paul was teased by co-workers at his last part-time job when one of them discovered that Paul has a learning disability. Paul has thus decided to keep his disability a secret from people at his next job.

Table 4.1 summarizes considerations for helping youth to decide when to disclose personal information about their disability. It is important to reiterate that the decision to disclose is ultimately and appropriately up to the youth; however, a teacher, job coach, transition professional, or advocate may need to prepare the youth to not only decide whether or not to disclose the disability, but also when, how, and to whom. The youth may need some preparation, perhaps through self-advocacy and self-determination training, and opportunities to practice disclosure, which will result in an increased level of comfort with and knowledge of their disability. The self-examination questionnaire in Appendix 4.1 can help youth to examine what they know about themselves and their disabilities as a prelude to deciding whether or not to disclose. The youth may also benefit from learning the most effective way to discuss disability and related accommodation needs. The next sections address these considerations.

Table 4.1. Deciding to disclose disability

It helps to disclose disability when it	It may not be a good idea to disclose disability when it
Is necessary in order to receive legally available accommodations	Can cause discrimination to occur
Enables supports for better workplace performance	Leads to stereotyped reactions or misperceptions about the youth's ability
Allows additional accommodations when job duties or supervisors change	Results in the youth being treated differently or unfairly
Improves self-advocacy skills	Makes the youth feel embarrassment or sensitivity
Promotes comfortable interactions with co-workers when they understand disability	Is possible that co-workers resent accommodations as special treatment

WHEN TO DISCLOSE

There are several possible junctures at which youth may have an opportunity to disclose their disabilities: during the initial contact with an employer, such as in a request for an interview, the scheduling of an interview, or during the interview itself; after the interview or acceptance into a work experience; or anytime after the work experience placement begins. Alternatively, the youth may decide to never disclose. No single "right" time or way to disclose disability exists, but there are important contexts to consider. When a youth has decided that disclosing a disability is necessary, helpful, or simply an empowering way to take proactive control of his or her life, certain settings and circumstances are more appropriate than others for disclosure.

When youth are pursuing unpaid work experiences such as job shadowing, work sampling, or unpaid internships, the issue of disclosure is different than when they are seeking a paid job. First, less is at stake in a volunteer situation because there are theoretically fewer expectations on the part of the employer for productivity. Also, a company may have fewer legal considerations in volunteer situations as opposed to when it is considering compensating the youth. Nevertheless, accommodation needs will often necessitate disclosure at various times in the work experience. The need for wheelchair access, for example, may have to be discussed on the telephone with a company prior to a volunteer experience for a particular youth. A youth who is deaf may require interpreters, in which case disclosure will be not only useful but necessary. A youth may require a teacher or job coach to accompany him or her to the worksite; disclosure about such a need may best be done during the initial contact with the company.

Alternatively, the youth may not want anyone at the worksite to know about the disability—or at least certain aspects of it. Youth may choose not to disclose at any juncture of the experience, whether it is while applying for it, at the first contact with the company, at the interview, or after the experience begins. Youth, however, can change their minds at any of these junctures for reasons both personal and practical. For example, they may become comfortable with certain supervisors or co-workers and feel safe disclosing their disabilities. Or, youth may find that asking for an accommodation, such as written rather than verbal instructions, is necessary to keep up with assignments. The choice to disclose is personal, but it is helpful to have someone available to counsel the youth on these decisions.

If a youth is applying for a paid job, the stakes may be a little higher—both for the youth, who benefits from the compensation, and for the employer, who has job performance expectations. For paid employment experiences, the decision about when to disclose varies with the phase of the job search or employment experience. When looking for a job, the considerations are different than when the youth has already started working. Ultimately, it is important to remember that accommodations in the workplace are only provided when a worker discloses his or her disability and requests job accommodations from the employer. Table 4.2 provides some contexts and examples about when youth may want to disclose their disabilities.

HOW AND WHAT TO DISCLOSE

Building self-awareness is critical. Each youth who is contemplating a work experience should be fully prepared to identify strengths, skills, and accommodation requirements. Disclosure of disability is a personal choice, but with or

Table 4.2. When to disclose a disability

Circumstance	Example
In a third-party phone call or reference	Employment specialists at the local One-Stop Career Center or other community agencies may have strong connections with local employers and may be willing to refer youth to a job opening. Youth should be counseled to decide about whether they want the counselor to disclose the youth's disability and, if so, how to represent it.
In a letter of application or résumé	Some individuals choose to disclose their disability in their résumé or letter of application. Having a disability may be viewed as a positive trait by some companies with disability recruitment programs. However, we generally recommend counseling a youth against this practice as it may cause an employer to decide not to interview the youth.
Preinterview	Disclosure prior to the interview is encouraged only when an accommodation is needed for the actual interview (e.g., wheelchair accessibility, sign language interpreter, a job coach to accompany the youth).
On the employment application	Youth may have several options if the employment application form asks something such as, "Do you have a limitation that may affect your performance on the job?" A youth may believe his disability is not a limitation on work performance and would therefore respond by answering, "No." On the other hand, the youth might decide that this is an opportunity to indicate he has a disability that will not limit performance if properly accommodated. Finally, he might decide not to answer the question and address the issue in an interview. There is always the risk that employers will discount the application if a disability is disclosed.
At the interview	A youth may or may not decide to disclose his or her disability during an interview. If the disability is visible, the youth may want to discuss the disability in the context of how it will not be a barrier to doing a good job, especially with proper accommodations. If the disability is not apparent, the youth will need to decide whether or not to disclose based on comfort level and self-confidence in the ability to articulate about it and potential accommodations.
After the job offer	Some youth will choose to disclose their disability after they have been offered the job. They want to be selected for their skills and positive attributes and worry that disclosure prior to selection may influence an interviewer's decision. Once hired, however, they may need accommodations to do essential functions of the job, so disclosure is necessary. Also, if the job requires medical or drug testing and the youth is taking medication that will show up in a screening, it will be an important time to disclose this to the employer.
During the course of employment	Sometimes youth will not recognize that aspects of their disability will negatively affect job performance without accommodations. This is especially true of youth with little job experience. It is always better to ask for an accommodation before job performance is questioned, but sometimes, after discussion with the employer, and maybe a teacher or job coach, an accommodation might be jointly identified that will improve the youth's ability to meet employers' performance requirements.
Never	If youth are able to perform job tasks to the satisfaction of the employer without accommodations or supports, it is not necessary to disclose disability.

Source: National Collaborative on Workforce and Disability for Youth (2005).

without specific reference to a disability, a discussion of relevant accommodations or alternative methods for completing work can take place. Employers are already arranging accommodations such as job restructuring, job sharing, and alternative methods of providing instruction and training to workers without disabilities. If such accommodations facilitate employee productivity, they are readily made. Thus, it is especially useful to present the need for accommodation in such a way that the company sees the benefit far more readily than they see the disability. Here are a few points of consideration that will help youth decide what personal disability information to disclose and how to disclose it.

- Prepare ahead of time. Youth will need to understand and be comfortable with their disabilities and accommodation needs so that they are prepared to discuss how these needs translate into what companies need to do to make it work for all involved. The activity in Appendix 4.1 is a useful place to start with youth if they decide to disclose.

- Be honest, be straightforward, and give factual information to make it easy for employers or co-workers to understand what the disability means for the youth and what it means for interactions with the youth.

- Relate comments to the immediate situation, such as how the youth's disability will affect (or not affect) the tasks assigned to the youth—not what it means in school or at home.

- Decide if it is necessary to name the disability or just identify accommodations. For example, youth can say either "My learning disability makes it hard for me to understand written directions" or "I learn better when I hear the directions than when someone writes them."

Often, it is useful to help youth develop a "script" they can practice with friends, teachers, relatives, or mentors. Most people find it easier to talk about the impact of a disability and how it will relate to a particular situation if they can practice it with people they know and trust. To prepare a disclosure script, youth can write or orally list positive attributes or strengths, identify challenges that they might expect at work or have experienced in the past at work, identify accommodations that have worked in the past and why, and consider how disclosing a disability can help the business or co-workers. The script should end with positive points about the youth or the requested accommodation. See Appendix 4.2 for a guide to preparing scripts.

TO WHOM TO DISCLOSE

To whom people choose to disclose their disabilities may depend a great deal on the position or role of the individual who will be the recipient of that information. Youth may choose and/or need to tell a prospective employer, a workplace supervisor, a workplace mentor, or a co-worker. When deciding to whom to disclose a disability, youth should consider the following questions.

- Does the person have the power or authority to help implement an accommodation?

- Can the person provide the accommodation?

Examples of Disclosure Scripts

"I'm really looking forward to this interview. I've heard so much about your company. I am checking to make sure the interview room can accommodate my wheelchair. That way I can more comfortably present my qualifications for this work experience."

"I like to stay busy, but I learn new jobs slowly. If my teacher comes with me to the job the first few times, I can learn what I need to do and stay busy at it."

"I am a very fast worker and get along with people well. In spite of my hearing impairment, I can lipread in face-to-face interaction. But I will need to communicate with my co-workers using email frequently and use TTY services and devices when using the phone."

"My energy and attention to detail would make me good at this job, and I would be very productive. I have an oral processing disability, which means that it helps when instructions are in writing rather than verbal. With this small accommodation, I know I can do the job quickly and then make myself available to help out others with their tasks."

"I really like this job, but I get anxious when there is so much noise. I work best in a more isolated area. I know I can do it better if I can move my workstation to another part of the office."

- Is the person responsible for hiring, promoting, or evaluating workplace performance?
- Is the person someone who can help provide support at the workplace?
- Can the person be trusted to keep disclosed information confidential?

If the answer is yes to any of these questions, then the person is probably someone to whom youth can consider disclosing disability information. Even if the answer is yes, however, youth may still choose not to disclose for reasons discussed previously.

A youth may also choose to disclose through a third party such as a job coach, teacher, or other transition professional who might act as an intermediary or "agent" when the youth cannot or is not prepared to do it for him- or herself. The next section outlines how this might be pursued.

REPRESENTING A YOUTH'S DISABILITY TO EMPLOYERS

Many youth will decide that it is necessary or desirable for someone to represent them in finding and negotiating work experiences because of communication challenges, significant support needs, or simply lack of confidence. By virtue of being a special education, transition, employment, or rehabilitation professional, many youth advocates are already readily identified as "disability" professionals.

Thus, anyone to whom these professionals introduce themselves already knows that they represent youth with disabilities. In that sense, any youth represented by these professionals are already "outed" as having a disability, and some measure of disclosure has taken place. Therefore, a youth's association with a transition, school, or employment service may, however indirectly, identify him or her as having a disability.

Youth, however, should still be empowered to exercise control over what, how, and to whom information about their disability should be disclosed, as discussed in previous sections. Importantly, professionals who represent youth in the pursuit, negotiation, and support of work experiences have an obligation to disclose information about youth's disabilities in a manner that is both respectful and appropriately presented. Third-party disclosure—that is, disclosure via a youth advocate—should always start with as a positive rendering of the youth's traits: "Jared is a fast worker when he gets the hang of a job," "Charley is really interested in technology and is well versed in computer applications," or "Jonelle can stay on task for long periods of time." Then, challenges that youth might expect at work or have experienced in the past are presented in the context of how they can be accommodated while sharing successful solutions: "Jared needs a job coach at the worksite to help him learn his tasks," "Charley needs a special keyboard for his computer," or "Jonelle will need a quiet place to work."

It helps to show how these accommodations or supports have worked in the past, as well as why and how these accommodations can be implemented to provide minimum intrusion on the company's operation: "I will be Jared's job coach and will work with him to learn the work tasks," "Charley will bring his own keyboard, and I will help him set it up at his workstation," or "Jonelle knows when to ask for help." In fact, it does not hurt for professionals and advocates who represent youth to prepare and practice their own disclosure script!

Remember that the disability label does not define the youth. It is not useful to say, for example, that "Dolores has an intellectual disability and can't read." Instead, one should say, "Dolores will take time to learn new tasks, but once she learns them she performs them well. And I will help teach her." It might be necessary or useful to explain the disability in terms of how to interact with youth: "Andrew has autism. Often people with autism have trouble with social interactions, particularly subtle meanings or metaphors. It is most effective to avoid teasing and be direct in your communication with him."

Whether representing the youth or helping youth learn how to represent themselves when making disclosure about a disability, there are some general considerations to keep in mind. Buchanan (2003) provided some guidelines to helping youth with issues related to disability disclosure (see page 75).

COUNSELING YOUTH ABOUT THEIR DISCLOSURE RIGHTS AND RESPONSIBILITIES

It is worth adding a final word about helping youth to decide if, when, and how to disclose personal disability information to employers or anyone else. The law provides certain rights designed to prevent discrimination, and widely accepted good transition practice provides guidance to professionals about ensuring that youth have a self-determined voice in disclosure decisions. Youth, however, must assume certain responsibilities to make effective decisions regarding disclosure.

Disclosure Guidelines for Youth Advocates (Buchanan, 2003)

Do

- Link discussion of disclosure to self-determination and self-advocacy
- Engage the youth in a discussion regarding thoughts and feelings on disclosing personal information
- Determine the reason and need for disclosure
- Weigh advantages and disadvantages of disclosing and not disclosing
- Plan and/or practice with youth on how to disclose personal information
- Determine who needs to have the personal information and why
- Limit information sharing to essential persons
- Assure the youth that both written and verbal information will be maintained in a confidential manner
- Get the permission of the youth (and parent/guardian, if necessary) to share personal information before disclosing to an employer or anyone else
- Relate disclosure comments to the actual situation, for example, in the context of how it will affect specific work situations or accommodations
- Get to know the youth well enough to be aware of accommodation needs
- Discuss private information in a private setting

Don't

- Share personal information about the youth without his or her consent (or the consent of parent/guardians when the youth is a minor)
- Discuss personal information about the youth with people who are not involved in his or her education or service delivery
- Ask personal questions in a group or public setting
- Leave written information in an area where it may be read by others not involved in delivering services to the youth
- Use confidential information for any reason(s) other than the purpose for which it was collected, disclosed, and indicated to youth and/or parent/guardian

Professionals and youth advocates will find it useful to counsel youth on not only their rights, but also their responsibilities to themselves and their employers, supervisors, mentors, and co-workers. The National Collaborative on Workforce and Disability for Youth (2005) provided guidance on this issue, as summarized in Table 4.3.

Table 4.3. Rights and responsibilities

Youth have the right to	Youth have the responsibility to
Have information about their disability treated confidentially and respectfully	Disclose their need for accommodations if they desire any work-related adjustments
	Search for jobs that match skills and interests
Seek information about hiring practices from any organization	Inform hiring managers or interviewers about the need for interview accommodations prior to an interview
Choose to disclose their disability at any time during the employment process	
	Identify appropriate and reasonable accommodations for an interview
Receive appropriate accommodations in an interview in order to demonstrate skills and competencies	Negotiate accommodations with an employer at the point of job offer and any time after beginning work
Be considered for job positions based on skill and merit	Demonstrate their skills and merits
	Be truthful, self-determined, and proactive
Have respectful questioning about their disability for the purpose of reasonable accommodation	
Be self-determined and proactive in disability disclosure decisions	

Source: National Collaborative on Workforce and Disability for Youth (2005).

SUMMARY

This chapter presented considerations about whether and under what circumstances youth may disclose personal information related to a disability. It also provided considerations and activities that professionals and advocates may use to help prepare youth to make disclosures of disability information. In all of these interactions, youth self-determination and self-advocacy should drive disclosure decisions. In addition, when it is important for employers and/or co-workers to know about a youth's disability and accommodation needs, it is the youth who should determine the method of disclosure.

The issue of disclosure is pertinent to any work experience, but more is at stake if disclosure decisions are related to a paid job. Hiring decisions are less likely to be influenced by the presence or absence of disability than by potential contribution of a job candidate to the company, especially when it is clear that value is being added to the employer's enterprise (Hernandez, 2000; Luecking, 2004; Magill, 1997; Unger, 1999). This has significant implications for planning for work experiences, individual job searches, identification of supports and accommodations, and managing job tasks. Youth self-awareness of strengths and support needs can significantly enhance the pursuit of the right job and related advocacy for accommodations, well beyond their initial exposure to work experiences and into their adult life.

LEARNING LAB: *Disclosure or No Disclosure?*

Read the following examples and consider how youth may be counseled to respond to the questions about disclosure. First consider the issues that might determine whether or not to disclose the disability, then consider why, when, what, to whom, and how. There are no right or wrong answers in this exercise, but use the information presented in this chapter when considering possible answers. (*Note:* Adapted from National Collaborative on Workforce and Disability for Youth, 2005.)

1. Andrea's anxiety has recently worsened around people, and it has affected her ability to concentrate on aspects of her work experience. Her psychiatrist has changed her medications and has made some recommendations to her regarding changes in her schedule.

   Disclose?

   Why?

   When?

   What?

   To whom?

   How?

2. Jolena has arranged an interview with the supervisor of a large department store to discuss a position as a sales clerk. She wonders how much her learning disability in math will affect her ability to run the cash register and make change.

   Disclose?

   Why?

   When?

   What?

   To whom?

   How?

3. José has scheduled an interview for an internship at a small technology company. He wonders if the building and the interview room will be accessible for his wheelchair.

   Disclose?

   Why?

   When?

   What?

   To whom?

   How?

4. Mi Ling has seizures that are mostly controlled by medication. She has mild cerebral palsy that affects her gait. She also has a mild speech impairment. Her co-workers have started to imitate her walk and her speech.

   Disclose?

   Why?

When?

What?

To whom?

How?

REFERENCES

Americans with Disabilities Act of 1990, PL 101-336, 42 U.S.C. 12101 *et seq.*

Buchanan, L. (2003). *The disclosure dilemma for advocates.* Washington, DC: George Washington University HEATH Resource Center.

Hernandez, B. (2000). Employer attitudes towards disability and their ADA employment rights: A literature review. *Journal of Rehabilitation, 16,* 83–88.

Luecking, R. (2004). *Essential tools: In their own words: Employer perspectives on youth with disabilities in the workplace.* Minneapolis: University of Minnesota, Institute on Community Integration, National Center on Secondary Education and Transition.

Magill, B. (1997). ADA accommodations: Don't have to break the bank. *HR Magazine, 42,* 84–89.

National Collaborative on Workforce and Disability for Youth. (2005). *The 411 on disability disclosure workbook.* Washington, DC: Institute for Educational Leadership.

Unger, D. (1999). Workplace supports: A view from employers who have hired supported employees. In G. Revell, K. Inge, D. Mank, & P. Wehman (Eds.), *The impact of supported employment for people with disabilities.* Richmond: Virginia Commonwealth University Rehabilitation Research and Training Center on Workplace Supports and Job Retention.

Appendix

- Just What Do You Know About Yourself and Your Disability?
- Practice Disclosure Script Activity

APPENDIX 4.1

Just What Do You Know About Yourself and Your Disability?

Complete the questionnaire below. For each question, check the box (yes, sometimes, or no) that best describes you.

Questions	Yes	Sometimes	No
1. Do you know what you do well in school?			
2. Do you know what you do well outside of school?			
3. Can you easily explain your skills and strengths to other people?			
4. Do you know how you learn the best?			
5. Do you inform your teacher how you learn best?			
6. Do you inform your employer how you learn best?			
7. Do you ask for help when you need it?			
8. Do you take responsibility for your own behavior?			
9. Do you feel proud of yourself?			
10. Do you set long-term and short-term goals for yourself?			
11. Do you create lists for yourself to help you achieve your goals?			
12. Are you present at your own IEP or 504 meetings?			
13. Do you participate in your own IEP or 504 meetings?			
14. Do you disclose your disability to others?			
15. Do you like the reaction you get when you inform someone about your disability?			
16. Do you practice disclosing your disability to others?			
17. Do you describe your disability differently depending on the setting or the people?			
18. Are there times you choose not to tell someone about your disability?			
19. Do you know what "reasonable accommodation" means?			

APPENDIX 4.1 *(continued)*

Questions	Yes	Sometimes	No
20. Do you know what accommodations you need in school in order to be successful?			
21. Do you know what accommodations you need on the job in order to be successful?			
22. Do you practice asking for the accommodations you need in school?			
23. Do you practice asking for the accommodations you need on the job?			

If you answered **YES** to many of the questions, you should be very proud of yourself! You definitely have a good sense of yourself and your disability. This means you're on the road to being a very self-determined individual! Of course you realized that there will always be room for improvement. Reflect on the questions you answered with a NO, and create some short-term goals designed to strengthen your areas of limitations.

If you answered **SOMETIMES** to many of the questions, you possess some very good skills in understanding yourself and your disability, but you have some specific areas that need to be developed. Once you have identified your strengths (the questions you answered with a YES), list the others areas that need work (the questions you answered with a NO) and prioritize them. Decide which areas of need are most important to focus on right now, and create some short-term goals to begin to strengthen your weaker spots.

If you answered **NO** to many of the questions, you are at the beginning stage of understanding yourself and your disability. Take the next step and seek out others whom you trust and who know you well; ask them to help you sort out your areas of strengths and needs (you probably have more strengths than you realize). Share the results of the questionnaire with these individuals and ask them for assistance in developing some short-term goals for the purpose of gaining a better understanding of yourself.

Practice Disclosure Script Activity

To help youth practice explaining their disabilities, it helps to have them write out, or memorize, a script. It should say what the youth wants to communicate in a way that someone who knows very little about disabilities will understand.

Here are some steps to follow to help youth prepare and practice a script:

Step 1 Have the youth write or say things about his or her positive attributes.

Examples: "I am friendly."

"I work fast."

"I am organized."

Step 2 Have the youth identify the limitations or challenges he or she faces because of the disability.

Examples: "I need help learning new tasks."

"I need to work in a quiet place."

"I need more breaks."

"I need wheelchair access."

"I type with one hand."

Step 3 Help the youth identify which accommodations have worked best in the past.

Examples: "When my teacher shows me how to do a new job I do well."

"Written instructions help me remember what I'm supposed to do next."

"When a keyboard is placed higher on the desk, I can reach it from my wheelchair."

Step 4 Help the youth put him- or herself in the employer's shoes, and consider how disclosing will make it easier or better for the company.

Examples: "I will work faster if I have a quiet work station."

"I will not get tired if I get a short break every hour."

"If I can show you how I work with my own keyboard, you will get an idea of how well I can type."

Step 5 Help the youth create a script and practice it!

The Way to Work: How to Facilitate Work Experiences for Youth in Transition by Richard G. Luecking

5

...

Supporting Families to Support Work Experience

Richard G. Luecking and Karen Leggett

This chapter provides the reader with

- A review of common challenges for families of youth in transition
- Strategies for involving families in preparing and planning for work experiences
- Strategies for helping families support transition work experiences and employment
- A Learning Lab on supporting families to support transition work experiences

---

"We, as parents, are also benefiting… by gaining a truer insight into exactly what strengths and weaknesses [our son] has on the job."

Parents of a 19-year-old participating in a paid internship

"Without [the transition specialist's] help, I would never have thought that Eric could hold a job, much less get there on his own."

Mother of a 20-year-old working at his first job

Daryll was 16 years old when his special education teacher suggested that he try an unpaid work sampling experience. He was interested; however, his mother did not think Daryll could work because of his disability. She was also worried that working would cause him to lose his Supplemental Security Income (SSI) and Medicaid. Daryll's teacher met several times with his mother at her home to explain the objective of the volunteer work experience—that eventually Daryll would able to hold a paying job. The teacher also put Daryll's mother in contact with another family whose daughter was working. This family not only helped Daryll's mother see the value that work had for their daughter, but they were also able to give her advice about special SSI provisions that allowed their daughter to earn money without losing all of her SSI benefit. Daryll's mother's feelings on the work experience eventually changed from reluctance to support. She even helped the teacher to identify Daryll's traits that would be assets on the job, including a pleasant disposition, good organizational skills, and steady attention to a task. After several unpaid work experiences, Daryll now works as a paid part-time employee at a grocery store—a job he hopes to keep long after he exits school.

When Sean expressed an interest in finding a part-time job after school, his transition specialists and his parents worked with him to come up with ideas for jobs he might like. Because he was an avid sports fan, together they came up with several ideas including employment at a sporting goods store and health club. The transition specialist worked with Sean and his parents to identify a network of contacts, including several relatives, friends, and neighbors who might provide ideas and potential job leads. The father of one of Sean's friends knew of a part-time opening at a large sporting goods store, where Sean was able to land a job as an associate clerk, unloading deliveries of merchandise and helping customers to load large purchases in their cars. Not only was being around other sports fans fun for Sean, but he was able to add another positive experience to his work portfolio, thanks to his family's network.

It would be an understatement to say that families can make a significant positive impact on the success of youth as they pursue and participate in work-based learning experiences in the earlier years of secondary school, as they obtain employment, and as they leave school and pursue their careers. As in the cases of Daryll and Sean, the ways in which families support youth in work experience may vary, as will the ways in which families are supported by transition specialists.

Parents and families are as diverse as the transitioning youth. For this book, we use the broad definition of *parent* and *parent surrogates* as provided by the National Parent Teacher Association (1997) to include not only legal parents but also: "[T]he adults who play an important role in a child's family life, since other adults—grandparents, aunts, uncles, stepparents, guardians—may carry the primary responsibility for a child's education, development, and well-being" (p. 5).

The family—meaning broadly anyone living under the same roof, be it, siblings, other relatives, or unrelated persons—can significantly influence transition-age youth. This chapter primarily addresses the roles of the primary adults in the youth's life. Therefore, the term *family* will refer to those people who exert the most direct influence on the youth, recognizing that the makeup of families encompasses a wide spectrum of possibilities including traditional two-parent households; single-parent families; and homes where grandparents, guardians, or other adults have the primary responsibility for a youth's development.

This chapter highlights the challenges that families face and the critical roles they play in supporting youth work experiences. It also discusses how transition specialists can promote family involvement in a way that is respectful and considerate of this supportive role and the diversity of the people who fill this role.

WHY FAMILY SUPPORT IS IMPORTANT

Family support of youth in transition is critical to youth work success for several reasons. First, the family knows the youth best—an obvious but often under-appreciated fact. The family is an important source of information about a youth's likes and dislikes, talents, and accommodation needs. They are also likely to be an important source of support—however modest or intense—long after the youth has made the transition to adulthood. Most families will at the very least remain in contact and will have some influence over the youth indefinitely after school exit. The preparation of youth for transition from secondary school to adulthood is an important time to make good use of this support so that the family has a positive influence in the long term.

Most families are already involved in the youth's life and therefore are already positioned to help. The National Longitudinal Transition Study 2 (Newman, 2005) found that 9 of 10 families reported participation in at least one individualized education program (IEP) meeting in the current or prior school year, which suggests that they are not only interested in their youth's educational program but also willing to contribute.

Finally, professionals cannot—and should not—do everything for the youth. Only 21% of families say that the youth, and by extension the family, is the primary developer of the IEP during secondary school, meaning that almost 80% of families still rely primarily on the special education professional to develop the IEP (Newman, 2005). There is indeed a lot more room for family advocacy for (and family input into) effective transition, especially as it relates to planning for and supporting work experiences that should be an integral part of the IEP and transition plan.

Emerging evidence suggests that schools and transition programs are more effective in achieving their goals when there is a presumed importance of families in educational service delivery (Epstein, 1996; Pleet, 2000; Wandry & Pleet, 2003). As a result, many educators are adopting a new paradigm: Because families are important, schools should help families to conduct activities that will help their children. In other words, the schools should be in partnership with families, rather than dictating how to support their children's education to them. The paradigm has therefore shifted from mere "parent involvement" to a concept of "shared responsibility" through school, family, and community partnerships (Epstein, 1996). In the context of transition and work experience, families are now viewed as critical partners who are not simply informed, but also contribute to the planning for work experiences.

Furthermore, for the extent to which families contribute to students' educational planning and activities, Pleet (2000) has shown that practitioners' efforts to involve families are at least as important as family background variables such as race or ethnicity, social class, income, and marital status. Therefore, when transition professionals reach out to families and include them in planning for transition activities, the results should be uniformly improved, regardless of family background. Evidence also suggests that family expectations influence the achievements of youth with disabilities, regardless of the nature of their disabilities (Grigal & Neubert, 2004; Newman, 2005). Elevating and cultivating these expectations are therefore important to a youth's workplace success. Transition professionals can play a significant role in shaping family expectations as well as family influence on work experience.

Finally, there is the law. The Individuals with Disabilities Education Improvement Act of 2004 (PL 108-440) requires state special education plans to ensure parents' rights for input; provide joint trainings of education personnel, parents, and related service providers; and use parents' feedback to monitor local school systems and student placement. Special education administrators must show how parent involvement was obtained and used in evaluation and improvement plans. Most important to transition specialists, provisions mandate parent involvement in and approval of students' IEPs. These requirements illustrate recognition of the important role of families as educational partners.

Thus, practice, research, and the law all reflect the importance of the family–educator partnership. In the end, the most compelling reason to promote family participation is that transition activities, especially work experiences, are well served by facilitated partnerships between families and practitioners. This chapter explores many of the ways to enhance and encourage these partnership activities.

KEY ISSUES FOR FAMILIES IN SUPPORTING YOUTH WORK EXPERIENCES

It is universal for family members to worry about their child's future, regardless of whether the child has a disability. For families of youth with disabilities who are in transition, these concerns are likely to be more intense and be the result of more challenging circumstances. These challenges will influence the planning for and the success of youth in work experiences. For families of youth with disabilities, common challenges include the following (Chambers, Hughes, & Carter, 2004; Cooney, 2002; Grigal & Neubert, 2004; Timmons, Whitney-Thomas, McIntyre, Butterworth, & Allen, 2004; Wandry & Pleet, 2003):

- *Balancing expectations*—Low expectations about work are common, especially among families of youth with low-incidence disabilities, because of lingering traditional disability stereotypes that focus on deficits. On the other hand, unrealistically high expectations are not unusual due to such circumstances as misunderstanding the nature of the disability or high-achieving siblings who set a standard for expected achievement. One of the best ways to achieve a balance is for families to learn from the work experience of the youth. Learning what kinds of work environments, tasks, and supports the youth needs is just as valuable for families as it is for the youth.

- *Available time and energy*—The demands of parenting, jobs, and myriad other family issues may tax the ability of family members to be available for planning and supporting work experiences. In these situations, transition professionals need to be prepared to facilitate family involvement in such a way as to minimize the demands on family time and resources, while maximizing family input. In addition, other complications such as poverty, low educational levels, illness, and substance abuse can adversely affect the capacity for some families to focus on youth work experience support.

- *Understanding and gaining access to resources and services*—Many families are unaware of the array of services that exist during school and after school exit. Moreover, the complexity of many of the service systems is overwhelming to some families. These families will need considerable assistance in navigating necessary transition and postschool services and programs, which will support or affect the ability to pursue work experience and employment goals. At various times, youth may need or benefit from services such as vocational rehabilitation, One-Stop Career Center youth programs, developmental disabilities and mental health programs, and various other social and health services. Even the savviest family member may struggle to understand and obtain these services without help from transition professionals.

- *Understanding the role of transition professionals*—Many families will passively defer to transition professionals, thinking that professionals "know best." On the other hand, some families have experienced disagreements and conflicts with the school system. It will take some time under these circumstances to gain the trust of these families so that they see the role of transition professionals as partners rather than adversaries. In either case, communication is necessary to build trust and understanding of how the family and professionals can work in partnership to promote work experience success.

- *Diversity challenges*—Families from various ethnic and racial groups and speakers of English as a second language may be intimidated when dealing with school systems and education professionals. They may possess cultural values that conflict with usual approaches taken by schools and professionals. Sensitivity to these circumstances and to family cultural background is essential for youth to successfully participate in and benefit from work experiences.

STRATEGIES FOR INVOLVING FAMILIES IN PREPARATION AND PLANNING

Recall the work experience schemata introduced in Chapter 2 that features three phases of work experiences: identifying goals and objectives for work experiences, negotiating the work experience, and implementing an individualized support plan. Families can play important roles in all three of these phases of implementing work experiences. In fact, it is never too early for families to promote career- and work-focused activities, and it is never too late for families to reinforce the value of work experience. Families can become strong assets to planning for work experience. For example, family members can be encouraged to

- Bring the youth along to visit them at their jobs
- Give the youth tasks and household chores to do at home
- Help the youth to pursue volunteering opportunities, as these opportunities provide experience in "soft skills" (e.g., dependability, appearance and behavior on the job, following directions, attitude)
- Help the youth to decide what type of job and work environment he or she really wants
- Talk to the youth about his or her dreams, as this helps to identify areas of interest and ways to draw the youth into making decisions about and planning for work experiences

By talking positively about the youth as a future worker, the transition professional can draw families into the planning process. This helps to minimize discussions about the youth that focus on a disability. Talk as much as possible in a positive context about the youth's positive personality traits, notable skills, and expressed interests. One family was dismissive about their son's dream to pursue a job in professional sports—until his transition teacher helped him to land a part-time job with a minor league baseball team. From October to March, the youth works part-time sorting and delivering mail, labeling donation request cards, recording the inventory of autographed balls and jerseys, and filling goody bags for fans. From April to September, the youth is living his dream: working right in the dugout, polishing and preparing helmets and bats, getting towels and Gatorade, and making sure there are enough balls for practice. This family now regularly speaks to other families about elevating expectations about their youth's career plans.

Chapter 3 discussed various strategies and methods for gathering information on youth's preferences, traits, skills, and needs for support. Not only can families help to gather this information, but they can also be significant partners in using this information to plan for work experience. In most cases, families will be interested and willing to participate in this process. Beyond the development of an IEP, families can contribute to any and all planning that takes place to identify directions for a work experience plan.

Families can make valuable contributions by

- Identifying preferences, hobbies, and leisure activities that might point to a possible career or job interest for the youth
- Identifying tasks that the youth performs at home that illustrate potential work skills and work behavior
- Identifying networks of relatives, friends, and neighbors who might help in finding a potential employer to host an identified type of work experience, as with Sean at the beginning of this chapter
- Identifying accommodations and supports the youth will need at work, including supports with which the family may assist (e.g., transportation)

Family participation in the planning process can be facilitated by holding discussions at times (e.g., before or after school) and places (e.g., family home, nearby public meeting place) that are most convenient for the families.

STRATEGIES FOR INVOLVING FAMILIES IN NEGOTIATING AND ORGANIZING WORK EXPERIENCES

When prospective worksites are identified, family input is useful—and often essential—to negotiating with employers and organizing the schedules, tasks, supports, and other important features of the work experience. The work experience is likely to be more successful if transition specialists are careful to communicate with families, solicit their input, and involve them in decisions before the youth begins the work experience. Several activities are recommended for transition specialists to solicit the highest level of family support in organizing work experiences:

- Inform families of schedules and work expectations about prospective worksites
- Work with families to plan ways they can support prospective work experiences, such as making sure the youth has the proper clothes and is ready on time
- Inform families about the status of conversations with prospective worksites so that they are not surprised by any development, are ready to support the work experience when it starts, and are ready to support the continued search if necessary
- Be prepared to fully explain to families the advantages and disadvantages of prospective worksites (e.g., location, type of tasks, accommodation possibilities)

Family Roles for Supporting Work Experiences

- Attend individualized education program (IEP) meetings, contribute to the IEP and transition plans, and contribute to individualized work experience and work support plans
- Share the youth's preferences, talents, skills, interests, and goals
- Help the youth negotiate with transition professionals about his or her preferences, skills, interests, wants, and goals
- Advocate for the youth's goals
- Provide networks and contacts for potential work experience sites
- Provide feedback to transition professionals about the work experience
- Reinforce work expectations to the youth
- Work as a partner with transition professionals in establishing, monitoring, and evaluating the work experience
- Offer help in solving challenges to the work experience, such as alternative transportation and special accommodation needs

- Be prepared to fully explain the reasons a particular worksite is targeted for the youth (e.g., what it offers in terms of potential tasks that are matched to the youth's skills, what can be learned from the experience, what features are suited for the youth's circumstances, the level of employer interest)
- Seek family feedback about and input into what supports and accommodations might be needed in a particular prospective worksite
- Make sure families are fully aware of attendance expectations for a prospective worksite so that their support in getting youth to the site is assured

STRATEGIES FOR INVOLVING FAMILIES IN IMPLEMENTING WORK EXPERIENCE SUPPORT

Once a worksite is identified and it is time to begin the work experience, families can be strong influencers of the success of the work experience. They can provide ideas about how to improve the experience, ensure proper support and accommodations, and evaluate and assess the benefit of the work experience. Transition specialists can seek family input throughout the work experience, recognizing that some families will expect more involvement or be able to contribute more than others. In any case, there are several ways family support will help the success of the work experience. To solicit and use this support, transition professionals can

- Ask family members to identify accommodations and supports that work at home and that might be useful in the workplace (see Chapter 8 for a detailed discussion of workplace supports)
- Communicate regularly with families about progress at the worksite by telephone, e-mail, or written notes—whichever is most convenient for the family

Promoting Youth Self-Advocacy and Work Experience: An Interview with a Savvy Parent

Haydee de Paula is a parent on a mission. She has been very active as an advocate for youth in transition, especially for her son, Ramon. She and her family have talked to Ramon since he was very young about his dreams and wishes for the future, including what he wanted to do in his work life. As a consequence, he had multiple work experiences while in secondary school. He exited school with a part-time job at a dentist's office that he later left to take the full-time federal job he now has held for 3 years. He excels at the job and likes it.

Ms. de Paula agreed to be interviewed about her role as a parent and Ramon's path to employment. Below are the two questions we asked and a summary of her answers.

What did you do to promote the idea of work to Ramon when he was in high school?

Here is an abbreviated list:

- Helped and encouraged Ramon to share his interests with his teachers and job coaches
- Made sure he continued to have at least one chore at home since he was in elementary school
- Helped him volunteer in the community—one volunteer job was to make copies of documents, a task he now has at his real job at the Department of Veterans Affairs
- Taught him that every job is noble—always do your best
- Showed him what his friends in "general education" were doing— like working and participating in sports—and encouraged him to go after the same opportunities
- Worked closely with his teacher and employment agency so that they spent time with Ramon to learn all about his interests and skills so that they could help him find the right job

How did you empower Ramon to make decisions about work?

When we found out that he had Down syndrome, we decided that we would expect the same from him as we would have before the diagnosis. We want for Ramon the same thing we want for our other son: that he be the best he can be, that he continue to discover and use his gifts to make a contribution and to help others. We taught him that it was alright to *not* like to do something and that many times people have to be flexible and patient, but persistent. Sometimes we have to do things that we don't like but they have to be done. We also encouraged him to speak up for himself, like he did when he was given a job in high school that he didn't like because they did not give him the right tools! Now, every year for his annual individual service plan meeting, we have him invite the service coordinator to our house for dinner so that we can work together planning his supports.

We need to pay attention to what he does, and coach him sometimes to make decisions. But we need to let him do it. We also need to pay attention to what his support staff does and coach them to help Ramon in the right way, including keeping high expectations for Ramon. And we helped him be very active with classmates and friends. We find that his friends can sometimes be his best advocates! We model and verbalize to him that he always needs to do his best and put his heart into whatever he does.

- Invite family input for solving problems related to accommodations or other issues that arise during the work experience
- Help link the youth and family to services and supports necessary for the youth to continue to pursue work (e.g., health and social services, vocational rehabilitation)
- Help link the youth and family to resources that can explain the effects of earnings on income support, such as SSI, and that can assist with the reporting and management of work experience income when necessary
- Celebrate success

Nothing gives parents and family members more pride—and nothing better sets the stage for ongoing collaboration about work experience—than providing information and elaborating on a youth's successes in the workplace. Make special calls to the family to report workplace gains and successes, mark successes with special occasions (however small) to celebrate them, and send notes and cards home telling of particular gains made by the youth at the workplace.

At all junctures of the work experience, remember that family input and participation is facilitated when planning and other meetings about the youth are conducted at places and times that are convenient and comfortable to families. Transition professionals should also support families to encourage youth to speak up for themselves. Promoting youth self-advocacy does not mean abdicating parental responsibility, but rather it encourages youth to exercise informed choice over their work experience planning and implementation.

PARENT-TO-PARENT SUGGESTIONS FOR SUCCESSFUL WORK EXPERIENCES

One of the most useful strategies for promoting family support of work experiences is to facilitate opportunities for families to talk to each other for support, information, and guidance. Few experiences have more immediate influence than when other families who "have been there" lend advice to families who are seeing their youth go to a worksite for the first time—or even the second, third, or fourth time! The following are some recommendations that you—or better yet, families who have already experienced the process—can share with those families who are new to supporting youth's work experiences (Montgomery County Transition Work Group, 2008).

- Help build a résumé that includes volunteer and work experience, skills, and strengths
- Know the youth's strengths, interests, and preferences
- Help the youth to speak for him- or herself
- Network with friends, neighbors, and colleagues, and let them know that the youth is looking for a certain kind of work opportunity
- Don't expect to find the one perfect job that will last a lifetime—everyone changes jobs at some point
- Talk early and often about the benefits of working
- Seek information on what factors the youth should consider in deciding when or how to disclose a particular disability when planning for a work experience
- Avoid being "helicopter parents," hovering nearby while the youth attempts to work
- Model, discuss, and share soft skills with the youth (e.g., appropriate attitudes and dress on the job, showing up on time, taking directions, working with co-workers, eagerness to work and to learn skills)
- Be creative and take advantage of as many learning opportunities as possible—you never know when one might lead to a work experience

Other strategies for supporting families include formal and informal parent-to-parent support groups where family members talk about shared experiences, lessons learned, helpful resources, and other pieces of useful information and advice about how to support work experiences and employment. Transition seminars and fairs are also occasions for families to convene for mutual learning about what to expect as youth prepare for and engage in work experiences. Finally, it is often useful to individually link experienced families with families who are new to transition issues and to the prospect of their youth working.

One transition teacher keeps the names and telephone numbers of the families of previous students who agree to be available to talk to other families of students who are new to her class each year. She begins each school year by sharing these names and contact information with new students' families. She often tries to purposefully match new families to experienced families with similar backgrounds or to youth with similar circumstances and disabilities. She asks the experienced families to share information about what to expect from the work experiences that are a major part of the year's curriculum. This information runs the gamut: how to help youth dress for work, identifying alternative transportation ideas, preparing for unique scheduling due to work hours, what to expect from the teacher, where to go to report earnings to the Social Security office, and many more areas of greater or lesser importance. Many times, the families develop a mutual bond as a result. The result is a group of families who are extremely supportive of their working youth. It is no surprise to the teacher that almost all of the students who exit her program have paid employment at the end of their secondary school education.

RESPECTING FAMILY CULTURE

A family's ethnic and/or cultural background may affect transition planning and relationships with transition professionals. Similarly, family diversity also affects

Setting the Stage for Family Support

A transition specialist from a local school district holds a group meeting with students' families at the beginning of each school year. The purpose of the meeting is to inform the families about how work experience will be incorporated into each student's schedule. The specialist has the following agenda for the meeting:

- Introductions
- Review of the importance of the work experiences and how they have helped previous students (usually a family member of a previous student also speaks)
- Overview of the process for arranging the work experiences, including how family members can support and participate in the process
- Discussion on communicating information about the work experiences
- Suggestions on how families can contribute to student success in the work experience
- Questions and answers
- Contact information and wrap-up

This transition specialist reports that this meeting sets the stage for strong family support of the work experience throughout the school year. In all but the rarest circumstances, she has found family members to be extremely cooperative and helpful as a result.

views of youth independence and pursuit of work (Kalyanpur & Harry, 1999; McGinley, 2003). Some cultures respond to disability by extended family support, which may provide a great deal of caring support; at the same time, some family members may be reluctant to support work goals or independent living (Wandry & Pleet, 2003). Others will see a youth's disability through the lens of culturally influenced stigma and thus will not believe that work is a suitable goal. Still others will have to cope with ethnic, racial, and linguistic inequities that make access to information about work and disability more difficult. It is thus important for transition professionals to be sensitive to and respect the cultural values of families of transitioning youth. Professionals should be ready to accordingly lend more or less help to the families as they begin to identify work goals and expectations for their youth.

Diverse families can be accommodated in the planning and implementation of work experiences. Here are a few strategies that, when possible to implement, can be helpful.

- Identify and use people from diverse cultural backgrounds in trainings and meetings.
- Assign staff from the same ethnic or linguistic group to work with the youth and family when possible.

- Provide information in the family's native language so as to insure greater ease of communication with families who are less fluent in English.

- Arrange meetings and contacts so that they are held in familiar community settings.

- Match family members of successful youth from the same cultural background to provide family-to-family support, encouragement, and information about the value of work and the impact it has had on their youth and family.

- Respect disagreements about work goals.

- Don't hesitate to promote the value of work in the context of the family's culture. For example, assure overprotective families that you will initially accompany the youth to ensure the safety of transportation and work arrangements.

When it is not practical to pursue many of these strategies, transition specialists can still be very effective when working with diverse families. Kalyanpur and Harry (1999) discussed three levels of cultural awareness that lead to successively higher likelihoods of effective relationships with diverse families. They refer to the lowest intensity of cultural awareness as the *overt level,* in which professionals are aware of clear external differences such as how people dress, their skin color, or that they speak a language other than English. This level of awareness is superficial and therefore limited in its helpfulness because stereotypes might be common. Thus, judgments made about the families and the communications with them are based on limited understanding of the culture. The resulting misperceptions will then create difficulties in establishing a productive partnership with the families, complicating the likelihood that the families will effectively support the youth's work experience.

The next level of cultural awareness is called *covert awareness.* At this level, professionals have more background knowledge of a culture and observe individual differences, such as communication styles. They may even ask families to explain the differences or they may acknowledge wishes of families as they make plans for work experiences. This background knowledge, however, is still often based on common stereotypes; professionals may still not be sensitive to cultural differences and how they affect a family's willingness to support work experiences.

The highest level of cultural awareness is called *subtle awareness,* when transition professionals understand that work and disability each mean different things to different cultures. These cultural values sometimes differ from those of the schools or transition programs. Without judging the families' motives, beliefs, or values, the transition professional operating at a subtle level of cultural awareness will find ways to communicate necessary information in the context of the families' cultural value system and accept that a family may not want to do things exactly the way things are generally done.

One transition professional made arrangements to meet a family at their home to communicate about a prospective work experience. This not only made the family more comfortable with the professional in spite of the language differences, but it gave the professional an opportunity to observe the youth and family interacting. In addition, for every visit, the youth's mother would prepare food, a gesture this family's culture makes to every visitor to the home. The professional quickly realized that turning down the food would be insulting to the family, so she ate all that was offered in spite of its copious amounts. During the meal, they would talk informally about the work opportunities she was helping the youth to pursue. It was during these discussions that the youth's mother came to trust the transition professional. A reluctant mother became a strong supporter of her son's work experience as a result of the professional's cultural awareness.

RECOGNIZING SUCCESSFUL FAMILY–PROFESSIONAL PARTNERSHIPS

How do we know when we are successful at engaging families? How do we know when there is a true partnership between families and transition professionals as youth pursue work experiences and jobs? And, as important as any aspect of family–professional partnership, how do we know whether families are satisfied with the partnership or if they view it as a successful relationship?

DeFur (2003) offered several markers useful for recognizing that families are involved, satisfied, and engaged in transition activities. These indicators reflect how transition partnership success might be viewed by families and can be easily adapted so that they apply to partnering for work experiences. Thus, from the family's point of view, an effective partnership between a family and transition professional would include the following aspects:

- Transition professionals listen to the family's perspectives and concerns and then cooperatively identify supports that are needed for the family in its efforts to support the youth's pursuit of work experiences.
- Meetings are held at times and places that are convenient to the family and considerate of its circumstances (e.g., in the home, with child care provided, at a faith community, in their native language).
- Transition professionals demonstrate a belief that youth can achieve work experience goals.
- Transition professionals suspend judgment of family status or past actions. They avoid blaming the family when there are problems at the worksite or external problems that affect the work experience.
- Families trust that the transition specialists have the best interest of the youth in mind.
- Transition specialists use family feedback when planning for, implementing, and evaluating the work experience.

These indicators are useful barometers for how effective transition professionals are when working with families. Building on these indicators, transition specialists can ask themselves the following questions when evaluating their own ability to engage families:

- Do I solicit and am I receptive to family feedback?
- Do I give families all of the necessary information to make decisions about youth in the workplace?
- Do I let families function as experts on their child's disability and their child's talents? That is, do they contribute to the planning, implementation, and evaluation of work experience?
- Do I provide regular communication about the status of the youth's work experience?

- Do I provide regular structured as well as informal opportunities for families to review the youth's progress?
- Do I consider the youth and his or her family as full team members when planning for and implementing work experiences?

SUMMARY

This chapter outlined many of the issues families face as they are engaged to help plan and support youth work experiences. The importance of a family's influence on the transition process is well documented. Transition specialists have the opportunity to make this influence as useful as possible for successful work experiences. This requires the kind of shared partnership espoused by Epstein (1996) and Pleet (2000), in which families and transition specialists have a shared responsibility and partnership with respect to the youth's pursuit of work experience and employment.

Strategies were presented that help transition specialists involve and accommodate families so that relationships are nurtured and so that families become partners in supporting work experience pursuits. Families are as unique and diverse as youth in transition. Thus, transition specialists are encouraged to develop a strong understanding and keen sensitivity to diverse family cultures and family circumstances. Ultimately, success in the workplace will be enhanced and reinforced when families are active supporters of the efforts involved in the youth's work experiences. Therefore, transition specialists are well advised to understand how families may view the partnership with transition professionals; in other words, see the relationship through the families' eyes.

Transition specialists cannot be all things to all families. On many occasions, family needs will be considerable, and it is not practical to solve every issue that might affect the youth's ability to participate in a work experience or to hold a job. The family's support of the youth's work experience may not be optimal or simply is not feasible because of factors outside of the control of transition professionals. Some families will need a gentle prodding, and others will need to be coaxed into partnering for the work experience effort. Still other families will require help to moderate their input, but all families will be somehow involved as youth pursue work experience. One way or another, families are almost always important influencers of a youth's workplace success. This chapter offered strategies to take advantage of and nurture the family support that will contribute to this success.

USEFUL RESOURCES FOR FAMILIES

- *Parent Advocacy Coalition for Educational Rights (PACER) Center* (http://www .pacer.org)—PACER is a parents-helping-parents organization that provides assistance, information, and materials for parents, families and professionals throughout the nation.
- *Parent Educational Advocacy Training Center (PEATC)* (http://www.peatc.org)— PEATC offers training opportunities for parents and professionals who are interested in developing courses for families. Of particular note, PEATC offers

a training series called NEXT STEP that focuses on skills and information to help students achieve transition goals.

LEARNING LAB: *Seeing Work Experience Through Family Eyes*

Imagine you are the parent of a child with a significant disability.

1. Role-play with another professional or write a brief dialogue for one of the following situations, in which you initiate a conversation about the possibility of a part-time job or volunteer work experience for your child with the following people.

   a. A neighbor who works in a local, medium-sized private business

   b. An acquaintance in your church or synagogue who works for a government agency

   c. A leader in an organization or company in an area of interest for your child (e.g., sports team, theater, law enforcement, retail)

2. List the traits you would want in a transition specialist who is facilitating a work experience for your child.

REFERENCES

Chambers, A., Hughes, C., & Carter, E. (2004). Parent and sibling perspectives on the transition to adulthood. *Education and Training in Developmental Disabilities, 39,* 173–188.

Cooney, B. (2002). Exploring perspectives on transition of youth with disabilities: Voices of young adults, parents, and professionals. *Mental Retardation, 40,* 79–94.

DeFur, S. (2003). Parents as collaborators: Building partnerships with school-based and community-based providers. In D. Wandry & A. Pleet (Eds.), *A practitioner's guide to involving families in secondary education.* Arlington, VA: Council for Exceptional Children.

Epstein, J. (1996). Perspectives and previews on research and policy for school, family, and community partnerships. In A. Booth & J. Dunn (Eds.), *Family-school links: How do they affect educational outcomes?* (pp. 209–246). Mahwah, NJ: Lawrence Erlbaum Associates.

Grigal, M., & Neubert, D. (2004). Parents' in-school values and post-school expectations for transition aged youth with disabilities. *Career Development for Exceptional Individuals, 27,* 65–85.

Individuals with Disabilities Education Improvement Act of 2004, PL 108-446, 20 U.S.C. §§ 1400 *et seq.*

Kalyanpur, M., & Harry, B. (1999). *Culture in special education: Building reciprocal family–professional relationships.* Baltimore: Paul H. Brookes Publishing Co.

McGinley, V. (2003). Defining the family: Changing demographics. In D. Wandry & A. Pleet (Eds.), *A practitioner's guide to involving families in secondary education.* Arlington, VA: Council for Exceptional Children.

Montgomery County Transition Work Group. (2008). *A parent's guide to helping career seekers with disabilities find jobs.* Rockville, MD: Author.

National Parent Teacher Association. (1997). *National standards for parent/family involvement programs.* Chicago: Author.

Newman, L. (2005). *Family involvement in the educational development of youth with disabilities.* Menlo Park, CA: SRI International.

Pleet, A. (2000). *Investigating the relationship between parent involvement in transition planning and post-school outcomes for students with disabilities.* Ann Arbor: University of Michigan Dissertation Services.

Timmons, J., Whitney-Thomas, J., McIntyre, J., Butterworth, J., & Allen, D. (2004). Managing service delivery systems and the role of parents during their children's transitions. *Journal of Rehabilitation, 70,* 19–26.

Wandry, D., & Pleet, A. (Eds.). (2003). *A practitioner's guide to involving families in secondary education.* Arlington, VA: Council for Exceptional Children.

6

...

Workplace Partners

Strategies for Finding and Recruiting Employers

This chapter provides the reader with

- Reasons why employers might consider bringing youth with disabilities into their workplaces
- Strategies for meeting employer expectations when recruiting them to provide work experiences
- Complementary strategies for finding and recruiting employers
- A Learning Lab on employer recruitment

"Nothing beats showing me how you can help me!"

An employer who agreed to host youth work experiences

"Like any other service or business partner, we are more apt to work with people who take the time and interest to learn what we do and how we do it."

Vice president of a publishing company who hired a youth intern

Like any other service or business, *Macworld* magazine is more apt to work with people who take the time to learn about their operations. For that reason, after meeting a professional from a transition program serving youth with significant accommodation needs, the *Macworld* vice president for human resources agreed to host a youth named Wynton for a paid work experience. The transition professional found out through a meeting with the vice president that there were needs in the magazine's circulation department to update customer marketing databases, as well as discard and shred outdated documents. She proposed that *Macworld* could meet these needs by hiring Wynton, who had an interest in information technology. Although the particular accommodations needed for a power wheelchair and communication board caused initial concerns, *Macworld* hired Wynton when the company realized the benefit his work could provide to them.

Every good museum depends on a cadre of committed and well-trained volunteers. Port Discovery, a children's museum in the heart of downtown Baltimore, is no exception. For that reason, the museum was willing to include as a partner a local transition program for youth with various disabilities. This transition program agreed to support and coach youth through the mandated volunteer training and to help identify volunteer assignments throughout the museum during regular weekly shifts. After 3 years of the partnership, Port Discovery continues to make youth with disabilities a part of its volunteer program. The museum will continue doing so as long as it receives competent help in identifying meaningful assignments that work for both youth and the museum.

One large grocery store chain has provided numerous paid internship experiences in its various stores to youth served by a transition program with a strong reputation for competent and responsive assistance in matching youth with assignments in the many stores the chain operates in the community. This partnership meets an ongoing need of the chain to keep certain departments fully staffed, and it helps the chain to identify future employees. For example, one youth who completed an internship stocking shelves in the bakery department was immediately hired into a full-time job as bakery assistant.

A manufacturing firm that produces portable generators and power washers offers its manufacturing facility as a worksite and a classroom for youth apprentices in manufacturing processes. It partners with a local school district to build a skilled manufacturing workforce, to reinforce a good work ethic in its community's youth, and to attract future workers to its facility. Apprentices include youth with and without disabilities who spend 1 year working for 36 hours per week onsite—6 hours of classroom instruction to complete their high school diploma requirements and 30 hours working and learning in the workplace. This company "graduates" six apprentices per year, many of whom are offered long-term full-time employment by the company.

The value of work experiences for youth with disabilities as a necessary springboard for eventual adult employment success has been well documented. These experiences, however, can only happen if there are available and interested employers, like those presented previously, who are willing to include youth in their workplaces. Without cooperating employers, everything else discussed in this book will have limited impact on the ability of youth to succeed as future workers and to enjoy successful careers.

This chapter discusses how to attract employers to host work experiences. It provides specific strategies to recruit and appeal to employer partners so that work experiences are as plentiful and as varied as youth's interests and circumstances require. Chapter 7 discusses how to keep employers interested in working with transitioning youth and transition programs.

WHAT EMPLOYERS WANT

Employers have various operational and economic stakes in the success of programs that bring them in contact with youth with disabilities. Regardless of their motivations for hosting these youth, employers still have to make sure they meet deadlines and satisfy their customers so that they make a profit, save money, and/or run their operation as smoothly as possible. Thus, as educators, transition specialists, workforce development professionals, family members, and youth organize and establish work experiences, it is essential to understand employers' needs, circumstances, and perspectives.

According to employers who have successfully brought youth with disabilities into their workplaces, three main reasons exist for employers to host youth with disabilities (Luecking, 2004). In order of importance, these reasons are

1. To meet a specific company need, such as filling a job opening or addressing a production or service need

2. To meet an industrywide need, such as preparing potential new workers in a technology industry

3. To meet a community need, such as helping youth become productive citizens

Although many employers are willing and interested in hosting youth in the workplace out of good citizenship, the order of these reasons suggests that it is more effective to appeal to employers' self-interest than it is to appeal to their potential altruistic interest in helping youth. It is therefore best to avoid appeals to an employer's benevolence by trying to convince employers of the value of helping youth with disabilities. It is more important to find out what employers want and then determine how an individual youth can help the employers.

Employers typically do not have the time or resources to seek out youth on their own. However, with proper information, support, and access, employers can be recruited effectively for partnerships with transition programs and professionals. Generally, employers identify four key factors that contribute both to their decisions to bring youth with disabilities into their workplaces and to their satisfaction with the contribution youth make in the workplace (Luecking, 2005).

1. Competent and convenient assistance in receiving youth referrals

Educators and transition personnel who are professional and responsive when interacting with employers are likely to get the most positive employer reaction to their contact. Although this seems intuitive and self-evident, employers have long been known to complain about disability program representatives who do not respect business needs and who do not present themselves as reliable professionals (Fabian, Luecking, & Tilson, 1994; Kregel & Unger, 1993; Locklin, 1997; Luecking, Fabian, & Tilson, 2004). In addition, for busy employers to react positively to solicitations and involvement with transition programs, the arrangement must be easy to manage and not interfere with the pressing demands of their workplace.

2. Matching of youth skills and interests to job tasks

Although it is often tempting to guide a youth into the first workplace where there is a willing employer partner, it can be a disaster if the youth is not matched well to what the workplace has to offer. If the student-centered approaches discussed in Chapter 3 are used as a basis for identifying potential workplaces for individual youth, then the likelihood of making that good match increases. At the same time, if the care is taken to fully understand the operation and the culture of the workplace, then the likelihood increases that the employer will be happy to consider being matched with a youth whose interests and skills fit with that workplace.

3. Support in training and monitoring the youth at the worksite

Employers do not appreciate what one employer described to the author as a "drop off and see you later program." If transition professionals truly understand that employers are partners to be treated well, then they will deliver whatever follow-up support the employer wants and needs to provide an effective work experience for the youth. This support is related to the time-tested concept in business that is called *service after the sale.* In the context of arranging work experiences, making sure the employer is comfortable and happy with the arrangement is a necessary aspect of the service provided to the employer after the youth is situated in the workplace. Much more will be said about this in Chapter 7.

4. Formal and informal disability awareness and training for the youth's co-workers (when the youth chooses to disclose a disability)

As discussed in Chapter 4, the decision on whether or how disability is disclosed is a personal one. However, when the youth gives permission to disclose and is involved in the disclosure process, it is often important for the youth's co-workers to receive at least a basic orientation on how best to interact and communicate with the youth. More will also be said about this in Chapter 7.

There are several key strategies that are useful in addressing each of these factors so that employers become willing participants in programs and services that help youth pave the way to work. The next section outlines and discusses those strategies.

HOW TO GIVE EMPLOYERS WHAT THEY WANT

There is an old business marketing maxim that says, "It is better to find out what your customer needs and wants and then match it to what you have to offer than it is to try to get them to buy what you are selling." Considering employers as customers of transition programs, much can be learned from this wise advice. First, do not try to appeal exclusively to employer altruism by selling employers on helping youth with disabilities. Not only is this strategy ineffective, but it creates an image of youth with disabilities that does not do justice to their individuality and potential competence as workers. Second, neither the youth's nor the employers' needs can be met without first getting to know employers and their operations. Finally, long-term relationships with employers depend on making sure they get what they want from the arrangement; otherwise, they will bail out at the first sign of trouble.

Table 6.1 provides a list of strategies that can be incorporated to meet each of the four employer expectations. This chapter discusses the first nine of these strategies, which are designed to identify and recruit employers. Chapter 7 discusses the remainder of the strategies, which address ways to keep employers happy that they "signed on," satisfied with the service from the transition program, and willing to stay involved for as long as they are needed.

Competent and Convenient Assistance in Receiving Youth Referrals

• • • STRATEGY 1

Conduct informational interviews.

Table 6.1. Strategies to address employer expectations

Employer expectation	Strategies
Competent and convenient assistance in receiving youth referrals	1. Conduct informational interviews. 2. Use business language. 3. Establish a single point of contact. 4. Maintain professional and responsive contact. 5. Underpromise and overdeliver.
Matching of youth skills and interests to job tasks	6. Know both the youth's capabilities and interests and the employer's circumstances thoroughly. 7. Identify tasks that are important to both the youth and the employer. 8. Customize assignments as necessary. 9. Propose and negotiate task assignments.
Support in training and monitoring the youth at the worksite	10. Clarify employer expectations about job training, coaching, and follow-up. 11. Follow through on agreed follow-up procedures. 12. Solicit employers' feedback on service from the intermediary. 13. Adjust support and service to employers based on their feedback.
Formal and informal disability awareness (when the youth chooses to disclose a disability)	14. Deliver information about specific accommodations required by the youth. 15. Ask what further information and help the employer desires. 16. Provide disability awareness information based on what the employer requests. 17. Model interaction and support appropriate for the youth. 18. Provide periodic guidance and information as necessary.

Armed with information about what types of workplaces and work experiences individual youth are seeking (see Chapter 3), transition professionals should be ready to contact prospective employer partners to find out about their human service and operational needs. Informational interviews are easy and effective ways to show interest in potential employers, as well as to identify opportunities for work-based experiences that may exist in their workplaces. They are a great way to meet new employers and learn their needs without the pressure of trying to convince them to make a placement. Few employers will refuse a request for a meeting to share what they do if they are approached with a genuine sincerity to get to know them better—as opposed to an approach that feels like a sales call. Consider the following tips on how to conduct such interviews.

- Ask to meet with a knowledgeable person in the business. This might be someone who has been recommended by a friend or acquaintance, or simply someone you learn about by contacting the company and asking who is responsible for hiring.

- Make the meeting request easy to fulfill. For example, you might say, "I would like to find out more about your business so I can better understand the human resource needs in your industry." Alternatively, you could say, "Many of my students are really interested in [industry type]. Is it possible for me to visit briefly and get more information?"

- Be prepared. Thoroughly research the business and prepare questions for the meeting, such as: What are the most pressing production or business operation challenges? What are some of the biggest staffing challenges? What kinds of

skills do your workers need? What are anticipated future workforce requirements? What are the ways in which you like to be approached by applicants
or by schools/programs representing youth?

• Indicate an interest in understanding the staffing and operational needs of the
business and learning how you may be able to help meet them. Request a
tour. During the tour, be conversational, asking questions about how things
get done and about what you observe.

• Keep it short. Respect the employer's time—15–20 minutes should be more
than enough.

• Thank the employer for his or her time. When you get back to your office,
send a written thank-you note or e-mail acknowledging the employer's time
and interest.

Not every informational interview will directly yield work experience opportunities. At the very least, however, each interview adds to increasing numbers
of contacts for future reference, as well as a growing knowledge of what employers are looking for and how they operate. Importantly, your foot has been in the
door of another workplace.

• • • STRATEGY 2
Use business language.

Education and transition jargon is likely to generate more confusion than not
when used to describe professional roles or transition programs. It is important
to be able to talk about what transition programs can do in terms the target
employers understand. For example, say that you offer help with *recruitment assistance* or *prescreened applicants* or *access to an expanded labor pool,* rather than promoting your work as helping youth with disabilities achieve employment. Emphasize
that you are helping prepare the future labor force rather than promoting the
work you are doing to develop work-based learning opportunities for youth.
Phrases such as *customized responses to human resource needs, reduction in recruiting
costs,* and *help in managing a diverse workforce* are much more meaningful ways to
describe your value to employers than trying to sell them on the importance of
youth work experience.

Finally, avoid using language, terms, and acronyms such as *vocational experience, work-based learning, IEPs, WIA, supported employment, work study,* and *cooperative learning.* Not only are they usually meaningless to employers, but they also
tend to take the focus off the needs of the employer partner.

• • • STRATEGY 3
Establish a single point of contact.

Remember that convenience and easy access to youth is important to employers
who have hosted youth with disabilities in their workplaces. It is therefore important to minimize the number of people employers have to interact with so that they
have an easier time understanding and relating to schools and transition programs.
A single individual should be designated to act as an account representative for
each employer contact established. This allows the transition professional to
become thoroughly acquainted with the employer's needs and circumstances and
thus to be more responsive to these needs. It is easier and more convenient for

employers when one representative handles all youth referrals to each company, which avoids duplicative and time-consuming interactions. For employers, having a single point of contact also considerably decreases the confusion and duplication that typically occur when multiple people from one organization or program come in and out of an employer's operation to place and supervise youth on the job.

• • • STRATEGY 4
Maintain professional and responsive contact.

It is important to observe basic courtesies such as keeping appointments and being on time, dressing professionally, returning telephone calls promptly, and thanking employers for their time. Not only do these courtesies make a good first impression, but they also indicate ongoing regard and respect for employer partners that will keep employers interested in working with transition professionals. In fact, ongoing responsiveness to any employer request is important for maintaining productive relationships, as Chapter 7 will discuss. After an initial informational interview, one transition professional sent occasional notes and even a holiday card to one employer with whom she had a particularly informative and pleasant conversation during the interview. Although there was no immediate job opening for youth at the first meeting, this responsive contact resulted in the employer eventually calling the transition professional 9 months later to tell her of a job opening. Needless to say, it was filled by a youth she represented.

Appendix 6.1 provides a form for organizing and maintaining information on employer contacts.

• • • STRATEGY 5
Underpromise and overdeliver.

"Underpromise and overdeliver" is a longstanding hallmark of customer service in any business relationship. It simply refers to giving customers more than they expect so that they will come back for more, as well as tell others about the service. In the context of youth transition activities, prospective employers should receive service that is over and above what was promised. It can be a simple matter, such filling an employer's request before an agreed-upon deadline, or it can be more involved, such as helping an employer recruit employees from another source such as another program or agency if the transition professional cannot provide applicants for a specific position.

In the figurative sense, such additional service essentially acts to build credit with the employer. That is, the employer feels grateful to the point that it is easy to later ask a favor of the employer—to consider a particular youth for a work experience, for example. One transition professional helped an employer implement an application process for applicants who could not read English but were fluent in another language. Although this process applied to other people besides youth with disabilities, the assistance was very helpful to the employer. Guess who the employer called first whenever there was an opening in the company? In effect, this extra assistance opened many doors to youth with disabilities who had a first shot at these employment opportunities. The transition professional delivered far more than promised to this employer, and the result was a long-time partner who brought many youth with disabilities into that workplace over several years.

Matching of Youth Skills and Interests to Job Tasks

The remaining strategies help to ensure that the youth is well-matched to the prospective job.

• • • STRATEGY 6
Know both the youth's capabilities and interests and the employer's circumstances thoroughly.

Although this is a basic requirement, many transition professionals are tempted to bring a youth into a workplace just because an employer expresses an interest or a need without full knowledge of what the youth and the employer require. Short-term expediency of a quick placement can lead to dire consequences if the match is not a good one. Never try to force the match. If a youth is interested in health occupations and dislikes loud environments, then a placement in a shopping mall food court emptying trash is obviously not a good idea.

Ideally, transition professionals will have a thorough knowledge of the youth's interests, skills, preferences, and needs for accommodation (see Chapter 3). Indeed, this should be the basis for the employer contact in the first place. Informational interviews, for example, with retail clothing store managers are in order if a youth has strong interest in that area. This interview will yield a thorough knowledge of an employer's operation so that matching is considered well before a youth is presented for an employer's consideration.

• • • STRATEGY 7
Identify tasks that are important to both the youth and the employer.

To ensure that both the youth and employer stay interested and engaged after the placement, it is useful to clearly identify and outline the possible assignments and likely performance expectations before the work experience begins. This closely follows the previous strategy and represents an important next step after knowing the youth's interests and employer's needs. Regardless of the type of work experience a transition professional is seeking for a youth, it is important to look simultaneously at the youth's interests and the employer's tasks. "Make-work" situations are not likely to keep employers any more interested than the youth.

Tasks that may be identified in a workplace run the gamut from simple, such as shredding paper, to complicated, such as operating high-tech equipment. Regardless of the relative complexity of the task, it is important to ensure that youth are performing a task that will teach something of value. Just as importantly, and especially if the employer is to become and remain a partner in transition work experiences, it is necessary that the employer sees the youth performing tasks that either need to be done or will eventually produce the kinds of skills and work behaviors that will ultimately benefit the employer's operation.

Appendix 6.2 provides a tool for identifying and taking an inventory of an employer's needs, which can be used to match to a youth's circumstances.

• • • STRATEGY 8
Customize assignments as necessary.

The availability of employer resources will be an important determinant of how youth assignments are organized. For example, will a co-worker mentor be available

---

Mutual Benefit in Proposing an Employer–Youth Match

After an in-depth informational interview and tour of a nationally known retail chain store, a transition teacher was able to recognize areas of operation that needed significant improvement. The most crucial problem areas included the mismatching of sizing tags on clothing with the size nubs on hangers (the local store was fined by national headquarters 3 months in a row after failing secret tests), the disorganization of the toy department (the only department to go down in sales profits since last quarter), and disorganization in the stock room (requiring personnel to work overtime at least once per week).

Based on this information, the teacher proposed a list of tasks that would address these key problems:

- Weekly accuracy checks of tags to size nubs to reduce incidence of fines and make shopping easier for customers
- Weekly clean-up and organization of the toy department to make it more accessible and appealing to shoppers and therefore increase sales
- Evening clean-up and preparation in the stockroom for the morning shift to make all employees' jobs run more smoothly and to reduce unnecessary overtime

The teacher further proposed that these tasks be done by a youth who liked to work with people and excelled in detail work. After organizing the necessary supports to train the youth to do these tasks, the youth began the work. The manager is very pleased and has noticed the increased sales as well as reduced fines and overtime pay.

---

to be assigned to the youth? How much supervisor time will be available? Will the youth need to receive standard in-house training? What are the employer's preferences for onsite support, such as job coaching, from the transition program?

Determine how the tasks can be monitored most effectively through any combination of employer and transition professional oversight so that youth receive effective task training and performance feedback once they are at the workplace. It will be different for each youth and each employer. Again, success of the future work experience is more likely when as much of this as possible can be determined before a youth is presented to an employer for consideration.

• • • STRATEGY 9

Propose and negotiate task assignments.

As all of the previous strategies are pursued, there should always be an eye on closing the deal for individual youth work experiences. Negotiating a work experience placement is obviously a critical step in the employer recruitment process. Ultimately, the negotiation with employers will hinge on proposing and negotiating task assignments based on how they will help the employer. Typical steps in such negotiation include the following:

1. Presenting tasks that might be performed by the youth in the workplace

2. Outlining how these tasks might be assigned to the youth

3. Highlighting how the tasks match the circumstances of the youth (e.g., interests, previous experience, skills)

4. Presenting the possible benefits to the employer for assigning a job or tasks to the youth (e.g., getting the job done if a paid job, preparing the future workforce if a career exploration experience)

5. Clearly describing the role of the program in supporting the youth (e.g., training, coaching, follow-up)

6. Making the "ask," such as

"Does this look like it will work for you?"

"Do you have any more questions?"

"Is there anything else I can do to make this work for you?"

"Can we set a start date?"

7. Reiterating the potential benefits to the employer. In the end, this will be what "sells" the employer on the relationship.

Each youth—including those requiring significant support from transition professionals—brings a range of competencies to any given workplace. Almost always, tasks can be identified that offer some benefit to an employer when performed by a youth worker. Employers may get involved with transition programs because they see it as an important means of addressing a community need, but most often employers' involvement is based on addressing an immediate or projected workforce need. Negotiating with employers for a youth placement is most successful when employers see a clear advantage for participating—that is, "what's in it for them." Wise transition professionals will keep this in mind during all stages of their relationships with employer partners.

Proposals to employers are most often informal, verbal presentations. However, sometimes it helps to have a prepared format to make a proposal to an employer. This can help organize one's thoughts about what to say to the employer or can serve as a formal adjunct to the "ask" that is given to the employer. Appendix 6.3 provides a sample proposal template.

COMPLEMENTARY STRATEGIES FOR FINDING AND RECRUITING EMPLOYERS

In addition to the strategies provided, there are a host of strategies that transition specialists can draw on to help in their search for potential employers. Networking and developing an effective "elevator speech" are two of the most common and useful.

Networking

Nothing beats having a large network of connections. As the old saying goes, it is not what you know, but who you know. In fact, the task of finding employers who are willing to offer their workplaces to youth with disabilities involves, if nothing else, "prospecting" for potentially interested employers. Networking is essential to finding leads for potential youth work experience (Griffin, Hammis, & Geary, 2007; Hoff, Gandolfo, Gold, & Jordan, 2000; Luecking et al., 2004). In fact, many seasoned work experience and job developers would say the strategies outlined previously are only useful as complements to networks of potential employer contacts. Still others would say that having a network of people who can put you in contact with employers trumps all other methods for identifying potential work experiences and jobs.

When thinking about networking, transition professionals should ask themselves:

- Who do I know who can identify an employer contact?
- Who do my friends know?
- Who do the youth and the youth's family and friends know?
- Who do my colleagues know?
- Who do my transition partners know?
- Who do employers with whom I have already worked know?
- What business organizations might I join?

In effect, *everyone you know is part of the network* that can put you in touch with potential employers. Research has shown that the larger the network, the more likely that work opportunities can be found (Granovetter, 1974; Hagner, 2003). It is not just who you know, but also how many people you know.

Therefore, the task is to always be on the lookout for expanding your network and meeting new people, no matter the venue. Joining business organizations such as the Chamber of Commerce is useful; they provide a place to meet more people outside the usual circle of educators, transition professionals, and human service professionals. Your network is also expanded when you meet people at church, at the grocery store, at the gym, at cocktail parties—basically everywhere.

The Elevator Speech

When you meet new people, will you be ready to answer the inevitable question of what you do for a living? You need to be ready with a concise explanation that represents what you do in an interesting, yet brief way—something that is suitable for any encounter with each new member of your network. You need to have an *elevator speech.*

Can you explain your work with youth concisely and compellingly enough to get your message across to a stranger in the time it takes to ride an elevator a few floors— using language that puts you and the youth in the best possible light, and in a way that causes people to want to learn more? If you can, then the world waits to become your network! The concept of an elevator speech is simply that it is useful to have a straightforward way to get a message across to a new acquaintance in any spontaneous encounter. When you have someone's attention and exchange information, there is a chance to follow up with another contact. The person becomes someone you might call on later as you add to your network. This person might know someone you can contact, who might know someone else you can contact, and so on.

Here are a few examples from colleagues who have used elevator speeches to great effect.

> *"Our school is working to really improve the ability of the students to be good workers. I work together with many of the community's employers so that youth have the opportunity to learn good work skills and so that employers find good people to fill their jobs."*

Networking Opportunities Are Everywhere

One transition teacher, when buying a house, established an excellent relationship with the law office that handled the settlement. After meeting several times, she noticed the busy activity in the office and the multiple tasks that she observed being performed by the staff. She thought such an office would be a great place for youth to find out about jobs in the legal profession specifically, but also to find out about the types of tasks and responsibilities that office jobs entail generally. She mentioned this to the lawyer during the settlement and asked if the lawyer knew of places like his office where this might be possible and where there might be some interest in hosting youth for work experiences.

Not only did the lawyer introduce the teacher to two other law offices, but the lawyer also arranged for the office manager to help the teacher identify tasks in his office. Eventually, this office and another became active partners in providing work internships for youth in the teacher's school.

"I love it when young people grow up and become responsible employees! At my school I spend a lot of time helping them to learn on the job."

"I work with area companies to identify ways to meet their future workforce needs by linking them with youth. It's exciting to see youth perform and to see companies happy about it!"

There is no exact formula for the best elevator speech, but there are three basic rules: keep it short, keep it concise, and keep it positive. The speech should be one that you are comfortable with and that communicates positively what your work is all about. You can introduce the fact that you work with youth with disabilities, but it should not be the main thing emphasized. It may not be useful to do it at all during a very brief, first-time encounter.

If you do mention that you work with youth with disabilities or in special education and you get a response such as, "It must be *sooo* rewarding," you may have given the wrong impression. You should phrase it so that you create a positive image—or at least prevent a negative or stereotyped one: "Many of the youth I work with require some modifications to the workplace or to work assignments because of a disability. My school is really good at matching their skills to an employer's needs to make them and the youth's co-workers as productive as possible." This communicates competence and professionalism. Remember, you never get a second chance to make a good first impression. Use a good elevator speech to make that impression.

SUMMARY

This chapter introduced the importance of focusing on employer needs as work experience and jobs are pursued with and on behalf of youth with disabilities. It discussed reasons why employers might consider participating as partners with transition programs and what they want from these partnerships. Employers are motivated mostly by their self-interest to find people to fill their present jobs or to help develop the workforce that will meet their future needs (Luecking, 2005). They are least motivated by opportunities to meet a community need to improve youth circumstances. The implications of these motivations are that appeals to employers to host youth in their workplace must emphasize how the partnership will benefit the employers. We also saw that employers want competent and convenient ways to receive youth referrals, and they want youth who are well matched to their tasks and workplaces.

Based on these factors, several proven strategies to interact with and recruit employers were introduced. The strategies discussed in this chapter are basic to developing relationships with employers. For those readers who want to dig deeper into the bag of employer recruitment tricks, a host of additional helpful resources are available (e.g., Bissonnette, 1994; DiLeo & Langton, 1994; Griffin et al., 2007; Luecking et al., 2004).

Transition specialists must elevate their level of professionalism when interacting with employers and must increase the opportunities for interactions with employers, no matter the strategies used. Ultimately, the success of linking youth with work is as much about meeting employers' needs as it is about serving youth. Otherwise, the entry of youth with disabilities into the labor market will continue to be only sporadically successful and characterized by low-wage, low-skill jobs. Therefore, greater emphasis needs to be placed on making transition programs for youth with disabilities more attractive and friendly to employers. Chapter 7 continues this discussion about meeting employer needs and keeping employers involved.

LEARNING LAB: *Becoming an Employer Recruitment Pro*

1. *Introducing yourself*—Can you grab the attention of strangers when they ask what you do? Compose an elevator speech that you can use to describe your work with youth. Remember to keep it short, keep it concise, and keep it positive!

2. *Expanding your network*—The opportunity to recruit employers grows with the number of people you know who can put you in touch with persons in their line of work. Make a list people you know in each of the following types of industries:

   Animal care

   Automotive

   Construction

   Finance

   Government

   Hospitality

   Information technology

Legal

Manufacturing

Medical and health care

Recreation

Retail

Science and technology

Security

Social Services

Other

3. *Contacting someone from the list*—Schedule and conduct an informational interview using the questions presented in the discussion of Strategy 1. Record your experience on the Employer Contact Sheet in Appendix 6.1, and file the form away for future reference!

REFERENCES

Bissonette, D. (1994). *Beyond traditional job development*. Chatsworth, CA: Milt Wright & Associates.

DiLeo, D., & Langton, D. (1994). *Get the marketing edge*. St. Augustine, FL: TRN Publishing.

Fabian, E.S., Luecking, R.G., & Tilson, G.P. (1994). *A working relationship: The job development specialist's guide to successful partnerships with business*. Baltimore: Paul H. Brookes Publishing Co.

Granovetter, M. (1974). *Getting a job*. Chicago: The University of Chicago Press.

Griffin, C., Hammis, D., & Geary, T. (2007). *The job developer's handbook: Practical tactics for customized employment*. Baltimore: Paul H. Brookes Publishing Co.

Hagner, D. (2003). Job development and job search assistance. In E.M. Szymanski & R.M. Parker (Eds.), *Work and disability: Issues and strategies in career development and job placement* (2nd ed., pp. 343–373). Austin, TX: PRO-ED.

Hoff, D., Gandolfo, C., Gold, M., & Jordan, M. (2000). *Demystifying job development: Field-based approaches to job development for people with disabilities*. St. Augustine, FL: TRN Publishing.

Kregel, J., & Unger, D. (1993). Employer perceptions of the work potential of individuals with disabilities. *Journal of Vocational Rehabilitation, 3*, 17–25.

Locklin, D. (1997). *Community exchange*. Knoxville, TN: Community Rehabilitation Program, Rehabilitation Continuing Education Program.

Luecking, R. (Ed.). (2004). *Essential tools: In their own words: Employer perspectives on youth with disabilities in the workplace*. Minneapolis: University of Minnesota, Institute on Community Integration, National Center on Secondary Education and Transition.

Luecking, R. (2005). Strategies for youth workforce programs to become employer-friendly intermediaries. *Info Brief, 12*, 1. Washington, DC: Institute for Educational Leadership, National Collaborative on Workforce and Disability/Youth.

Luecking, R.G., Fabian, E.S., & Tilson, G.P. (2004). *Working relationships: Creating career opportunities for job seekers with disabilities through employer partnerships*. Baltimore: Paul H. Brookes Publishing Co.

Appendix

- Employer Contact Sheet
- Inventory of Employer's Needs and Tasks
- Work Experience Proposal Template

APPENDIX 6.1

Employer Contact Sheet

Name of company/employer: _____

Date of contact: _____

Company contact person: _____

Address: _____

_____

Telephone number: _____

E-mail address: _____

Nature of contact

☐　Telephone call

☐　Informational interview

☐　Company tour

☐　Other _____

Describe contact:　_____

_____

_____

_____

Next steps:　_____

_____

_____

_____

_____　　_____
Transition specialist's signature　　　　　　　　　　　Date

APPENDIX 6.2

Inventory of Employer's Needs and Tasks

Name of company/employer: _____

Address: _____

_____

Description of business: _____

Contact person: _____

Telephone number: _____

E-mail address: _____

Are there?

	Yes	No	Explain:
Logjams in work areas	☐	☐	Explain:
Backlogs of unfinished work	☐	☐	Explain:
Rush times	☐	☐	Explain:
Seasonal fluctuations	☐	☐	Explain:
Highly paid employees doing administrative tasks	☐	☐	Explain:
Sporadic but important tasks	☐	☐	Explain:
Areas of staff turnover	☐	☐	Explain:
Future workforce needs	☐	☐	Explain:

Potential tasks that youth interns/workers could do

1. _____

2. _____

3. _____

4. _____

5. _____

6. _____

7. _____

8. _____

9. _____

10. _____

Additional comments

_____

_____

_____

_____

_____

_____   _____

Transition specialist's signature   Date

APPENDIX 6.3

Work Experience Proposal Template

1	*Recap visits or contacts* "Thank you for the time you took to show me your operations last week. It was interesting to observe your employees at work!"
2	*What did you see?* "During my visit, I heard several of your colleagues say that there were often backlogs due to increased customer orders."
3	*Tasks that could be assigned to youth* "I realized that there are tasks such as delivering documents across departments, assembling customer packets, copying documents, and sorting incoming mail that people are spending a lot of time doing."
4	*How the tasks match the youth intern* "One of my students, Joseph, is good at clearly organized tasks and would love to work in an office."
5	*How would this help the company* "If Joseph assembles and delivers the packets to each department, workers could attend to other tasks. This might help reduce the backlog of work."
6	*How will you help?* "I will accompany Joseph to get him oriented to his new tasks and check in every day to see how he is doing."
7	*Make the "ask"* "Can I bring Joseph in for an interview?"
8	*Reiterate the benefits to the company* "With my help, Joseph can learn these tasks and the other employees will not have to worry about their tasks. He can help move the work along."

7

$\bullet\ \bullet\ \bullet$

Workplace Partners

Strategies for Retaining
Effective Employer Participation

> **This chapter provides the reader with**
>
> - Strategies for helping employers to provide effective work experiences for youth
> - Strategies for keeping employers pleased and willing to continue hosting youth in the workplace
> - Strategies and resources for helping employers to accept and understand disability and accommodations
> - A Learning Lab on managing employer partnerships

"My chief recommendations to programs that represent youth with disabilities are to make sure youth are doing 'real' work and to guarantee to help work through any issue that the youth's presence might create."

An experienced employer partner

As mentioned in Chapter 6, Port Discovery managed a program through which youth could volunteer for various activities associated with museum operation. A transition teacher learned of this program and realized that such volunteer experiences would be useful for some of her students. She negotiated with the museum manager to have these students volunteer in various areas of Port Discovery. The teacher constantly solicited feedback from the museum staff about how she could make sure that she was supervising and supporting the students in ways that made their experience at the museum productive for Port Discovery. As a result, she could quickly help to reassign students who were not performing well, counsel students who were not adhering to dress codes, or work with students who were not meeting time commitments. The museum manager was so pleased with the teacher's responsiveness that she contacted that teacher for new volunteers before she advertised openings.

Every time the manager of one large department store has a job opening, he calls the transition teacher from a local school to see if she has a student available or if she knows someone who might be interested. This is because in the 2 years the manager has been hosting youth in his workplace, this teacher has been extremely responsive to his requests and questions about the youth; has been on the site frequently to check on the youth working there, especially when a problem arises; and has offered to help with other staff recruiting needs.

When employers are treated like customers of transition programs, opportunities for work experiences can be plentiful, as in these two examples. After all, getting employers interested and willing to host youth in the workplace is only half the battle. Keeping them interested is just as important. As with any partnership, the best partnerships with employers are those characterized by trust, mutual benefit, and durability. In other words, can the partners count on each other to do what they say they will do, will they each get something out of it, and will the partnership last beyond the initial relationship? Having these features built into the partnership can mean the difference between employers going away mad or raving about how great it is for them to provide work experience opportunities for youth. This chapter focuses on strategies that promote ongoing employer partnerships after the initial relationship is established.

REVISITING EMPLOYER EXPECTATIONS

Employers are primarily motivated by their self-interest when choosing to partner with transition programs. They are not in business to host youth with disabilities for work experiences or to hire them. For the most part, everything employers do is to make a profit, save money, or make their enterprise operate as well as possible. This applies to all employers, whether they are in the private, government, or nonprofit sector. Interest in having youth in the workplace may come from the need to fill immediate job openings, to deal with future workforce shortages, or to address a perceived community need such as promoting constructive development of its citizens—in this case, youth with disabilities. Even in the latter situation, in which employers want to become corporate good citizens, it is still self-interest that drives their participation. But whatever the reason, strategies that show respect for employers' needs and interests are necessary to convince them to enter into and maintain partnerships with transition programs that represent youth with disabilities.

Chapter 6 discussed four expectations that employers have when deciding to host youth in their workplaces:

1. Competent and convenient assistance in receiving youth referrals
2. Matching of youth skills and interests to job tasks
3. Support in training and monitoring the youth at the worksite
4. Formal or informal disability awareness (when the youth chooses to disclose a disability)

Years of experience of colleagues around the county working with employer partners on behalf of youth with disabilities bear out the validity of these expectations.

Table 7.1. Strategies to address employer expectations

Employer expectation	Strategies
Competent and convenient assistance in receiving youth referrals	1. Conduct informational interviews. 2. Use business language. 3. Establish a single point of contact. 4. Maintain professional and responsive contact. 5. Underpromise and overdeliver.
Matching of youth skills and interests to job tasks	6. Know both the youth's capabilities and interests and the employer's circumstances thoroughly. 7. Identify tasks that are important to both the youth and the employer. 8. Customize assignments as necessary. 9. Propose and negotiate task assignments.
Support in training and monitoring the youth at the worksite	10. Clarify employer expectations about job training, coaching, and follow-up. 11. Follow through on agreed follow-up procedures. 12. Solicit employers' feedback on service from the intermediary. 13. Adjust support and service to employers based on their feedback.
Formal and informal disability awareness (when the youth chooses to disclose a disability)	14. Deliver information about specific accommodations required by the youth. 15. Ask what further information and help the employer desires. 16. Provide disability awareness information based on what the employer requests. 17. Model interaction and support appropriate for the youth. 18. Provide periodic guidance and information as necessary.

More importantly, employers themselves who have successfully hosted youth in their workplaces have expressed these expectations in their own words (Luecking, 2004).

Chapter 6 introduced strategies to address these expectations, as summarized in Table 7.1. This chapter details those strategies not covered in the last chapter—strategies 10 through 18—which primarily relate to retaining employer participation and keeping employers happy with the arrangement. Happy employers contribute to successful work experiences for youth, and the strategies discussed in this chapter will help to make that happen.

STRATEGIES FOR KEEPING EMPLOYERS HAPPY

Most people have heard advertisements with such tag lines as "It's not yours until you like it," "We give service after the sale," and "Backed by the best warranty in the business." Often, our decision to purchase a product or service is influenced by how well we think a company will honor such promises. More importantly, the likelihood that we will remain a customer of that business—and that we will tell our friends about how good that company is—depends on how we are treated after we buy its product or service. Simply stated, we are loyal to companies that treat us right.

This same concept applies to maintaining good, productive relationships with employers who participate in transition programs and provide work experiences for youth. It is one thing to get the employer to "buy into" the idea of hosting youth in their workplaces but quite another to help them do it well and stay committed to doing so. Transition professionals should therefore think of each employer as one of their customers.

Use the strategies from Chapter 6 to attract employers to your service and to hosting or hiring youth. Use the strategies in this chapter to generate satisfied and therefore repeat employer partners for transition and youth employment programs. By keeping the employer satisfied, the work experience is more likely to be successful for the youth, the employer is often willing to host additional youth, and the employer is likely to tell other employers about his or her positive experience. After all, many marketing experts will tell you that excellent customer service is the best marketing strategy of all (e.g., Patton & Bluel, 2000; Zemke & Anderson, 2002). Satisfied employers will tell other employers how good your service is and therefore how beneficial it is to provide work experiences for youth.

The following sections provide some useful and effective strategies to meet— and in most cases exceed—employers' expectations. The strategies have been shown to lead to satisfied and long-term employer partners (Luecking, Fabian, & Tilson, 2004). These strategies build on those introduced in Chapter 6 and are extrapolated from Table 7.1.

Support in Training and Monitoring the Youth at the Worksite

• • • STRATEGY 10
Clarify employer expectations about job training, coaching, and follow-up.

Just as each youth requires specific supports and accommodations to learn and perform in the workplace, each employer presents a unique set of circumstances that affect the employer's willingness and ability to host youth. Regardless of whether the youth will require minimal support or a lot of support, it is important to involve the employer in deciding how the support will be provided. It should not be left to chance. Make sure employer preferences are considered in deciding when, how often, and under what circumstances transition program support is provided on the jobsite. Decisions about how much training or coaching a youth may require are certainly driven by individual youth circumstances; however, these support activities will take place in the employer's workplace. Thus, the employer should be involved in deciding how the support activities are implemented. The rule of thumb is to provide as much follow-up as you can until the employer says otherwise; err on the side of providing too much follow-up. It is better for the employer to ask that you reduce follow-up than for the employer to be frustrated because the transition professional has dropped a youth into a workplace without any support.

Often, it is useful to develop a written plan for follow-up after the youth is placed. Such a plan identifies the agreed-on responsibilities of the employer, the youth, and the transition professional; basic contact information; the nature of the expected follow-up, such as initial training, coaching, and/or decision making; the expected frequency and duration of the follow-up; contingencies for increasing or decreasing follow-up contact; the basic expectation of all parties; and other factors that might be important for clarifying roles. Chapter 8 will offer more discussion about this as well as provide a sample Work Experience Agreement for this purpose.

• • • **STRATEGY 11**
Follow through on agreed follow-up procedures.

Once everyone agrees on how the work experience will be monitored, it is important to do what was promised: *service after the sale*. This follow-up includes being on the jobsite as often as the employer expects or requests. It does not hurt to be there more often than expected, as long as it is not an imposition, but it is never good to be there less than expected or promised.

This strategy also presumes that transition professionals will be as responsive as possible to all employer requests, including attending immediately to requests for assistance with a youth.

One employer was concerned that a youth was not keeping up with his tasks during his work experience and was disrupting the workplace by constantly talking to himself. After receiving the call from the employer about the situation, the transition professional arranged to be at the jobsite first thing the next day to observe the youth and identify strategies to intervene. Upon observation, it was quickly determined that the youth was simply talking himself through the steps of his tasks because he could not remember them. Consequently, he was slow to complete his work. Both problems were solved when the transition professional developed a picture prompt notebook that the youth followed to move through his tasks. This action not only made the work experience more successful for the youth, but it also showed the employer a high level of responsiveness to his request for help and a high level of competence in resolving the situation. The work experience ultimately lead to a full-time job for the youth at that worksite, as well as an employer who was happy with the performance of a productive employee.

Other "rules" of responsive employer relationships include

- Return telephone calls and e-mail messages within 24 hours—or better yet, before the end of the business day.

- Confirm appointments 1 day ahead of time. This communicates that you respect the employer's time and also provides an opportunity to quickly prepare for any additional requests the employer might make in advance of a scheduled meeting.

- Drop everything and respond immediately in cases of emergencies or pressing situations. Such responsiveness communicates a concern for the circumstances of the employer and may in fact make the difference between keeping and losing that employer as a long-term partner.

- Underpromise and overdeliver. The most effective transition professionals who have the best relationships with employers work to "dazzle" employers with postplacement service.

In Chapter 6, the customer service concept of underpromising and overdelivering—doing more or giving more service than promised—was introduced as a strategy to deliver competent assistance to employers as they consider receiving youth referrals. The application of this concept is so important to winning employer goodwill and garnering their positive regard that it bears repeating here in the context of ongoing support to employer partners. People always want to work with people they like and trust and who offer to make the situation better than it was before they met. It adds value to the relationship in the eyes of the employer partner. Underpromising and overdelivering is a proven way to get employers to like you, to trust you, and to think they are better off for having known you. Here are some examples of overdelivering on promises:

- After helping a company to hire a student he represents, a transition teacher promises to assist the company's human resource director in advertising additional openings to other schools and employment agencies in the community.

- A transition professional stops by a company's office just to bring cookies for the co-workers of a student doing an internship there.

- One teacher arranged for a youth to participate in an internship at a local printing company. She recommends the printing company whenever she hears that other companies where she has students in work experiences need printing jobs completed.

- An employer requested that a transition professional contact her by the following week with useful accommodation information about a youth at the workplace. The transition professional provided the information the following day.

- A teacher offered three potential times to be available for a meeting after the employer asked for one.

The gesture does not have to be grand or significant. It only matters that the employer gets more than expected because it communicates to the employer that there is clear interest and respect for the enterprise by the transition professional. It also demonstrates the thoughtfulness of the professional, something that is likely to be greatly appreciated. This strategy is probably one of the most important to maintaining a long-lasting and positive relationship—and it is usually easy and inexpensive. In each of the previous examples, it is easy to guess who the employer will call for future job openings and who will tell other employers that this transition professional is more than "on the ball."

Responsiveness to Workplace Problems

What happens when things go wrong? Another aspect of follow-up on agreed-on procedures is being responsive to problems that arise. Invariably, there will be a situation when a youth performs or behaves badly in the workplace. Many youth will have had few, if any, previous experiences in the workplace, and they may not—in spite of the best efforts to prepare them—fully understand workplace expectations or know how to handle new situations. Sometimes, there are even mistakes in matching individual youth with the right workplace environment. So how do you keep the employer as a partner under such circumstances?

Think again of the employer as a customer of transition services. Most customers tend to have a higher tolerance for mistakes if there is a timely and genuine response that communicates that the situation will be addressed. Attending to the problem immediately and encouraging feedback from unsatisfied customers are essential customer service activities that the business world has long adopted (Connellan & Zemke, 1993; Zemke & Anderson, 2002). Often the customer knows exactly what the solution might be to "fix" the problem. But even for situations in which this is not the case, identifying how the problem can be addressed, and then coupling that action with a service that adds value to the encounter, breeds strong customer loyalty (Patton & Bluel, 2000). This added value is often important because simply fixing the immediate problem is not always sufficient to make the customer happy. This strategy was effective when a potentially serious problem arose in a transition program workplace.

A transition specialist helped to secure a work trial for a youth at a local grocery store that is part of a large national chain. The purpose of the trial was to expose the youth to a few stock clerk tasks to see if he could perform them in an authentic environment, to see if he would like the type of work and the environment, and to determine the best type of job coaching support. This information would help to identify future employment goals and would be a stepping stone for later job development.

The trial did not go well. In fact, on the second day at the store, the youth erupted with loud yelling and threw items from an entire shelf on the floor, breaking most of them. The store manager called the transition specialist, who immediately went to the store. He not only helped to clean up the mess, but he also solicited another colleague to take the youth home because the store manager no longer wanted him there. The transition specialist offered to pay for the damages (an offer that the store manager refused). The manager was impressed with the responsiveness of the transition specialist and the genuine concern he expressed for the problems the youth created for the store.

The manager was even more impressed when he received a sincere note of apology from the transition specialist, who took responsibility for not being aware that the youth may cause such problems. In the note, he also asked what else he could do to remedy the problems that were created by the situation. Although the youth was not permitted to return to the worksite, the manager remained willing to host other youth for work trials because the transition specialist was responsive in addressing the problem, helped to correct the problem, apologized for the problem, and offered to make up for whatever the problem caused.

Remember that a well-handled problem or complaint has the potential to lead to more customer loyalty than existed before the complaint. That store provided work experience opportunities for many years following this episode as a result. The store may not have remained a partner with the transition program after the episode, but the response to the problem certainly increased the likelihood that it would.

The failed trial work experience was not really a failure because the youth and his teacher learned from it. The most important lesson for them was that a work environment with the constant presence of people moving—like a grocery store—was not a good match for this youth. He subsequently found a job in a home improvement store warehouse, where he could work with few people interrupting him.

• • • STRATEGY 12
Solicit employers' feedback on service from the intermediary.

It is obviously important to get employers' feedback on how youth are performing. However, it is even more important from a customer service perspective for transition professionals to ask for feedback from employers on what employers think about the transition program's service. To elicit useful feedback, ask these basic questions of employer partners:

1. What does the employer like about the transition program's service?
2. What does the employer not like about it?
3. What can be improved?

These questions can be asked informally during a telephone call or a visit, or in a more formal way through a brief written survey such as the Employer Satisfaction Questionnaire provided in Appendix 7.1. No matter how employers' views are solicited, the key is that they be solicited in some way. This communicates concern for the employers' operation, impresses on employers that there is concern, and most importantly gives the transition professional the chance to act on the feedback so that he or she can improve employer service. Many work experiences can be saved by acting on employer feedback.

It is also useful and important to solicit feedback about the youth's performance so that the proper support can be provided to the youth. A useful performance appraisal for soliciting employer feedback on youth performance is included in Appendix 7.2. Ensuring effective support to youth in the workplace goes hand in hand with keeping employers happy with the experience; Chapter 8 will explore this subject.

••• STRATEGY 13
Adjust support and service to employers based on their feedback.

Feedback is only useful if it is acted on. If employers want more follow-up on youth on the job, provide it. If employers want less, back off. If employers ask for faster response time to a youth problem, be there quicker. Again, such service improvement efforts impress employer partners. They also increase the likelihood that the employer will do two things: continue the partnership with the transition program and tell other employers about the program's responsiveness. Good service is also good marketing!

Implementation of high-quality support to employer partners involves a continuous process of delivering service (i.e., facilitating youth placement in the workplace), soliciting feedback about the service, responding to the feedback, and adjusting the service accordingly, as in the feedback loop in Figure 7.1.

As employers provide feedback, transition professionals need to be ready to address occasionally negative feedback. This is what helps to improve and sustain relationships with employers. So how should you handle employers' complaints?

- Listen. Do not argue or be defensive. Ask for or offer solutions to fix the problem. Nobody ever wins an argument with customers. Even if you know the customer is wrong, make him or her feel that he or she is right. Sometimes a complaining customer just wants to be hcard. The same concept applies to employer partners, whom you should regard as your customers.

- Never ignore or minimize employers' concerns or complaints. Doing so is delivering a message that you do not care about them as partners, in which case you might as well forget them because they will not likely do business

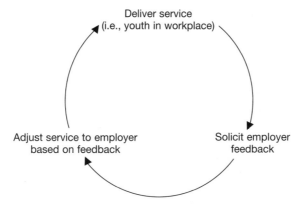

Figure 7.1. Feedback loop of implementing quality service to employers. (*Source:* Luecking, Fabian, & Tilson, 2004.)

with you again. Chances are that they will also tell other employers about their dissatisfaction, spoiling your reputation and your opportunity to develop new employer partners.

• Offer to correct the problem, as in the previous example of the youth in the trial work experience at the grocery store.

• Improve and deliver service to the employer accordingly.

Formal and Informal Disability Awareness

Whether or not to disclose a disability is a personal decision that each youth should make, not teachers or transition professionals. The same is true about *how* a disability is disclosed in cases where youth want and need to disclose a disability. The remaining strategies are provided with the proviso that they be used only when youth have given permission to transition professionals or the youth's representative to disclose the youth's disability, and related needs for accommodation, to potential and current employer partners. Extensive treatment of the issue of disclosure was provided in Chapter 4. It is important that you are thoroughly familiar with how to help youth make decisions about whether, how, and to whom to make disclosures about their disability before proceeding with the following strategies.

• • • STRATEGY 14
Deliver information about specific accommodations required by the youth.

Any discussion about accommodations required by individual youth should be in the context of the specific work environment and specific work tasks. This is best done during negotiations with employers (see Chapter 6), but it can happen any time after the placement when accommodation needs are recognized. As with each of the strategies presented in this chapter, remember that it is the employer partner for whom these strategies are initiated. Accommodations might look very different through an employer's lens than through a disability advocate's lens. Therefore, it is important to describe accommodations in terms of how they will help the youth perform to the employer's satisfaction, rather than in terms of legal requirements.

It is important to understand that the employer is only legally bound to provide accommodations when the youth is hired for a defined company position, not necessarily for other types of work experiences, such as work sampling or unpaid internships, where the youth is not an actual employee of the company. Even then, accommodations are only required if they are necessary for the employee to perform the *essential* functions of the job—that is, those tasks that are required as identified in a formal job description. Some youth will be able to perform jobs with standard job descriptions with or without accommodations. Even if these accommodations might be extensive, such as wheelchair accessibility or modified keyboards, the employer must offer them if they are not an undue hardship on the company.

Many youth with disabilities, however, may only be able to perform some tasks within a standard job description. In these cases and in cases of unpaid work experiences, the employer is under no obligation to provide accommodations or to hire the youth. This is distinctly different from educational settings governed by the Individuals with Disabilities Education Act of 1990 (PL 101-476), under which schools must provide learning and physical accommodations. Thus, it is all the more important to be prepared to negotiate with prospective employers based on a youth's positive traits and potential contributions to the company. Then, whatever accommodations are necessary will be seen as minimally intrusive and ultimately beneficial to the youth's performance at the worksite.

Transition professionals should be direct and open about whatever accommodations might be necessary and should then work with the employer to identify the most effective way to provide the accommodations. Clarify what the transition professional's responsibility will be to arrange the accommodations and what the employer's responsibility or preference might be in providing them.

• • • STRATEGY 15
Ask what further information and help the employer desires.

Employers who are unfamiliar or new to youth with disabilities may not always know how to ask, or what to ask, about supporting and accommodating youth. How to properly communicate with youth about their disability and related accommodations is also a common employer question. It will, therefore, often be important and necessary not to wait for the employer to ask but to solicit his or her concerns so that he or she will be comfortable in supporting and accommodating the youth. This is easy when the accommodations are straightforward, such as giving written directions to the youth rather than verbal directions. When the accommodations are extensive or involved, however, much more help by the transition professional will be required so that the employer is comfortable.

From the very beginning of the placement and periodically thereafter, it may be useful to ask the employer the following questions:

• Do you feel comfortable with the accommodations we have in place?

• Are they helping the youth to complete the assigned tasks?

• Are the youth's co-workers familiar and comfortable with the accommodations?

• Is it easy for you to communicate with the youth? If not, how can I help?

Mutual Benefit Through Disability Disclosure and Accommodation

Cynthia's severe dyslexia is not readily apparent upon first meeting her; however, whenever she must read directions, she needs quite a bit of extra time to get through them. Without accommodating for this, Cynthia is prone to making problematic mistakes. She was fired from one job due to errors in following directions, but she really wanted to work and was interested in animal care.

Cynthia's transition teacher found a local veterinarian who also operated a boarding facility for dogs and cats and who was looking for animal attendants. The teacher explained Cynthia's love of animals. She also informed the veterinarian, with Cynthia's permission, that Cynthia had a reading disability. During a subsequent job interview, the teacher, the veterinarian, and Cynthia together talked about ways to accommodate her and to provide alternate ways to follow feeding and playtime directions on the boarding orders.

With the veterinarian's input, it was decided that the office assistant would read the orders aloud to Cynthia when an animal was initially brought in for boarding. This proved to be a very effective approach because Cynthia's excellent recall ability enabled her to remember each animal's care needs. She unfailingly carried out her tasks for the entire school year she worked at the boarding facility. This was made possible by disability disclosure to the veterinarian and the other co-workers, joint problem solving to determine an effective accommodation, and the attentive work of the transition teacher to make sure it worked for everyone.

Soliciting this information is similar in concept to Strategy 12 because it is a type of customer service issue. Of course, it is important for the youth to be properly accommodated, but the accommodation has to work for the employer. Employers' comfort with disability and accommodations is important to their ongoing comfort and satisfaction with partnering with youth transition programs.

• • • STRATEGY 16

Provide disability awareness information based on what the employer requests.

Transition professionals can and should offer to provide disability awareness information to employers, but that information should not be forced if it is not needed. If it is needed, then it should be based on a particular employer's needs and request.

One employer was particularly concerned about co-workers' responses to having a young man with a significant communication disability in the workplace. She asked the transition teacher to provide a general disability awareness training session to the staff, as well as to offer specific techniques to the co-workers on how to interact effectively with the youth. This employer-initiated awareness training was useful in the youth's eventual acceptance into that workplace. Just as importantly, it was useful in making the supervisor and the staff in that workplace comfortable with the youth.

Another teacher was asked by an employer who hired a youth with autism to provide some basic information on autism that he could share with staff and co-workers so they could better understand the youth's behaviors, particularly the youth's difficulty following social and verbal cues. She provided a basic one-page fact sheet on the nature of autism and the various ways it was manifested. It was particularly helpful in the case of this particular youth, whose social interactions were complicated because the youth often did not respond to nuanced communications or took them literally. The youth was confused and unresponsive if his supervisor said, "Hurry up or we'll have hell to pay." But once the supervisor learned to say, "Please finish five packets by 12 o'clock," the youth was very compliant. Teaching co-workers to communicate in concrete terms rather than using metaphors was a big help to this employer's ability to support the youth's placement in the workplace.

The format of providing disability awareness information—whether it is delivered informally as needed or formally through written materials or training sessions—is often based on what the employer asks for, on feedback solicited from the employer by transition professionals, and on the workplace environment. The important thing is for the transition professional to be ready to respond to what the employer needs to make the situation work for them.

• • • STRATEGY 17
Model interaction and support appropriate for the youth.

Every time the transition professional is at the workplace, he or she has an opportunity to show, by modeling, how best to interact and support specific youth workers. This is especially true when a youth has unique or involved accommodation needs. Although this helps to ensure that the youth will receive the necessary support in performing assigned tasks and interacting with co-workers, it is also important in helping supervisors and co-workers become comfortable in interacting with the youth.

• • • STRATEGY 18
Provide periodic guidance and information as necessary.

Follow-up, both self-initiated and based on employer feedback, is again useful and necessary here, just as in Strategies 11 and 12. It is important for the transition professional not to assume that everything is working fine as long as there is no request from the employer. Checking in periodically to see how accommodations are working gives the employer the impression that the transition professional wants the partnership to work for the employer as much as for the youth. In addition, there is always the possibility that new wrinkles will occur in the workplace that require adjustment of accommodation or reacquaintance with disability awareness issues after the youth begins the work experience.

BE A "CUSTOMER SERVICE STAR"

Like any customer who is subscribing to a service, employers know good customer service when they see it and when they experience it. From the moment transition professionals first meet an employer, they begin to convey their effectiveness—or

---

Modeling Interaction "Breaks the Ice"

Bill started working in a retail clothing chain store as a "markdown attendant." His job entailed going from section to section in the store using a handheld scanner to scan items on display. If it is time to lower the price on an item, the scanner prints a sticker with the lower price, which Bill then puts on the scanned item. Normally, this is a fill-in responsibility for other employees whose primary duty is waiting on customers. The job was customized for Bill through negotiation with the store manager so that more customers could be served in the store while he handled the markdowns.

The transition specialist inquired after a week on the job about Bill's performance and if there was anything she needed to do to help make the arrangements work. The store's sales associates knew Bill had a disability and were uncomfortable around him at first. They were not sure how to interact with him. The store manager asked if the teacher could come to a staff meeting before the store opened one day and explain Bill's disability to the sales associates. The teacher gladly complied. She also spent part of the day at the store with Bill modeling to the associates how to interact with Bill. Within an hour, the ice was broken, and the associates began to comfortably interact with Bill. It wasn't long before they were inviting him on breaks with them. Two years later, Bill is still working at the store.

---

ineffectiveness—as service professionals. The strategies discussed in this chapter ensure that employers see only competence, responsiveness, and a desire to meet the employer's need—in other words, good customer service.

As professionals begin to incorporate these strategies into their repertoire, they are likely to find increasing ease with the whole idea of working with employers as partners and are more likely to become outstanding facilitators of work experience for youth. Transition professionals should ask themselves the following questions as they work to improve their ability to attract and maintain employers as customers of transition programs:

- Do I listen to my employer partners and communicate clearly about what I do and what I can do for them?
- Is it easy for my employer partners to reach me?
- Am I pleasant to work with?
- Do I follow through on commitments I make?
- Do I anticipate problems before they arise and propose solutions?
- Are my proposed solutions easy to implement in the workplace, and are they as unobtrusive as possible?
- Do I respond quickly when my employer partners need me?
- Do I invite employer partners to give me feedback on how I am doing to meet their needs?
- Do I take ownership if something goes wrong?
- If my employer partner is not happy with my service, do I take steps to correct it?
- Do my employer partners see me as a valuable resource?

The aim, of course, is to be able to answer "yes" to all of these questions.

Outstanding performance rarely goes unrecognized by any customer. The same applies to employer partners of transition professionals who you should now be thinking of as your customers. Outstanding performers are able to develop and sustain partnerships with employers of all kinds. They are the transition "stars." They can readily answer the important question about customer service to employers: How does what I do look in the eyes of the employer? Seeing the situation from the lens of the employer will often clarify the best approaches to keeping employers interested in hosting youth in the workplace.

SUMMARY

As in Chapter 6, it is useful to emphasize that the success of linking youth with work is as much about meeting employers' needs as it is about serving youth. A corollary to this concept is that the success of youth in the workplace is as much about keeping employers happy with the arrangement as it is about supporting youth. One cannot happen without the other—youth cannot be successful, and employers cannot benefit, unless there is a simultaneous recognition that both have something to gain by good service from transition professionals who are supporting the work experience.

Persuading an employer to commit to bringing a youth into the workplace may seem like the goal, but it is really just the beginning. Delivering promised services in a timely, convenient, effective, responsive, and value-added way so that the employer remains satisfied is in fact the larger goal. It is not sufficient to simply convince employers to host youth in their workplaces. Responsive post-placement service to employers will keep them convinced. This chapter provided strategies to significantly increase the likelihood that employers remain willing to stay involved and provide youth with the kind of work experience they need to advance their career progression.

Once employers are recruited to be partners who will willingly provide their workplaces for youth work experiences, and once there are approaches in place to ensure the employers' ongoing satisfaction with the arrangement, there is still the critical matter of making sure the experience offers the best opportunity for youth to benefit from the work experience. This will require effective accommodation and support strategies so that youth have access to tasks they need to learn. Youth will also need to perform the tasks in a way that not only meets the expectations of the employer but also accommodates their individual learning styles. Finally, youth will frequently need feedback from transition professionals about how they are performing and how the work experience relates to other school and academic goals. Chapter 8 provides considerable detail about making sure youth are supported effectively on the job and are receiving maximum learning benefits.

LEARNING LAB: *Keeping Employers Happy*

1. Contact an employer with whom you have worked in the past. Or through a colleague, find an employer who has hosted youth in the workplace. Arrange

to interview the employer using the Employer Satisfaction Questionnaire in Appendix 7.1. After completing the survey, answer these questions:

    a.   What can you learn from what the employer found most important?

    b.   What can you learn from what the employer found least important?

    c.   What does the response to the question about recommending services to other employers tell you about how to keep employers happy with participating in transition programs?

2.   List five things that you or any transition professional can do to ensure that employers stay interested in maintaining a partnership.

REFERENCES

Connellan, T., & Zemke, R. (1993). *Sustaining knock your socks off service*. New York: AMA-CON.

Individuals with Disabilities Education Act of 1990, PL 101-476, 20 U.S.C. §§ 1400 *et seq.*

Luecking, R. (2004). *In their own words: Employer perspectives on youth with disabilities in the workplace*. Minneapolis: University of Minnesota, Institute on Community Integration, National Center on Secondary Education and Transition.

Luecking, R.G., Fabian, E.S., & Tilson, G.P. (2004). *Working relationships: Creating career opportunities for job seekers with disabilities through employer partnerships*. Baltimore: Paul H. Brookes Publishing Co.

Patton, J., & Bluel, W. (2000). *After the sale: How to manage product service for customer satisfaction and profit*. Rego Park, NY: Solomon Press.

Zemke, R., & Anderson, K. (2002). *Delivering knock your socks off service*. New York: AMACON.

Appendix

- Employer Satisfaction Questionnaire
- Youth Performance Feedback

APPENDIX 7.1

Employer Satisfaction Questionnaire

1. How would you rate your overall relationship with our program?

   ☐ Excellent   ☐ Good   ☐ Not very good   ☐ Poor

   Suggestions/comments

2. How would you rate our ability to help make the student's placement work for you?

   ☐ Excellent   ☐ Good   ☐ Not very good   ☐ Poor

   Suggestions/comments

3. How would you rate our program's willingness to listen to and respond to your interests and needs?

   ☐ Excellent   ☐ Good   ☐ Not very good   ☐ Poor

   Suggestions/comments

4. What aspect of our program's services is most important to you?

5. What aspect of our services is least important to you?

6. What changes could we make to enhance our relationship with you or other employers?

7. Would you recommend our services to other employers in our community?

   ☐ Yes   ☐ No

   Why or why not?

8. Other comments?

Thank you for taking the time to share your thoughts with us!

APPENDIX 7.2

Youth Performance Feedback

Date: _____

Student: _____ Transition specialist: _____

Job site: _____ Supervisor: _____

Start date: _____ Date of last appraisal: _____

Please rate the student's performance in each of the following areas on a 1–5 scale with 5 being *Outstanding* and 1 being *Unsatisfactory*. Comments by the supervisor, student, and employment specialist are encouraged.

	Rating	Comments
Appearance		
Attendance		
Punctuality		
Interaction with supervisor		
Interaction with co-worker(s)		
Response to criticism		
Initiative		
Independent problem-solving		

APPENDIX 7.2 *(continued)*

	Rating	Comments
Productivity/timeliness		
Quality of work		
Safety		
Other:		
Other:		
Overall performance		

Recommendations

Signatures

Student: _____   Date: _____

Supervisor: _____   Date: _____

Transition specialist: _____   Date: _____

8

• • •

Supporting Youth in the Workplace

Richard G. Luecking and George P. Tilson

This chapter provides the reader with

- Considerations for planning how best to support youth in the workplace
- Strategies for identifying and implementing effective supports and accommodations in the workplace
- Considerations for adjusting accommodations in various workplace contexts
- A Learning Lab on supports and accommodations

"I love my volunteer job. I get to be around animals a bunch during the week. Only thing is because I can only use my one arm, I couldn't open those gigantic bags of dog food. So my teacher suggested someone else empty the bags into those barrels, and I scoop out the food. Works great. And we figured out ways to store the leashes and other stuff so I can get at them easy. Actually, I came up with that idea myself."

Gina

"I guess you could say I have an attitude sometimes. My teacher helped me figure out things I could do to control my temper. We sort of worked out a system—if I feel like I'm gonna get angry, I take a quick break. My boss is cool with that, a long as I get the work done."

Salvador

Derrick is participating in a cooperative work experience with a large law firm. His primary tasks are to assist the librarians in delivering and retrieving books and other resource materials from attorneys, entering basic information into the database, and replacing updated pages in three-ring binders. The attorneys enjoy having Derrick at the firm and feel he has demonstrated his eagerness to learn from the experience.

Derrick has succeeded in this workplace despite that fact that he has multiple disabilities, identified in his school record as cerebral palsy, epilepsy, and intellectual disabilities—information that was of little value in determining the kinds of workplace supports Derrick needed. Instead, his transition specialist knew the following was important: Derrick uses a wheelchair, is unable to stand unassisted, has severe tremors in one arm, and has not had a seizure in over a year. Also, Derrick's speech is quite difficult to understand until you get to know him, he reads on a fourth-grade level, and he will often indicate that he understands something when he does not. He has access to public transportation, but that system is not always reliable. In addition, Derrick cannot feed himself or use the toilet independently. There is no question that Derrick needed considerable support and accommodation to make his work experience a successful one.

Jonetta is an intern with a custom kitchen design company. Because she had extensive experience in woodworking through her father's business, Jonetta is working directly with the custom millwork division of her host company as an assistant. Her school records identify her as having specific learning disabilities and attention-deficit/hyperactivity disorder. She receives special education services, which include a reading resource teacher and testing accommodations. Like Derrick, this information was of little value in determining the kinds of workplace supports she would need. It is, however, important to know that Jonetta has trouble concentrating when seated for longer than 15 minutes, needs to be physically active, and requires directions in written form because she frequently misses steps and gets confused when instructions are presented orally. This information was critical when it came time to help Jonetta set up her work experience.

To be successful in the work experience, many youth will require carefully planned processes, supports, equipment, and/or adaptations to the work environment. Whether these work supports are extensive, as in Derrick's case, or relatively straightforward as with Jonetta, they must address specific issues related to accessibility and work performance. All youth benefit from oversight and guidance from education and transition personnel when on a worksite. This is because anyone new to a workplace may need help learning new skills, following directions, taking initiative, making judgments, communicating with co-workers, fitting in socially, or any number of other aspects of functioning successfully in a work setting. For effective learning to occur at the workplace, for the youth to perform to the satisfaction of employers, and/or for potential problems at the workplace to be addressed, careful and well-planned intervention from transition specialists will be necessary.

Supporting youth with disabilities in the workplace requires two general areas of attention. The first is oversight during the work experience itself, which includes such basic activities as teaching someone how to do various job tasks, giving feedback on performance, and providing regular follow-up. The second area is facilitating accommodations that might be necessary because of barriers related to disability, such as modifications or adjustments to the work environment and/or the conditions of work. This chapter addresses both issues, discussing and providing strategies for assistance, guidance, advice, modifications, and adjustments that may be necessary or useful for ensuring effective work experiences for youth.

POSSIBILITIES AND
IMPORTANCE OF WORKPLACE SUPPORTS

For all youth, with or without disabilities, who are new to or inexperienced in the workplace, there are important considerations about making sure the whole thing works. How comfortable will they be in the new environment? How confident will they be in their ability to learn and perform work tasks? How competent will they be in performing the assigned tasks? For youth with disabilities, there may be additional considerations. What barriers to work performance might there be? How well will they be able to address barriers through specific accommodations so they can perform at their best? These youth are likely to need some kind of help from school or transition program staff, job coaches, workplace mentors, supervisors, and/or co-workers to best organize support for the experience.

The successes of people with disabilities who are strategically supported in the workplace are well documented. Effective accommodations for youth and adults with disabilities range from supports afforded by rapidly advancing assistive technology to straightforward and low-tech workplace adaptations. On the high-tech end of that spectrum, for example, augmentative communication supports—including a range of specific computer-aided devices as well as carefully crafted methods of e-mail communication—have provided much wider access to workplaces for people with communication disabilities (Costen, 1988; Zielinski, 2000). Behrmann and Shepis (1994) reported that, with in vivo design and application of assistive technology, youth with significant mobility disabilities experienced improved employment access and success. Numerous other examples illustrate the application of very complex computer adaptations that have supported workers with a variety of disabilities and accommodation needs, allowing them to accomplish a variety of work tasks (e.g., Fisher, 1999; Inge, Wehman, Strobel, Powell, & Todd, 1998).

In addition to technology-related supports, there are numerous studies and documentation of employment success when specially trained and assigned job coaches are available for people requiring a high level of support (Wehman, 2001). Methodology has also been widely reported that draws on naturally existing and internal workplace supports, such as co-worker mentors, that contribute to successful work performance by youth with high support and accommodation needs (DiLeo, Luecking, & Hathaway, 1995; Mank, Cioffi, & Yovanoff, 1997; Rogan, Banks, & Howard, 2000). In fact, the literature is replete with anecdotal illustrations of workplace supports that contribute to successful job performance for workers with disabilities (e.g., Ford, 1995; Sunoo, 2000; Targett, West, & Anglin, 2001).

Combining well-considered workplace support with suitable accommodation for disability-related barriers increases the likelihood that *any youth* can experience success in the workplace. To help them do so, transition specialists need to be familiar with the context of workplace supports and well versed in ways to implement these supports and accommodations.

CONTEXT FOR WORKPLACE SUPPORTS

As a work experience is being developed and negotiated between the youth and the host employer, the goals, strengths, and needs of the youth should be matched to the goals, expectations, and requirements of the employer. During this time, it is essential that the youth's support needs also be outlined. These needs should not come as a surprise to the transition specialist or youth because challenges and support strategies were identified while planning for the work experience and development of the Positive Personal Profile (described in Chapter 3). In Chapter 2, we introduced the work-based experience process. We restate it here in Figure 8.1, which depicts the entire process leading up to the Individual Support Plan.

Once a work experience has been negotiated, there are many facets to this experience that may require supports, including

- Setting up specific goals
- Determining timelines and other logistics
- Orienting the trainee to the worksite (and vice versa)
- Teaching new skills and providing opportunities for applying the new skills
- Encouraging development of social skills and fitting into the culture of the workplace
- Teaching employability skills
- Providing regular feedback and evaluation of performance

Clearly the type, level, and amount of support will vary from person to person and across situations. In addition, it is very important to note that the youth is not the only one who will require some level of support. Supervisors, co-workers, or anyone who might be at the worksite may also need support from the transition specialist so that they, in turn, can comfortably and effectively support the youth work experience and also benefit from the experience. After all, this experience should ideally be beneficial to all involved parties.

It is helpful to think of workplace support on a continuum from minimal to extensive. Only very basic support will be necessary for youth who are very independent and for whom accommodations are relatively easy to implement. Support may consist of a series of check-in calls and visits; supervisors and co-workers typically provide the primary supports under these circumstances. Moderate support may be necessary for youth who require a more structured approach, whereby the transition specialist or other external provider attends the worksite on a regular basis and may provide hands-on assistance to the youth, especially at the beginning of the work experience. Specialized accommodations may or may not be needed for these youth.

Extensive support is needed for youth whose support and accommodation needs are significant. Such support may include frequent hands-on involvement of the transition specialist (e.g., full-time job coach). These youth may also need complex accommodations. Whether the supports are basic, moderate, or extensive, it is always important to involve supervisors and/or co-workers in the process of deciding how the supports will be arranged. In all cases, it is ideal to assist the company in providing its own supports to the youth, to the maximum extent possible. This is often referred to as *natural* (or *typical*) *supports* (DiLeo et al., 1995).

Accommodations are a part of any support strategy. Legal definitions of *accommodation* will be covered later in this chapter. For now, *accommodation* will be defined simply as any strategy that alleviates or lessens the effects of a specific

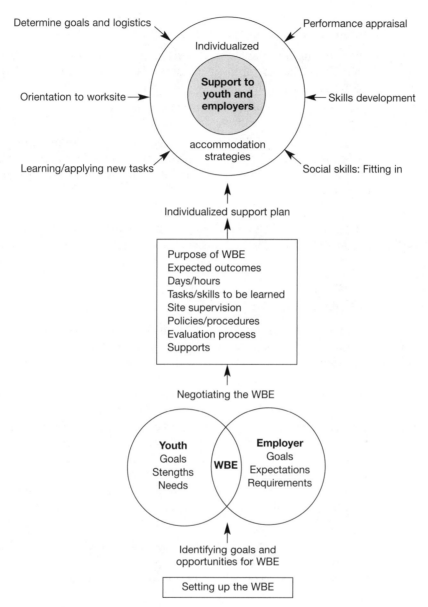

Figure 8.1. Work experience model.

barrier. Accommodations are a way to make a person feel competent, confident, and comfortable in a given environment. When organizing a successful work experience, you might ask:

• Does the youth have the skill and know-how to accomplish a given task (competent)?

• Can the youth apply those skills consistently and with a sense of certainty (confidence)?

• Does the youth enjoy doing the work and being in that particular work environment (comfortable)?

Accommodations can be categorized in three primary areas:

1. *Physical*—adaptive equipment; assistive devices; and changes to facilities and equipment such as putting in ramps, providing assistive or adaptive equipment, making materials available in large print, and so forth

2. *Specialized services*—sign language interpreters, readers, job coaches, and personal care attendants, for example

3. *Creative problem solving*—changes in procedure, reading an employment test to someone who cannot read, task restructuring, task reassignment, giving instructions in different formats, flexible schedules, and assigning a workplace mentor, among others

In other words, accommodations can be high tech, low tech—or no tech! The next section examines the specific issues of providing responsive support to youth in the workplace and considers a process for ensuring effective support.

SIX STEPS TO PROVIDING EFFECTIVE WORKPLACE SUPPORTS

By following a purposeful sequence of activities, transition specialists can proactively help youth to approach the work experience with the highest probability of valuable learning occurring. They can also anticipate and therefore avoid or minimize problems in youth work experiences. As a result of the kinds of advanced planning discussed in Chapter 3, particularly completing a Positive Personal Profile, you will already know what types of support and accommodation youth might need prior to the work experience. Once the site for the work experience is negotiated, it will be necessary to determine how these anticipated supports and accommodations will apply given the specific features and circumstances of that worksite. This process can be distilled down to six basic steps. Figure 8.2 provides a schematic representation of these steps for identifying and implementing workplace support, which are discussed in detail in the following sections.

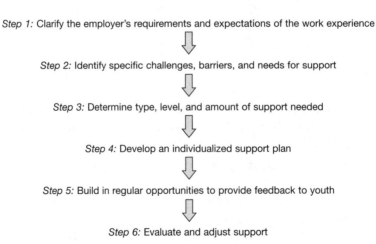

Step 1: Clarify the employer's requirements and expectations of the work experience

Step 2: Identify specific challenges, barriers, and needs for support

Step 3: Determine type, level, and amount of support needed

Step 4: Develop an individualized support plan

Step 5: Build in regular opportunities to provide feedback to youth

Step 6: Evaluate and adjust support

Figure 8.2. Six steps for effective workplace supports.

Step 1: Clarify the Employer's Requirements and Expectations of the Work Experience

Finding a suitable workplace experience for youth is only the beginning. It is important, but insufficient without postplacement support. In fact, leaving youth to fend for themselves once the work experience placement is made can have disastrous consequences at worst; at best, the experience will be only marginally useful for the youth's career development. In addition, carefully planned and responsive postplacement support is equally important to the employer. The last thing employers want to experience is the "dump-and-run syndrome," or as one employer calls it, "the drop-off-and-see-you-later approach."

From the outset, determine employer expectations. It is important that all requirements, policies, and procedures are spelled out clearly. Clarify general issues such as dress code, punctuality expectations, places in the worksite that pose safety risks or are off limits to the youth, and so forth. If it is a volunteer experience, the employer's expectations will likely be modest: when to be there, what to observe, general task assignments, and how to stay unobtrusive and safe. For paid employment, however, the expectations for youth performance will understandably elevate to include productivity requirements and higher standards of workplace social behavior. Accordingly, knowing these expectations is critical to implementing the next step of identifying needs for support so that the youth can meet these expectations. Without a clear grasp of what the employer expects, it will be difficult to know how to support and accommodate any youth in the work experience.

One way to clarify employer expectations is to provide a format for outlining them. A convenient tool for this purpose is a basic agreement between the company, the youth, and the supporting school or organization. The Work Experience Agreement included in Appendix 8.1 can be adapted for use in setting up the work experience so that, from the beginning, all parties have as clear an idea as possible about the expectations and goals of the experience. Once employer expectations are clarified, it is then possible to help the youth identify and implement the supports that will best enable the youth to meet the employer's expectations.

Step 2: Identify Specific Challenges, Barriers, and Needs for Support

As discussed in Chapter 3, individualized, person-centered, and self-directed planning precedes any activity that puts youth in the workplace. An essential aspect of this process is identifying potential work barriers and ways of compensating for them. Considering supports and accommodations early in the game will be invaluable once youth are in the workplace. From the moment transition specialists begin working with youth—using processes such as the Positive Personal Profile to ascertain their goals, skills, interests, and other attributes—they can begin to also pinpoint those areas that might pose a challenge to the youth's success in the workplace.

Derrick's accommodation needs were extensive and required considerable planning. Transportation had to be worked out; a personal attendant had to be at

Supporting Youth in the Workplace

Dennis loved movies and was ready for his first paid work experience at a local video rental store. The manager of the store agreed to hire Dennis after a job interview, during which Dennis impressed the manager with his knowledge of movies and his ability to read and sort DVDs by movie titles for reshelving. The expectations for his work experience were spelled out in an agreement signed by Dennis, the store manager, and the transition specialist who facilitated the arrangement. These expectations included Dennis's work schedule, the basic tasks he was expected to perform (reshelving returned DVD rentals, organizing the shelves for placing newly released DVDs, and stocking the snack area), how much he would be paid (standard store associate rate), and how often his performance would be reviewed by the manager and transition specialist (weekly).

As planned, a review was conducted after his first week on the job. He was able to meet most of the demands of the job; however, the manager wanted him to stock the shelves faster, especially the sections with popular movies, where customer demand was high. It was determined that Dennis had trouble carrying large stacks of videos and DVDs and had to make many trips to bring them to the correct shelf location. The manager and the transition specialist made arrangements for Dennis to use a small rolling cart to carry items to the shelves. After the second week, the manager and Dennis agreed that the easy and inexpensive accommodation helped bring Dennis's performance up to the manager's expectations. The expectations set at the beginning of the work experience, which included a designated performance review schedule, helped address early performance problems. Dennis successfully worked at the video rental store for the duration of the school year.

the workplace during mealtimes and for helping him in the restroom. He needed adaptive computer equipment and negotiated tasks. Most of these accommodations were clearly identified in advance of Derrick's placement in the work experience. Other accommodation needs emerged after the placement was made and specific tasks and situations were identified.

This is why it is so important to determine employer expectations before organizing specific supports and accommodations for youth. Each individual youth is unique, and each workplace is unique. Be prepared to make adjustments on the fly!

Step 3: Determine the Type, Level, and Amount of Support Needed

Potential considerations for individual support needs include the following.

- *Has the youth ever had a work experience or worked before?*—If not, then the transition specialist will need to ensure a thorough orientation to the new workplace. Additional oversight may be necessary at the beginning of the work experience. If the youth has had other work experiences, then the transition specialist should find out as much as possible about the circumstance of that experience: what went well, what did not, what supports worked, and so forth.

- *What is the youth's preferred learning style?*—Auditory learners will need verbal instructions from supervisors and co-workers. Hands-on learners will need to be shown the work tasks and given opportunities to try them, with feedback. Other learning styles will require other approaches. In each case, the transition specialist will need to make sure that the most appropriate presentation of tasks is available at the worksite.

- *Does the youth need a little or a lot of oversight?*—This has implications for not only how often the transition specialist visits the site (see Step 4), but also how much and what kind of orientation the worksite supervisor will need as he or she begins working with the youth.

- *If the youth has had previous work experiences, have there been problems?*—Inappropriate social behavior, tardiness, or poor task completion in previous work experiences will indicate a need to find ways to minimize their occurrence in the new experience. These problems might also determine how often the transition specialist visits the youth on site and/or how much assistance the worksite supervisor will need in organizing and overseeing work assignments.

- *How well is the youth able to speak up for himself or herself?*—Reinforcing self-determination training and/or preparing the workplace supervisor for eliciting youth responses may be a necessary support intervention for many youth.

- *How extensive will the support need to be?*—Jonetta's support needs were relatively basic. She needed to have minor adjustments made in the work setting to accommodate her specific learning challenges. People in the workplace were comfortable communicating and working with her, and the transition specialist made regular, brief check-ins. On the other hand, Derrick's support needs were quite extensive and involved assistive devices, the services of a personal care attendant, and a job coach to help him navigate the intricacies of the workplace.

The transition specialist needs to involve the youth and the host employer in determining the type, level, and amount of support that will be provided. In all cases, however, it is imperative that the transition specialist be involved at the start of the work experience and have a full understanding of how things are progressing through the duration of the experience. There are a host of other possible considerations when identifying potential support needs. Each youth is unique in this respect, and the previous questions are only examples of what might have to be considered. Although it is impossible to anticipate every potential performance hurdle or support requirement, the better acquainted the transition specialist and the employer are with the youth's specific support needs, the more likely it is that the work experience will get off to a good start.

Step 4: Develop an Individualized Support Plan

To keep the work experience on the right track and to ensure that individual youth receive the support they need for optimal workplace performance, a well-considered plan is helpful. An Individual Support Plan for conceptualizing and planning for work experience supports is included in Appendix 8.2. The plan does not have to be complex. It does help, however, to think about at least these three questions: Who will provide most of the support? What specific supports and accommodations need to be in place? How will they be implemented?

Who Will Support the Youth?   An obvious place to start is by identifying the designated supervisor of the youth during the work experience. The person supervising the youth, as well as the intensity of supervision, will vary considerably, depending on the nature of the work experience (e.g., unpaid or paid), who has time to devote to overseeing the youth's performance and communicating with the transition specialist, and the complexity of the work tasks to be assumed by the youth. Most often, identifying the youth's workplace supervisor is easy and self-evident, but it will be necessary to have a person on record who will supervise the youth, who oversees the youth's work, and who the transition program will count on for feedback about the youth's performance.

In addition to the person designated as the youth's supervisor, it is useful to identify co-workers who might be willing to serve as formal or informal mentors to the youth. There is much evidence to support the importance of workplace mentors for any new person on the job, especially youth with disabilities (Timmons, Mack, Sims, Hare, & Wills, 2006). The usefulness of this strategy is so important that the entire next chapter is devoted to identifying and developing mentor relationships at the workplace. A workplace "champion"—one who supports, encourages, guides, and helps represent the youth—can make all the difference in how well the youth is accepted in the workplace, how well co-workers respond to the youth, and how much the youth is able to learn during the work experience (Jekielek, Moore, & Hair, 2002). In addition, a workplace mentor can keep transition specialists apprised of the youth's progress and help identify emerging challenges before they become major problems. In effect, this person will be the "go-to person" for the youth when he or she has questions or needs direction at the workplace and the key contact with whom the transition specialist will communicate regularly about the work experience.

Face in the Place   Regardless of who is the designated workplace supervisor or if a workplace mentor is identified, the transition specialist will always have a need to have a "face in the place." Often in the crush of supporting multiple youth who are spread among many worksites, transition specialists are challenged to give each youth as much oversight and attention at the workplace as he or she needs. It is critically important, however, that scheduled and unscheduled visits to the youth in the workplace occur. Site visits should be noted in the Individual Support Plan. These visits are important because they provide

- Visual context for evaluating the work experience (i.e., seeing youth perform ensures that feedback is accurate and on target)
- An opportunity to identify the need for adjustments in task assignments or to facilitate specific accommodations
- An opportunity to solicit feedback from employers and co-workers
- An opportunity to troubleshoot and correct problems that arise in the workplace

Problem areas that might require the intervention of transition specialists include lack of production, task mistakes, work and social behavior, attendance, and taking direction/feedback, among a host of other possible matters. Being in the workplace to observe these things will enable them to be addressed in a timely fashion.

Two additional things to keep in mind when determining how often to visit youth at the workplace include the status of the work experience and the preferences of the youth and/or employer. Go more often when youth start at the workplace, go immediately and return as often as necessary when there are problems, and go less often when youth are more experienced and established. Go as often as the employer wants—some will be reassured by more visits; others will consider them an imposition. Go more when students seem to be more comfortable in the presence of the transition specialist, less when the youth does not want to stand out or be stigmatized because of the presence of a transition specialist.

What Supports Need to Be in Place? The type and extent of supports that may be necessary are based on both the assessed support needs of the youth and the expectations of the employer. Later in this chapter, possible accommodations for each phase of the work experience will be provided.

Required supports will also be dictated by the learning expectations—that is, how does the work experience relate to school coursework, and how does it relate, if at all, to specific individualized education program (IEP) goals? Chapter 11 will cover this in some detail. For the purposes of this chapter, it is sufficient to point out that the plans for work experience support should also be influenced by how the experience is linked to academic coursework and/or educational objectives.

How Supports Will Be Implemented Implementation of the Individual Support Plan will be guided in part by the decision of youth to disclose disability. As discussed in considerable detail in Chapter 4, disclosure is a personal decision that only the youth can make. Youth may decide to disclose a disability to receive specific accommodations. In that case, asking for and negotiating specific accommodations will need to be included in the plan. The absence of disclosure, however, does not mean the absence of support need. If the youth decides not to disclose, then supports will need to be implemented without reference to disability and in the context of what will need to be in place for the youth to perform at his or her best.

It is often helpful to have a checklist to provide direction to the activities of the transition specialists during worksite visits, as well as to create a record of the purpose and results of the visits. A format for this purpose is the Worksite Visit Checklist provided in Appendix 8.3.

Regardless of the nature or duration of the work experience, youth will better internalize learning from the experience if there are goals for the experience that the youth and transition specialist jointly identify. It is common practice—and certainly very useful—to work with the youth to incorporate these goals into a learning contract that specifies these goals and expectations for performance (see the Work Experience Agreement in Appendix 8.1). A formal agreement of this nature will not be necessary or appropriate for all youth, but it is a useful tool when organizing the work experience and structuring the oversight provided by the transition specialist.

Finally, to increase the likelihood of work experience success, the company and its operation needs to be considered. The best workplace supports:

- Reflect the business environment
- Are as unobtrusive as possible
- Ultimately help the youth contribute to the employers' operations

Step 5: Build in Regular Opportunities to Provide Feedback to Youth

It is natural and appropriate to solicit feedback about the youth's performance from the person designated as the youth's supervisor. In fact, the most organized and best work experiences include a formal process for evaluating the experience.

For this purpose a Work Experience Evaluation is included in Appendix 8.4. Proactive solicitation of employer feedback is necessary for all kinds of reasons. For example, employers may hesitate to be direct about a youth's performance, or they may not know how to best frame the feedback due to discomfort or inexperience with disability. In any case, organizing structured feedback allows the transition specialist to promptly address any problem at the worksite. Just as importantly, if the youth's performance is good or exceptional, it allows the transition specialist to provide positive feedback to the youth to both reinforce and celebrate the achievements along the way!

Much can be gained from soliciting informal feedback about the youth's work experience from mentors and co-workers. This chapter has already discussed the value of having a mentor as a "go-to" person. Because mentors are likely to be people with a vested interest in helping the youth get the most from the work experience, they tend to be keenly aware of how youth are doing and what issues have arisen at the workplace. Similarly, co-workers see and know how the youth performs and are therefore useful sources of information about the youth's progress in the work experience.

No matter the nature of the feedback—positive or negative—from supervisors, mentors, or co-workers, it is critical for the transition specialist to ask what else the specialist can do to help support the youth. By asking whether they can help the youth with learning task performance, help the supervisor explain and reinforce work rules, or discuss a workplace problem, transition specialists leave the impression that they care about how the workplace is benefiting from the experience and that the opinions of the people at the workplace are valued. Most importantly, this assistance encourages people at the worksite to suggest ways to improve the experience so that when feedback is provided to the youth, it is based on specific reports from those who know firsthand how the youth is doing in the experience.

Ultimately, this information is only valuable if it is passed on to the youth in some fashion to help him or her learn from it. When giving feedback, be direct, provide it regularly, look for opportunities to praise, and note exceptional performance. One helpful tool to structure feedback to youth is the Daily Work Report in Appendix 8.5.

Step 6: Evaluate and Adjust Support

What is working? What is not? Do you need to be at the workplace more or less often? Are there issues with supervision? Do the workplace supervisor and co-workers need help communicating with the youth? Are there issues that arose that you did not expect? Signs of difficulty may include spotty attendance, tardiness, poor task performance, slow production rate, inappropriate social interaction, or any number of things in work and social skill areas. Feedback from the workplace will help enable transition specialists to identify the kinds of supports that work well, work fairly well, or do not work at all for a particular individual. Chances are good that most youth will encounter some situations or problems that call for revising the approach to workplace supports.

Typical areas in which adjustment of the transition specialist's support might be necessary include the following:

- *Frequency of feedback to the employer or youth*—for example, provide more feedback when there is a specific problem such as attendance or provide less feedback when the employer or youth complains that the transition specialist is hovering over the youth too much

- *Nature of feedback to the employer or youth*—for example, model for the employer how to interact with the youth rather than telling the employer how to do it; meet with the youth off site rather than the workplace to discuss a problem that is sensitive in nature

- *Frequency of on-site visits*—for example, visit more when there are performance issues that need specific supports; visit less once an effective mentoring relationship is established

- *Refining the instruction given to the youth*—for example, replace a verbal prompt with a picture prompt when steps are missed, or break the task down into smaller steps

- *Adjusting or refining accommodation for accessibility and/or learning*—There are a host of considerations and options for facilitating and adjusting the type of accommodations that youth may require to fully participate in what the work experience has to offer and to fully take advantage of the learning opportunities it presents. The next section covers them in detail.

CONSIDERATIONS CONCERNING WORKPLACE ACCOMMODATIONS

At times, a youth may require an assistive device, equipment, specialized service, or other substantial accommodation to succeed on a worksite. In such cases, the transition specialist is called on to help the individual obtain this accommodation; ideally, this has been addressed long before the work experience has been negotiated. Most employers, unlike transition specialists, do not have experience with extensive accommodations. In all likelihood, they will be very receptive to your skills and knowledge in acquiring the necessary accommodation tool—and in helping the youth to integrate the accommodation in the worksite.

As was stated previously, an accommodation is essentially any strategy that eliminates or lessens the effects of a specific barrier faced by a person with a disability. A barrier is an obstacle that may exist at home, in school, at the workplace, in the community, or in getting to and from places. In the context of youth work experiences, an accommodation is any change in the environment or work process that makes it possible for a youth with a disability to enjoy access to and participate in a workplace opportunity.

Accommodations are used to help youth learn or demonstrate what they have learned, work as independently and as efficiently as possible, and get the help they need to be successful. Accommodations are not intended to justify or compensate for a lack of knowledge, skills, or abilities necessary to succeed at the workplace. Ideally, they are implemented so that they are based on the use and further development of existing skills and abilities.

Remember, the *obstacle* that the disability creates—not the disability itself—determines the accommodation. For example, stairs are barriers to a youth who uses a wheelchair, a fast-paced work environment is a barrier to a youth who needs to work at a deliberate pace, and reading below grade level may be a barrier for a youth who wants to work in a bookstore. Cerebral palsy is not a barrier for the youth who uses a wheelchair. Emotional disability is not a barrier for the youth who cannot work at a fast pace, nor is learning disability a barrier for the youth who reads below grade level. In other words, the disability itself does not indicate the accommodation, but the barrier that is shaped by the specific circumstances of the youth's disability, which is unique for each youth—even for youth with the same disability.

Legal Requirements and Workplace Accommodations for Youth

It is worth reiterating that accommodations employers make on behalf of youth in work experiences are not necessarily those required by law. Title I of the Americans with Disabilities Act of 1990 (PL 101-336) requires employers with 15 or more employees to make reasonable accommodations for qualified job applicants and employees with disabilities. Under the law, *reasonable accommodations* are adjustments and modifications that range from making the physical work environment accessible, to providing assistive technology, to offering flexible work scheduling for qualified individuals. They are not required if the applicant or the employee cannot perform the *essential functions* of the job—that is, those tasks ordinarily required of a position or that are outlined in a formal job description. Accommodations are also not required if their costs constitute an undue hardship for the employer.

Legally required reasonable accommodations in the context of youth work experiences only apply if a youth is being considered for a standard paid job, if the youth can reasonably be expected to perform the essential functions of that job if the accommodations are made, *and* if the costs of providing the accommodations are not considered excessive. For work experiences in which there is no legal employer–employee relationship (e.g., work sampling, unpaid internships, career explorations, job shadowing), employers are not required to provide accommodations, reasonable or not. In addition, even when there is a formal employer–employee relationship, the employer may still not be legally required to provide accommodation under conditions of unusual work circumstances, such as carved or restructured jobs for which no previous job description existed (ADA & IT Information Center, 2000).

This is distinctly different from education settings governed by the Individuals with Disabilities Education Improvement Act of 2004 (PL 108-446), under which schools must provide learning and physical accommodations if they are identified as necessary in the IEP. Thus, it is extremely important to be prepared to negotiate with prospective employers based on a youth's positive traits and potential contribution to the company. Necessary accommodations are then seen as minimally intrusive and ultimately beneficial to the youth's performance on the job.

Most employers are quite willing to work with youth and transition specialists in implementing necessary accommodations, no matter the circumstance of the youth or the presence or absence of a legal obligation, as long as they receive competent help and service from the specialist (see Chapter 7). This is the case even when accommodations far exceed any pertinent legal requirements and/or if the accommodations are extensive or complex, as in Derrick's case at the beginning of this chapter. Thus, the main issue of accommodating youth in work experiences is not a legal one, but a practical one. Can the accommodations be implemented in such a way that they will provide the youth an opportunity to get the most out of the work experience? Can they be implemented in a way that does not overly tax either the resources or the patience of the employer? Most often the answer is yes, but it requires planning. The individualized support plan should always include planning for accommodations if they are needed.

Accommodations for Each Component of the Work Experience

When there is a need for physical accommodations, such as wheelchair access, or service accommodations, such as sign language interpreters, the process of identifying these accommodations is relatively straightforward. However, when youth present other needs for accommodations that are less obvious or less common, careful analysis of these needs may be required—and perhaps even some creative problem solving. Furthermore, accommodations may be necessary at any phase of the work experience process. The following sections outline junctures in the work experience when such specific accommodations may be necessary, along with potential approaches to accommodations during these phases of the work experience.

Application and Interview Process   With the exception of career explorations and worksite visits, there almost always is a process for applying and/or interviewing prior to the start of the experience, whether the work experience is paid or unpaid. Many experiences, such as internships, apprenticeships, or paid employment, will require that the youth participate in a standard interview and selection process. In such circumstances, it may be necessary for youth to ask for (or receive help asking for) accommodations that will enable them to illustrate their suitability to perform in the prospective job. There are a number of alternative ways to accomplish this by lessening potential barriers in completing applications or participating in interviews. Several ideas for making accommodations that might help youth put their best foot forward to prospective employers are listed on page 154.

Initial Training and Orientation   Each youth's needs in this area are different, depending on the youth's learning style and the particular skill requirements of the tasks to which he or she will be assigned. The potential accommodations for worksite training and orientation listed on page 155 provide a menu from which the youth and transition specialist can draw to best match the needs of the youth

Potential Accommodations for Work Applications and Interviews

- Provide help and clarification in completing applications and arranging interviews.
- Allow the youth to take the application home.
- Obtain the application information through a verbal interview rather than in writing.
- Conduct interviews in an informal environment that is free of distractions.
- Minimize the number of introductions made or assure the youth that there will be time later to get to know everyone he or she meets.
- Describe the job tasks clearly and concisely, and break down tasks into steps.
- Demonstrate job tasks, in addition to or instead of describing them verbally.
- Allow the youth to demonstrate a task skill through a "working interview" rather than participate in a verbal interview.
- Adjust the interview length according to the youth's ability to concentrate and remain attentive.

with the specific demands of the assigned work tasks. Because starting a work experience is a potentially anxious time for youth, especially if experience in the workplace is limited, some of the potential accommodations might be useful for other reasons as well. They are additional ways to increase the youth's comfort, confidence, and competence as the youth starts a new work experience!

On-the-Job Performance It is common for anyone's performance on the job to occasionally fall short. When youth are inexperienced in the workplace and/or have specific barriers to performance due to disability, there are always ways to shore up performance. Several potential approaches to accommodations in any number of performance areas are outlined on pages 156–158. Accommodations are available for general work performance issues, attendance challenges, stamina and stress challenges, concentration issues, meeting deadlines, memory difficulty, visual limitations, reading and spelling challenges, and calculation limitations.

Workplace Integration and Interpersonal Relationships Inexperience in the workplace, youthfulness, and co-worker misunderstanding about disability can all contribute to difficulties for youth as they strive to feel comfortable and accepted by co-workers and others in the workplace. Often, the transition specialist is in a position both to provide guidance to youth about workplace socialization and to educate workplace supervisors and co-workers about the youth's need for accommodation. This is not necessarily an easy and clear task; however,

Potential Accommodations for Worksite Training and Orientation

- Tailor training to the youth's preferred learning style (e.g., verbal instructions, written instructions, demonstration, tactile prompting, or a combination).
- Break down tasks into clearly defined, smaller steps or components.
- Provide additional training time and additional training.
- Develop a consistent routine or sequence for the job tasks, and train the youth to follow the routine or sequence.
- Create pictures or diagrams to train and prompt the youth through a task sequence.
- Provide extra time to orient the youth to the employer's rules and performance expectations.
- Reinforce verbal training with written or visual material.
- Provide additional coaching, on-the-job training, or retraining as necessary.
- Supplement standard employer orientation and training procedures with coaching from the transition specialist.
- Discuss and role-play appropriate workplace social skills and behavior.

most often the transition specialist will encounter success in this regard with a little creativity and context. The list on page 159 is a place to start identifying strategies to improve the ability of youth to become socially integrated in the workplace and to establish appropriate social relationships with others at the workplace.

Chadsey (2008) suggested that social acceptance of youth with disabilities in the workplace is evident when co-workers are willing to work with the youth, eat lunch or take breaks with him or her, attend company-sponsored social functions with the youth (e.g., birthday parties, holiday gatherings), and invite him or her to socialize outside of work. Transition specialists should be alert to these signs. If they are not evident, then generating strategies to encourage them will be an important to step.

SUMMARY

The topic of supporting youth in the workplace could encompass an entire book. In this chapter, it has been covered in a few key strategies. All of the support strategies in the world would be rendered ineffective if one important element is overlooked: the match itself. No amount of on-site support, accommodations, personal attention, and effort by a transition specialist or host employer will address a situation in which a youth is ill-suited to a particular jobsite, where there is a poor match between the employee's skills and the required tasks, when the individual's personality and temperament are not suited to the workplace

Potential Accommodations for On-the-Job Performance

General

- Restructure or modify job tasks to include a few basic and essential tasks for completing basic assignments.
- Provide additional coaching.
- Arrange the assistance of existing workplace supports such as regular supervisor or co-worker feedback.
- Assign a mentor to provide daily guidance and to assist youth to set workplace goals.
- Provide praise, positive reinforcement, and constructive suggestions for improvement.
- Clearly define work performance expectations and responsibilities and the consequences of not fulfilling them.
- Provide written work agreements.
- Develop and use self-management and compensatory tools such as checklists, to-do lists, and picture prompts.
- Allow time for telephone calls to health care professionals, family members, and others needed for support.
- Monitor the effectiveness of accommodations and supports, and be alert to the need to modify or add supports.

Attendance Challenges

- Consider flexible scheduling or time off (when needed for medical, counseling appointments, etc.).
- Consider flexible leave for health problems.
- Arrange job sharing or task-sharing with another youth.
- Change the work schedule to less or different hours to accommodate personal circumstances, such as transportation or family issues.
- Alter arrival or departure times if transportation is problematic.
- Look for alternative transportation, such as a family member or co-worker.

Stamina and Stress Challenges

- Arrange flexible scheduling.
- Organize longer or more frequent breaks.
- Identify back-up coverage when the youth needs to take a break.
- Identify work assignments that include self-paced work.
- Organize ad-hoc breaks to use stress management techniques.

(continued)

Potential Accommodations for On-the-Job Performance *(continued)*

Concentration Limitations

- Minimize noise and visual distractions in the work area.
- Provide a separate work area, private office, or room partitions.
- Break down large assignments into smaller tasks and steps.
- Allow the youth to listen to soothing music on an MP3 player.
- Reduce clutter in the work area.
- Plan for uninterrupted work time.

Organizational and Deadline Challenges

- Make a daily to-do list, and check off items as they are completed.
- Develop a set routine or sequence for tasks.
- Arrange material in order of use.
- Write appointments and deadlines on a calendar.
- Arrange for a co-worker or mentor to remind the youth of deadlines.
- Provide an electronic organizer or personal digital assistant (PDA).
- Color-code items or resources.
- Avoid reorganizing the youth's workspace without his or her involvement.
- Label items and places where they are stored when not in use.

Memory Deficits

- Develop a set routine or sequence for tasks.
- Allow the youth to make an audio recording of meetings.
- Arrange for written minutes of meetings.
- Provide an electronic organizer, PDA, notebooks, a calendar, or sticky notes to record information for easy retrieval.
- Provide written or picture-coded checklists.
- Prompt the youth with written, e-mail, text message, or verbal reminders.
- Use cues such as color-coded labels, and post written or pictorial instructions on or nearby the work area or frequently used equipment.

Visual or Reading Limitations

- Provide information in large print.
- Use pictures, symbols, or diagrams instead of words.

(continued)

Potential Accommodations for On-the-Job Performance *(continued)*

- Arrange for someone to read written information.
- Provide an audio recording of the information.
- Use the voice output option on computers.
- Increase natural lighting or use high intensity lamps.
- Provide glare guard for computer monitors.
- Provide tools to assist with tracking while reading (e.g., ruler, card with a window cut in it).

Limitations with Writing, Spelling, Signing Documents, and Other Written Communications

- Use templates or forms to prompt the provision of needed information.
- Allow verbal responses instead of written responses.
- Use the voice input option on computers.
- Use spell check software tools.
- Use a scribe to assist with written communications.

Calculation Limitations

- Provide a calculator, large display calculator, or talking calculator.
- Provide a counter or ticker.
- Make a precounted or premeasured poster or jig.
- Provide a talking tape measure.
- Use liquid-level indicators or mark measuring containers with a "fill to here" line.

environment, or other discrepancies that should have been discovered early on in the process of seeking a work experience or job.

This chapter provided a six-step strategy for ensuring effective supports that are basic for any youth in any workplace. It also introduced considerations for determining and implementing necessary workplace accommodations for youth with disabilities in various stages of the work experience. The transition specialist must be thinking about the kinds of supports that will be needed from the moment he or she meets a job seeker. Identifying and implementing effective workplace supports cannot be an afterthought. The importance of continually soliciting feedback from the youth and his or her workplace colleagues was discussed, as well as the need for evaluating and adjusting supports and accommodations accordingly. In this regard, the most basic formula for facilitating effective workplace supports includes

Potential Strategies for Supporting Workplace Integration and Interpersonal Relationships

- Provide disability awareness and sensitivity training to co-workers.
- Model positive, nonpatronizing, and respectful social interaction.
- Teach the youth to ask a supervisor or co-worker for support and assistance.
- Identify a co-worker to be a workplace mentor.
- Ask a co-worker to support the youth in participating in and getting to on- and off-site meetings and work-related social activities.
- Model and help the youth practice appropriate workplace social skills and behavior (e.g., how to greet co-workers, when and where to eat at the workplace, how to answer the telephone, how to handle frustration, when to leave or not leave the workstation).

- Identifying supports and accommodation needs by starting with each individual youth and his or her circumstances, then matching them to an employer's requirements and expectations for the work experience
- Seeking continuous feedback from both the youth and the employer
- Making adjustments in support as necessary and as feedback indicates
- Renegotiating tasks, supports, production requirements, and other workplace requirements as necessary

This chapter offered a range of considerations when facilitating supports and accommodations during youth work experiences. Using the Individual Support Plan and with a little creative problem solving, transition specialists can put every youth in a position to learn from every work experience.

LEARNING LAB: *Solving Workplace and Performance Obstacles*

Scenarios are provided in Figure 8.3 that illustrate potential workplace support needs. For each scenario, identify the obstacle, and offer a potential solution or solutions to address the problem described. The first scenario is completed as an example for responding. You might want to brainstorm the obstacle and potential solutions for each example with colleagues.

Scenario	Obstacle	Potential solution(s)
1. Roberto has just been hired in an accounting firm. Although his office is accessible for his wheelchair, the conference room where all the staff meetings are held is not.	*The inaccessibility of the conference room (facility)*	*Hold staff meetings in a different office. Determine why the room is inaccessible (e.g., crowding, door) and if it can be modified without imposing an undue hardship to the company.*
2. Rebecca loves her work experience trial as a cooperative cataloging assistant. She gets along splendidly with her co-workers and her supervisor. Recently, Rebecca has had difficulty making it to work on time and has been missing days.		
3. Saundra, who is applying for a position as a data process entry clerk, requires a sign language interpreter for the interview. The supervisor has some concerns that the company will need to hire a full-time interpreter for Saundra to successfully perform the duties of the position.		
4. Tracy works for a company that maintains and repairs equipment for high-end coffee shops such as Starbucks. His primary tasks are to disassemble tools and sort them into specially marked bins. His supervisor has noticed that Tracy's level of productivity has declined steadily over the past week.		
5. Laverne is in a work-study job in a formal corporate office. She continually chooses not to use the office intercom to talk to her supervisor as requested. Instead, she frequently poses questions to him in a loud, boisterous voice that is an irritating disruption for her co-workers and supervisors.		

Scenario *(continued)*	Obstacle	Potential solution(s)
6. Brian uses a wheelchair and is interning at a major pharmaceutical company. One of his varied assignments is to photocopy and file time-sensitive insurance materials. He is unable to reach the selection button mounted on the rear of the photocopier.		
7. Theresa has the basic skills necessary for the job of administrative assistant, likes the work, and shows potential. When she finishes one task, however, she tends to stand in one place and look around, unsure of what to do next.		
8. Given a specific mailing job duty that occurs only once per week, Rayford is having difficulty remembering all the steps involved with the process. His supervisor is tired of having to repeat the directions each week.	.	
9. Marcy works for a small consulting group of hydrologists, who analyze water quality. She works closely with the scientists to collect water samples and files the samples in the laboratory van (quite an elaborate setup). Marcy cannot read or write; she was taught on the job how to "read" the many markings on the apparatus. Recently, the firm switched over to brand new equipment, essentially the same but with slight differences in the markings. Marcy filed a day's worth of samples incorrectly, causing a major error in analysis. The head of the company wants to fire her.		
10. John consistently receives praise from his boss for performing his job (as a car detailer) in an exemplary manner. When John is not busy, he will stand in one place, rock back and forth, and flick his fingers in front of his face. On several occasions, customers have complained to management about him.		

Figure 8.3. Learning Lab activity: Scenarios that illustrate potential worksite support needs.

REFERENCES

ADA & IT Information Center. (2000). *Civil rights and people with disabilities: Americans with Disabilities Act: A series of lesson plans for educators.* Rockville, MD: TransCen.

Americans with Disabilities Act of 1990, PL 101-336, 42 U.S.C. §§ 12101 *et seq.*

Behrmann, M., & Shepis, M. (1994). Assistive technology assessment: A multiple case study review of three approaches with students with physical disabilities during the transition from school to work. *Journal of Vocational Rehabilitation, 4,* 202–210.

Chadsey, J. (2008). *Social inclusion at work.* Washington, DC: American Association on Intellectual and Developmental Disabilities.

Costen, C. (1988). *Planning and implementing augmentative communication service delivery: Proceedings of the National Planners Conference on Assistive Device Service Delivery.* Washington, DC: RESNA.

DiLeo, D., Luecking, R., & Hathaway, S. (1995). *Natural supports in action: Strategies to facilitate employer supports of workers with disabilities.* St. Augustine, FL: TRN Publishing.

Fisher, S. (1999). Assistive technology. In S.H. DeFur & J.R. Patton (Eds.), *Transition and school-based services: Interdisciplinary perspectives for enhancing the transition process.* Austin, TX: PRO-ED.

Ford, L. (1995). *Providing employment support for people with long term mental illness: Choices, sources, and practical strategies.* Baltimore: Paul H. Brookes Publishing Co.

Individuals with Disabilities Education Improvement Act of 2004, PL 108-446, 20 U.S.C. §§ 1400 *et seq.*

Inge, K., Wehman, P., Strobel, W., Powell, D., & Todd, J. (1998). Supported employment and assistive technology for persons with spinal cord injury: Three illustrations of successful work supports. *Journal of Vocational Rehabilitation, 10,* 141–152.

Jekielek, S., Moore, K.A., & Hair, E.C. (2002). *Mentoring programs and youth development: A synthesis.* Washington, DC: Edna McConnell Clark Foundation. Retrieved April 6, 2008, from http://www.childtrends.org/what_works/clarkwww/mentor/mentorrpt.pdf

Mank, D., Cioffi, A., & Yovanoff, P. (1997). Analysis of typicalness of supported employment jobs, natural supports, and wage and integration outcomes. *Mental Retardation, 35,* 185–197.

Rogan, P., Banks, B., & Howard, M. (2000). Workplace supports in practice: As little as possible, as much as necessary. *Focus on Autism and Other Developmental Disabilities, 15,* 2–11.

Sunoo, B.P. (2000). Accommodating workers with disabilities. *Workforce, 2,* 86–91.

Targett, P., West, M., & Anglin, N. (2001). Corporate supports and mentoring in the workplace for persons with severe disabilities. In P. Wehman (Ed.), *Supported employment in business.* St. Augustine, FL: Training Resource Network.

Timmons, J., Mack, M., Sims, A., Hare, R., & Wills, J. (2006). *Paving the way to work: A guide to career-focused mentoring for youth with disabilities.* Washington, DC: National Collaborative on Workforce and Disability for Youth, Institute for Educational Leadership.

Wehman, P. (2001). *Supported employment in business.* St. Augustine, FL: TRN Publishing.

Zielinski, D. (2000). The age of access. *Presentations, 9,* 40–49.

Appendix

- Work Experience Agreement
- Individual Support Plan Template
- Worksite Visit Checklist
- Work Experience Evaluation
- Daily Work Report

APPENDIX 8.1

Work Experience Agreement

Student name: _____

Company: _____

Work experience location: _____

Company contact person: _____ Title: _____

Transition specialist: _____

Work schedule

Sunday	
Monday	
Tuesday	
Wednesday	
Thursday	
Friday	
Saturday	

Work experience goals/objectives

1. _____

2. _____

3. _____

4. _____

Primary duties

1. _____

2. _____

3. _____

4. _____

Student agrees to

1. Attend according to agreed-on schedule.

2. Conform to the rules and regulations of the workplace.

3. Notify my supervisor when I will be late or absent.

4. Notify my transition specialist if problems arise or if I have a concern.

_____   _____
　　　　　　　Student's signature　　　　　　　　　　　　Date

Employer/supervisor agrees to

1. *Host　Employ*　(circle one) student per the agreed-on schedule.

2. Conform to federal/state regulations regarding employment, safety, and wages (if applicable).

3. Designate a supervisor/mentor responsible for the student and work experience oversight.

4. Consult with the transition specialist about student performance and participate in evaluating the work experience.

_____   _____
　　　　Employer/supervisor's signature　　　　　　　　Date

Transition specialist agrees to

1. Provide/help with training and orientation to the student as necessary.

2. Visit the student at the worksite and provide regular feedback and assistance.

3. Assist the student and employer/supervisor to identify and resolve any performance problem that may arise.

4. Maintain contact with the student and employer/supervisor throughout the work experience.

5. Evaluate the work experience and provide appropriate credit as required.

_____   _____
　　　Transition specialist's signature　　　　　　　　Date

APPENDIX 8.2

Individual Support Plan Template

Student name: _____

Company: _____

Company contact person: _____ Title: _____

Transition specialist: _____

Who?

Role of workplace supervisor/mentor (e.g., training, supervision, coaching)

Role of transition specialist (e.g., coaching, acquisition of assistive devices)

Other primary contacts at worksite (e.g., co-workers)

What? *(check all that apply)*

☐ Mentor identified   ☐ Tasks clearly outlined

☐ Physical accessibility assured   ☐ Task modifications identified and in place

☐ Accommodations identified   ☐ Orientation and training arranged

How? *(check all that apply)*

☐ Disclosure decision determined with student

☐ Learning goals identified for work experience

☐ Site visit schedule determined

☐ Feedback/evaluation schedule determined

Other comments

APPENDIX 8.3

Worksite Visit Checklist

Student name: _____

Company: _____

Date of visit: _____

During today's visit

☐ Observed the student perform assigned tasks

☐ Coached the student in completing task

☐ Gave feedback to student on performance

☐ Spoke with supervisor/mentor about student's performance

☐ Helped make adjustment to task or assignment

☐ Checked on effectiveness of accommodations

☐ Spoke with co-workers about student

☐ Scheduled the next visit

Comments

APPENDIX 8.4

Work Experience Evaluation

Student name: _____

Company: _____

Learning objectives *(check if met)*

☐ 1. _____

☐ 2. _____

☐ 3. _____

☐ 4. _____

☐ 5. _____

Explanation/comments

Rate the student using the scale provided.

	Work habits and skills	Rating
4 *exceptional*	1. Accepts direction and feedback	
3 *better than average*	2. Maintains good appearance	
	3. Attendance is on time	
2 *comparable to average*	4. Shows enthusiasm for assignments and assigned tasks	
	5. Asks for help when needed	
1 *below average*	6. Follows instruction	
n/a *does not apply*	7. Follows rules	
	8. Stays on task	
	9. Meets employer's performance expectations	
	10. Interacts well with other co-workers	
	Overall rating	

APPENDIX 8.4 *(continued)*

Additional comments

I agree that this evaluation accurately represents _____ 's work experience.

_____   _____
Student's signature   Date

_____   _____
Supervisor's signature   Date

_____   _____
Transition specialist's signature   Date

Daily Work Report

Student name: _____ Date: _____

Company supervisor: _____

Transition specialist: _____

Today during a visit to the worksite, the following
was observed and discussed about the student:

☐   Came to work on time

☐   Was doing assigned tasks

☐   Stayed on task

☐   Performed to supervisor's expectations

☐   Had a good attitude about work

☐   Asked for help when needed

☐   Interacted well with co-worker

Comments

9

• • •

Workplace Mentors
for Youth Workers

Richard G. Luecking and Meredith Gramlich

This chapter provides the reader with

• Documentation of the value of workplace mentoring

• Strategies for identifying and recruiting workplace mentors

• Strategies for supporting workplace mentors

• A Learning Lab on workplace mentoring

---

*"Nobody gets through life without help. Young people
need help in every stage of their lives."*

Marian Wright Edelman, Founder, Children's Defense Fund

When Robert started at his part-time job at Starbucks, he was shy, unsure of himself, and often confused about what his duties were. When his job coach was with him, he could follow the coach's direction and perform his tasks well. He competently cleared and wiped tables, kept the napkin dispensers full, and emptied the waste bins, but only with the reassuring prompts of the job coach. When the job coach was not there, Robert struggled with staying on task and deciding what to do next.

One of the baristas, Liz, who worked during Robert's shift, took a special interest in Robert. She had a brother who, like Robert, was in a special education transition program. She gradually took it upon herself, with the job coach's encouragement, to provide simple reminders to Robert to move to the next task when he stood around after completing a task. She also took breaks with him, and they both enjoyed talking about their mutual interest in country music. With Liz's occasional prompts and with the frequent praise she provided when Robert performed his tasks correctly, Robert not only became a confident and competent worker at that Starbucks store but also was nominated as employee of the month several times.

Ashley also benefited from a mentor's guidance but in a more formalized way. Because of Ashley's interest in technology, her transition teacher helped her to arrange an internship at a federal agency that promotes and monitors the U.S. space program. The school has enjoyed a longstanding relationship with key managers at the agency through a local program that matches youth with disabilities to work experiences in high-tech companies. In addition to providing exposure to work in specific departments, the federal agency also has a formal arrangement where all interns are matched with an experienced employee who is designated as the intern's mentor.

Ashley's mentor, Bill, volunteered for the assignment after Ashley was assigned to his department and after the supervisor announced the mentorship opportunity at a staff meeting. Bill was given an orientation to the expectations of mentoring youth in the program, as well as a brief introduction to Ashley's accommodation needs that included large-print material and a screen enlarger for her computer due to her visual impairment. Throughout Ashley's semester-long internship, Bill provided guidance to her about everything from how to complete her timesheet to how to operate sensitive calibration equipments. As a result, the internship provided Ashley with a valuable exposure to work and to career opportunities in the high-tech field. The mentorship experience also helped Bill appreciate the importance of developing young talent in the field, not to mention giving him a renewed enthusiasm for his own work.

Whether the mentorship relationship is informal, as in Robert's case, or formally arranged, as in Ashley's case, mentors are significant contributors to the success of the youth work experience. Companies adopt many approaches with prospective and current employees to promote the development of the skills needed to enhance productivity and the quality of the workplace. Many of the top-performing organizations include mentoring as a specific strategy to nurture employee performance (Hansman, 2002; Simonetti, Ariss, & Martinez, 1999). There are important similarities between this concept and what occurred for Robert and Ashley. For the most part, mentoring youth workers offers the same benefit to the company and to the youth as mentoring does to regular employees of any age or level of experience. For youth who may have limited experience in the workplace, mentoring has a particularly useful function of acclimating them to job duties and performance expectations (Timmons, Mack, Sims, Hare, & Wills, 2006). Companies benefit in a number of ways, not the least of which is that mentoring youth workers contributes to the development of the future workforce. As we shall discuss later, in companies where there is mentoring for youth with disabilities, either formally or informally, there is an extra bonus of authentic, person-specific, disability awareness that is absent from most company diversity training programs.

Many definitions of *mentoring* and *mentor* exist. For the purposes of youth work experiences discussed throughout this book, *mentoring* is defined as a trusting and supportive relationship, formally or informally designated, which pairs youth with well-established individuals at the workplace. Similarly, a *mentor* is defined as a well-established person at the workplace who is given, volunteers for, or naturally assumes the role of mentoring a youth in the workplace.

An effective workplace mentor will model and reinforce behavioral characteristics that will contribute to the youth's successful work experience. However, an effective mentor relationship will benefit not only the youth but also the mentor, the company, and the transition program overseeing the work experience. This chapter discusses how mentoring relationships can provide valuable support to youth in the workplace as they build skills, confidence, initiative, and responsible work behavior. It will also discuss how everyone involved can benefit so that the experience works for everyone involved.

WHY MENTORING IS EFFECTIVE

The value of experienced and mature adults of any age mentoring and providing guidance to youth has long been recognized in a host of contexts, including at work, where effective mentors are able to model and encourage skills and positive behaviors (Sipe, 1999). In addition, strong relationships with adults have been shown to be of critical importance to youth, especially those with barriers to social acceptance, as is the case with many youth with disabilities (Beier, Rosenfeld, Spitalny, Zansky, & Bontempo, 2000; Jekielek, Moore, & Hair, 2002; Sipe, 1999). Furthermore, literature on the value of workplace mentoring—particularly on adult career development—has consistently shown associations between mentor support and career advancement (Hansman, 2002). Thus, it is clear that informal and formal workplace mentors have the potential to be key ingredients in shaping career development of all youth, but especially youth with disabilities (Timmons et al., 2006).

Among the many advantages of facilitating workplace mentors is the help mentors provide youth as they develop social and work competencies, make connections with co-workers, and navigate both the physical and social circumstances that are unique to each workplace. In short, having a workplace mentor provides a nonjudgmental, available, experienced helper who can impart crucial job-related and social skills, enrich and expand the youth's social connections both inside and outside of work, and enhance the youth's self-concept and optimism for the future. For youth with disabilities, workplace mentors provide two additional benefits. First, they can reinforce self-determination because the youth is able to try more at the workplace, which in turn will enable the youth to have a larger repertoire of experiences from which to draw important information about workplace likes/dislikes and career knowledge to make better-informed job and career decisions. Second, the help and guidance provided by mentors offer many youth with disabilities the opportunity to take more active roles in the workplace, allowing youth to learn to take a more active role in their own career planning process. In short, workplace mentors can open the doors to new opportunities and help youth establish and make use of connections in and out of the workplace. Five specific benefits of workplace mentoring for youth are outlined in the following sections. Additional benefits and benefits for mentors, companies, and schools are also discussed.

Increased Comfort and Acceptance in the Workplace

Anyone of any age at any point in their career who has ever started a new job experiences some anxiety. "How will I fit in?" "Can I do the job?" "Will my co-workers accept me?" and "What if I make mistakes?" are just a few of the questions that come up in the minds of people beginning a new job. The prominence of these questions is significantly magnified for youth who have had few, if any, experiences in the workplace. The presence of an experienced co-worker who can mentor youth on the job can go a long way in helping to minimize the anxiety that youth may feel in a new workplace.

As youth struggle to learn new tasks, meet and interact with co-workers, and acquire effective work behaviors, there are few better ways to ease their way than having an established and trusted co-worker act as a mentor. As we have seen, this relationship can be informal, in which an interested co-worker naturally assumes the role, or it can be a formally designated person who will guide the youth in managing the work tasks and the social relationships in the workplace.

Sam began a part-time volunteer work experience at an auto parts store. He was excited about the opportunity because he was a big NASCAR fan and loved cars. He told his teacher, however, that he was very nervous. His teacher worked with the store manager to identify a young employee, Mario, who shared Sam's interests in NASCAR. Mario became Sam's informal workplace mentor, showing him where to find parts and who to ask for help. They also took breaks together, during which they discussed their mutual interest. Not only did Sam become comfortable at the store, but he also eventually became a part-time employee when the volunteer experience ended.

Antonio was eager to work but was worried about his new job stocking shelves at a grocery store because he spoke limited English. He is proficient at his native Spanish but was not confident in an environment with mostly English speakers. His teacher identified a bilingual co-worker who became an informal mentor and who occasionally acted as an interpreter when Antonio had trouble understanding his supervisor's directions. As a result, Antonio has been very successful at his job, he has a person at the store who is his "work buddy," and he is one of the more popular employees on his shift.

Skill Acquisition

Almost everyone has learned new skills by virtue of association with someone already accomplished in those skills. Similarly, almost everyone needs help learning new job tasks. One of the best ways to learn a new job or new work task is from someone who already is doing the task. Here again, the value of a workplace mentor is significant. In almost every job, someone is taught and guided by a valued colleague or co-worker. These people—whether it is recognized as such or not—are mentors. The same concept applies to youth in work experiences, who will ideally interact with established workers, who will in turn play a role in helping these youth learn their job tasks and refine their task performance. Transition specialists and youth advocates who are facilitating youth work experiences will also be better able to manage the work experience when they can identify and encourage the involvement of workplace mentors who are skilled at their jobs to help youth with task proficiency.

Denise was hired as a veterinarian's assistant to help with cleaning cages in the kennel, walking dogs who boarded there, and checking in the animals that were brought in for boarding. She loved animals but had never worked in a paid job before this experience. A long-time assistant was assigned to help her to learn how to do all of these tasks and do them in the way the head veterinarian wanted them done. Without this person's assistance, Denise would not have lasted long on the job. With her co-worker's help, Denise not only learned her job well, but she also worked part time at this kennel for her entire senior year in high school.

Enhanced Work Performance

Learning work tasks is usually not the only expectation for workplace perform-ance. Becoming better at them is almost always a desired outcome. Of course, someone at the workplace who is already good at the task can help youth to gain proficiency at these tasks. Also, it is very useful for youth to have someone at the workplace who can provide feedback to them on what to do, how to do it, and how to correct errors. Even more important is someone who can praise and encourage youth as they are learning tasks. Effective mentors do all of this.

Effective mentors also guide youth about acceptable work behaviors that contribute to good work performance. These behaviors might include—among a host of others—how to manage criticism, how to interact with co-workers, how to work as part of a team, how to manage time, and how to correct errors. Even if the transition specialist is available to be on the job to coach youth on many of these work behaviors, it is beneficial that there be an additional experienced hand to guide youth as they strive to improve workplace performance.

Amy's transition teacher helped her to obtain a paid 3-month internship at a local insurance company. Among her assignments were mail preparation and filing. Her teacher helped her learn the fundamentals of her work tasks. However, when the teacher was not there, Amy would struggle to finish the tasks correctly. Darla, a co-worker, decided to help. She showed Amy how to organize the files alphabetically and gave her feedback as she improved both her speed and her accuracy. Not only was Darla an effective and valuable workplace mentor to Amy, but she also became someone the teacher could count on to make sure Amy's internship was successful.

Social Networking

It is common for youth to have difficulty integrating into the social network of the workplace (Chadsey, 2008). Although the transition specialist can and should play a role in facilitating social connections in the workplace, this can best be done by people who are already well established there. Workplace mentors can introduce youth to other co-workers, help youth interact appropriately with co-workers, and give youth status by virtue of association with a popular mentor. Mentors can also show youth the "ropes" around the workplace, such as when people take breaks, the informal rules about who to tease and who not to, and how to please the boss.

Nothing eases the anxiety and uncertainties of being in a new workplace bet-ter than being included in the social network of the workplace. Mentors can help include youth in workplace gatherings and even after-work gatherings.

Ryan's transition specialist helped him to obtain a work sampling experi-ence at a local nonprofit agency. It was his first work experience. He was assigned to a worker, Melissa, who prepared membership mailings. Melissa became an informal mentor to Ryan during his semester there. She made sure he participated in all of the office birthday celebrations and even made sure that the rest of the office celebrated his birthday when it occurred during his time there. Melissa also accompanied Ryan on his breaks and at lunch, where Melissa made sure that he was encouraged to join other co-workers as they gossiped about celebrities and chatted about their families. Ryan blossomed from a young man who would rarely try anything new and rarely got up before noon to someone who could hardly wait to get to work. Not only was this work experience an effective introduction to the workplace, but he still has contact with Melissa and other people at the agency.

Enhanced Self-Concept and Self-Confidence

Adolescents often view themselves through a "reflected appraisal"—that is, they tend to see themselves through others' judgments of them or others' perceived judgments (Sipe, 1999). In this regard, a positive mentoring experience can make a big difference in youth development. If mentors see youth in a positive light, youth's views of themselves can shift to a more positive self-regard as well as change the way they regard others' views of them. Hence, a mentor's positive appraisal can gradually become how the youth sees him- or herself. In short, it feels good to be positively regarded, which leads to increased self-regard, which leads to more confidence, which leads to more work and career success.

Richard disliked school, performed poorly academically, and was suspended from school several times due to disruptive and aggressive behavior. His self-image and self-confidence were extremely low. The owner of a heating, ventilating, and air conditioning (HVAC) company, Dell, recognized a kindred spirit in Richard when his transition teacher introduced the two during an interview for a work experience shortly before Richard exited high school. Dell soon became a friend and informal mentor to Richard. He helped Richard enroll in a community college program sponsored by the Air Conditioning Contractors of America (ACCA). Richard attended classes two nights per week and received on-the-job training at Dell's company as an apprentice. During his apprenticeship, Richard earned the respect of co-workers and graduated from the ACCA program. He eventually became a journeyman HVAC technician. Throughout the experience, Dell encouraged him, reinforced his performance, and gave Richard the confidence to succeed. Richard no longer sees himself as the guy who was labeled in high school as a troublemaker and poor student, thanks to Dell's mentorship.

Additional Mentoring Benefits for Youth

As youth develop more work experiences and pursue their career course, they will need both employment and social contacts. Relationships with mentors offer additional benefit beyond the work experience where they were first paired. In fact, there are several ways in which mentors can help youth outside of work. First, the mentor can recommend youth to potential future employers. Every person who a youth meets expands the network of contacts that is so important to adult job searches (Granovetter, 1995). Thus, mentors can expand the number of

people the youth knows who have work connections and who also may constitute a network from which to identify future work and career opportunities.

For many youth, the relationship with a mentor provides a benefit that goes
well beyond the work experience. Outside of work, mentors often help youth
become part of a more socially desirable or higher-achieving peer group (Jekielek
et al., 2002). As workplace mentors model mature behavior and informally connect and expose youth to others who exhibit mature behavior, they help youth
to expand their social behavior repertoire and resist negative influence (Sword &
Hill, 2002). It is hard to understate the potential value to youth who establish
relationships, either formally or informally, with workplace mentors.

Not every mentoring relationship works well for every youth. However, as
noted later in the chapter, factors that contribute to successful mentoring relationships include mentor training, clear expectations, and support from a transition specialist. In any case, it is clear that under the right circumstances, the
potential benefits are plentiful for the youth, not to mention self-evident.
Mentors, employers, and transition programs benefit for different reasons, which
will be discussed in the following sections.

How Mentors Benefit

Mentors may get involved for a host of reasons, and for the same reasons they
may gain as much as the youth from the experience. These reasons include,
among others, the chance to positively influence youth, a way to improve their
own job performance by showing someone else how to do it, recognition from
managers and supervisors for taking on extra work, and satisfaction from helping others (Sipe, 1999; Timmons et al., 2006). The wise transition specialist will
do well to keep these in mind when recruiting or identifying potential workplace mentors for youth on the worksite. It is also useful to keep in mind that
unless there is some direct benefit to the mentor, either tangible or intangible,
the mentor relationship either will not take root or will not work. Mentorship
relationships evolve in much the same way as negotiations with employers for
youth work experiences discussed in Chapter 6. That is, they require making the
proposition attractive to all involved parties, which will be discussed in a later
section.

What Companies and Schools
Gain from Mentoring Relationships

As discussed at the beginning of this chapter, many companies have already
adopted mentoring programs for existing employees, so it is not a foreign concept
in the workplace. Companies can benefit in many ways when experienced workers
are paired with youth workers: having more direct influence over the development
of the future workforce, potentially increasing productivity of both the youth
worker and the mentor, improving oversight and supervision of the youth, and
having useful conduits for communication with transition specialists involved
with the youth.

As for the transition specialist—and, by extension, transition programs—there
are obvious advantages to having someone mentor the youth in a work experience.
After all, transition specialists cannot be everywhere! Having someone to oversee the
youth's performance in the transition specialist's absence, directly help the youth

Mutual Benefits of Workplace Mentoring

For Youth

- Increased comfort and acceptance in the workplace
- Enhanced work performance
- Accelerated acquisition of skills
- Improved work and social behavior
- Increased self-esteem and self-confidence on the current work experience and for subsequent work experiences

For Transition Programs

- Increased likelihood of successful work experience for youth participants
- More clear connectivity of learning and work
- Improved, constructive workplace oversight for youth
- "Eyes and ears" of transition specialist, a key "go-to" person for the work experience

For Mentors

- Opportunity to improve the quality of life for young people
- Chance to hone communication and coaching skills
- Improved quality of education in the community
- Satisfaction in helping others
- Recognition and responsibility from supervisor; improved standing at work
- Continuous improvement in skills and effectiveness on the job by sharing and reinforcing knowledge

For Employers/Companies

- More direct and positive influence on youth
- Enhanced productivity by youth and other employees
- Improved workplace supervision and oversight of youth
- Additional way to recognize and promote workers who act as mentors
- Enhanced avenue for communication with supervising transition specialist
- Expanded avenues for influencing the future workforce

learn tasks, facilitate the youth's connection to co-workers, and report on the work experience are just a few of the advantages to the transition specialist. In short, a mentor becomes the "eyes and ears" of the transition specialist at the workplace and increases the likelihood that the work experience will be a successful one.

Again, under the right circumstances, workplace mentor relationships can benefit everyone. The next section provides strategies for organizing and monitoring mentor relationships so that the most favorable mentoring relationships can be facilitated.

BASICS OF IDENTIFYING AND ORGANIZING MENTORING RELATIONSHIPS

Workplace mentoring need not take a lot of time, nor does it need to be a formal designation. Mentors range from supportive co-workers who naturally guide and encourage youth during their time at the workplace to more formal and intensive interactions between an assigned mentor and a youth. Co-workers frequently guide and assist one another without the label of "mentor," but they are often in positions to do all of the things that a formally designated mentor would do: provide a role model, provide guidance as to work performance and work behavior, facilitate social relationships at the workplace, as well as any number of other useful roles. As a successful adult worker, a mentor is in a position to model and reinforce work skills and behavior for youth in the workplace.

Mentors are therefore potentially valuable for augmenting the work of specialists who are facilitating work experience for youth in transition. For the transition specialist, the effort that goes into fostering workplace mentoring may also vary in intensity, depending on the youth and depending on the workplace. It may involve careful recruitment, selection, and matching of a mentor with a youth that takes time and careful consideration. More likely, however, is the scenario in which a transition specialist merely offers support and guidance to a relationship that naturally evolves between youth and an interested or involved supervisor or co-worker. In any case, a prerequisite to fostering mentoring relationships is to carefully identify potential mentor roles from among many for an individual youth.

Finding Mentors

Once familiar with the support an individual youth needs and how that support fits with any of the various roles mentors can take on, transition specialists are ready to begin identifying potential workplace mentors, encouraging their participation with youth, orienting them to the particular needs of a youth, and supporting them in managing the relationship. Ways in which transition specialists can facilitate the matching of a mentor include the following:

- *Find a champion*—Often, there are people in the workplace who are naturally predisposed to help youth adjust to the workplace. This could be someone who is a younger worker him- or herself, someone who is familiar with disability through a family member, or someone who simply expresses an interest in a particular youth worker.

Summary of Mentor Functions

Workplace mentors perform many important support functions, including the following (Connecticut LEARNS, 2000; Gramlich, 1999):

- Provide the youth with an orientation to the workplace including rules, policies, and procedures, as well as unwritten rules such as when to take breaks and how to request help
- Help the youth understand his or her job or task responsibilities
- Help the youth resolve conflicts, clarify issues, and cope with stressful situations
- Make suggestions about appropriate work assignments and specifications of the work experience
- Model behaviors that lead to workplace success, including respectful communication and cooperation with co-workers and supervisors
- Guide the youth in work-related decision making and scheduling
- Provide feedback necessary for the youth to perform effectively, highlighting strengths and opportunities for improvement
- Coach the youth to improve work performance
- Informally evaluate the youth's performance
- Act as a liaison between the youth and school or transition personnel to share information about the youth's progress and performance in the workplace
- When appropriate, contribute to the design, development, and modification of the youth's work experience objectives
- Help the youth's self-esteem and confidence by encouragement and positive feedback

- *Solicit individual recommendations*—Managers or supervisors can be encouraged to recommend and solicit recommendations for potential mentors from people in the company, especially identifying people who have been mentors in the past. In addition, mentoring might be attractive for someone who wants to add the experience of supervising and mentoring fellow employees to his or her work résumé.

- *Observe co-workers*—Some people in the workplace may seem especially sympathetic to youth or exhibit good communication with them. These people can be tapped to be informal mentors. Also, it often happens that when youth are at the workplace, certain co-workers naturally gravitate toward a particular youth, and vice versa. Transition specialists can cultivate this interest so that the co-worker agrees to "keep an eye out" for that youth. Often this just happens naturally; all the transition specialist has to do is encourage and support the relationship by being available to the co-worker to provide information about how the youth learns, how to give feedback to the youth, or any number of specifics that apply to the youth.

A factor in helping to identify potential workplace mentors is the set of particular traits of established employees who could offer youth workplace support. Characteristics of an effective workplace mentor might include any combination of the following items (Connecticut LEARNS, 2000):

- Willing and able to commit the necessary time
- Interested in helping and teaching youth
- Able to communicate effectively with youth
- Able to see mentoring as an opportunity rather than an "assignment"
- Sensitive to different cultural backgrounds
- Capable of encouraging, supporting, motivating, and leading others
- Willing to share constructive criticism and feedback in a supportive, sensitive, and patient manner
- Capable of being nonjudgmental

In addition to these factors, there may simply be occasions when a straightforward expression of interest in the youth may open the door for a mentor relationship. Transition specialists alert to these situations are in a position to support and encourage a relationship that, as we have seen, can significantly contribute to the success of any youth's work experience.

When LaShaun started his volunteer work experience at a local children's museum, he was notably shy and unsure of himself. He rarely initiated a conversation; when he did talk, he kept his head down and talked very softly. In addition, he was almost always late getting to the museum for his assigned time. One of the museum docents, Shirley, made a point of saying hello to him every day he was there and asking him about the sports team T-shirt that he often wore. He smiled big when Shirley teased him that maybe he should play on the team, given its lousy record. The transition teacher noticed how LaShaun reacted to Shirley. She later approached Shirley about keeping an eye on LaShaun, introducing him to others at the museum, and showing him how to collate the museum's brochures. Due to this relationship, LaShaun became noticeably more confident, initiating conversations and performing his duties well. He was always early so he and Shirley could talk and get ready for the day. LaShaun completed his volunteer experience and is now working at a regular job, but he and Shirley, his onetime informal mentor, still maintain contact.

Supporting Mentors and the Mentoring Relationship

Mentors are helpful in any stage of the work experience, including initial orientation to the workplace, throughout the learning and performance of work tasks, and in the final evaluation of the work experience. These stages are each discussed next. Consequently, transition specialists should be ready to help mentors understand and fulfill their role, no matter if the mentoring relationship is a formal or an informal one.

Transition specialists and youth advocates are encouraged to offer an easy reference or brief handout to guide the mentor in his or her relationship with youth in the workplace, such as the one provided in Appendix 9.1. Mentors will appreciate continual communication, encouragement, and advice as they learn to instruct and guide youth. As a consequence, youth will benefit from the mentor's well-supported guidance.

Workplace Orientation

In the orientation phase, when youth are first beginning the work experience, mentors can play a key role. They are in a position to discuss employer expectations for the work experience, including performance, punctuality, attendance requirements, dress codes, and break times. Transition specialists can help mentors structure and/or deliver this information. It is important also to communicate to the mentor the objectives of the youth's work experience so that the mentor's support will augment the most important aspects of the experience.

Transition specialists will need to orient workplace mentors to each youth, addressing specific issues that may affect the success of the relationship, such as the best ways to communicate with the youth, individual learning styles of the youth, and issues of specific disability accommodation if the youth has agreed to disclose personal disability information (see Chapter 4).

Ultimately, the key orientation message that mentors ideally impart is fourfold: "We are happy that you are here. This is what we do here. This is what we expect you to do here. Let's work together to make this a success."

Learning and Performing Tasks

Many youth and their employers will rely on transition specialists to teach work tasks to youth. Some will need only some initial and occasional guidance from a workplace supervisor or co-worker. Others will need very little, if any, structured assistance in learning their workplace tasks. In any case, there are common strategies and activities that transition specialists can help mentors implement, including the following:

- Giving basic task instruction, based on the youth's learning style
- Guiding youth in decision making and prioritizing work tasks
- Helping youth resolve conflicts, clarify expectations, and cope with stressful situations
- Making suggestions concerning alternative work assignments if youth are ready to take on new tasks or if they are poorly matched to present tasks
- Providing feedback on youth work performance, especially highlighting performance strengths and constructively demonstrating specific areas that need improvement
- Modeling good work behavior
- Implementing supports and accommodations that might be necessary for an individual youth
- Acting as a liaison between the workplace and transition program staff
- Keeping it positive

Most importantly, we want mentors to stay positive. One of the best ways to do that is to model positive feedback to mentors.

Evaluating the Work Experience

As discussed in Chapter 8, a key support role of the transition specialist is to provide feedback to the youth during the experience and to ultimately evaluate the work experience performance of the youth. When there is a mentor involved, this responsibility should become much easier, not to mention more effective. Who better to provide the youth with feedback and encouragement than people who have had the best opportunity to observe and encourage the youth's work? It is thus useful to involve the mentor in periodic feedback sessions, as well as in the final evaluation of the youth's work experience. Getting feedback from the transition specialist is one thing, especially if it highlights the positive aspects of the youth's performance, but it is quite another to receive feedback from someone with whom the young worker has a good relationship at the workplace.

Finding Balance

Often, transition specialists will need to counsel mentors to refrain from getting too involved, overstepping their roles, or doing things that are more appropriately the role of the transition specialist. For example, it will be important for mentors to avoid asking personal questions or inquiring about a youth's personal life unless the youth brings it up. When they do, mentors should not act as counselors or therapists. If a thorny issue comes up, the mentor should be encouraged to let the transition specialist know. The transition specialist can then facilitate the necessary and appropriate response or service.

Similarly, mentors should be cautioned to minimize personal advice and/or judgment about issues the youth mentions. The possibilities are vast with adolescents who are just learning their way in the world. Youth have revealed issues as serious as criminal behavior, as life changing as pregnancies, as problematic as financial difficulties, and as innocent as what course to take the next semester. In each case, workplace mentors are advised to seek the help of transition specialists to make sure the youth receive appropriate counsel and are referred to suitable services when necessary or fitting. Mentors should always be encouraged to seek out the transition specialist whenever they are in doubt about handling any situation related to the youth, especially those related to personal or life crises. Finding the right balance between constructive guidance and excessive personal involvement sometimes requires a little tweaking, but the mentor relationship can be rewarding and effective for all when transition specialists are alert to these issues and ready to step in to help when necessary.

MENTORING AS A VEHICLE FOR DISABILITY AWARENESS

Some companies have embraced the concept of introducing disability awareness training in the workplace as an element of a diversity initiative. Similarly, many transition and rehabilitation professionals have promoted disability awareness training to companies to generate employer interest in hiring people with disabilities. These activities can be potentially effective tools to pave the way for people with disabilities in the workplace. However, these trainings are not likely to have much impact without an opportunity to apply what is learned. The reasons are twofold. First, diversity programs in companies often do not include disability as a diversity feature. Second, whether or not employers include disability in diversity initiatives, general diversity training by itself is minimally effective in changing hiring behaviors of employers (Hastings, 2007).

Employers who have hosted youth with disabilities and adult workers with disabilities, however, generally express a very positive opinion of these individuals

(Luecking, 2005; Unger, 2002). This suggests that planned exposure and contact with people with disabilities acts to dispel myths, stereotypes, and apprehension about disability. Clearly, work experiences that put youth in the workplace contribute to this phenomenon. Even more important, however, are those activities such as mentoring that purposely put co-workers in close proximate relationships with youth. In this respect, mentoring is an actionable way of promoting disability awareness. Sensitivity to disability occurs not by talking about it or by having presentations about it, but by actually interacting with a person with a disability on a regular basis. Consider these quotes from employers with whom our colleagues have worked.

> *"Before I met James, I had never met anyone as disabled before. I would never have considered such people employable. Now that I know James, I know better."*

> *"I was assigned to help Joey learn his assignments here. I had to be patient, but what a joy to see him become more and more confident as he became more and more proficient with his work."*

> *"Deborah was the first person I ever talked to with cerebral palsy. I was nervous talking with her at first, but after we got to know each other, I hardly noticed her disability."*

We have heard variations of these comments many, many times. Almost every transition specialist we have known can say the same thing. By promoting the development of mentoring relationships, transition specialists are also promoting— however indirectly or unconsciously—disability awareness. This is the type of disability awareness that can directly affect employers' future hiring behavior.

SUMMARY

This chapter identified why and how workplace mentor relationships benefit not only youth, but also the companies, mentors, and the transition programs that oversee youth's work experiences. Youth have the benefit of a supportive workplace relationship that is likely to significantly enhance the work experience. Transition programs have additional "eyes and ears" to observe youth workplace performance. Companies experience a higher likelihood that youth will contribute to the operations during the work experience and beyond as they shape the future workforce. Finally, the mentors have the opportunity to directly influence the career development of youth and to hone their own communication and work skills.

This chapter covered how to organize and facilitate mentor relationships. It illustrated examples of effective mentor relationships and how they benefited all involved parties. Finally, it discussed the value of mentoring as an element of company diversity training in that individual and direct contact with people with disabilities enables workers to develop relationships based on something other than disability and in a way that makes the understanding and awareness of disability easier and more effective. This is a potential advantage for companies and—in a larger context—has the potential to cultivate more workplaces that will be more accepting of young people with disabilities.

LEARNING LAB: *Examining the Value of Workplace Mentors*

Take a few minutes to reflect on your own past work experiences. Ask yourself the following questions:

1. Who acted as a mentor in your early career?

2. How did the relationship affect your experience then? What made it work?

3. What might have worked better?

4. How did it influence your later career?

Think of a youth you know well, someone you helped in the past or are helping now in any capacity. List five characteristics you think a mentor of that youth should have.

REFERENCES

Beier, S., Rosenfeld, W., Spitalny, K., Zansky, S., & Bontempo, A. (2000). The potential of an adult mentor in influencing high-risk behaviors in adolescents. *Archive of Pediatric and Adolescent Medicine, 154*, 327–331.

Chadsey, J. (2008). *Social inclusion at work.* Washington, DC: American Association on Intellectual and Developmental Disabilities.

Connecticut LEARNS. (2000). *Workplace mentoring guide.* Retrieved January 21, 2008, from http://www.state.ct.us/sde/lib/sde/PDF/DEPS/career/WB/mentoring.pdf

Gramlich, M. (1999). *How to facilitate workplace mentoring: A guide for teachers to support employers and student workers.* Rockville, MD: TransCen.

Granovetter, M. (1995). *Getting a job* (2nd ed.). Chicago: The University of Chicago Press.

Hansman, C. (2002). *Critical issues on mentoring: Trends and issues.* Columbus: The Ohio State University, Center on Education and Training for Employment.

Hastings, R. (2007). *The case for strategic diversity.* Retrieved September 9, 2008, from the Society for Human Resources Management web site http://www.shrm.org/diversity/library_published/nonIC/XMS_022037.asp

Jekielek, S., Moore, K.A., & Hair, E.C. (2002). *Mentoring programs and youth development: A synthesis.* Washington, DC: Edna McConnell Clark Foundation. Retrieved April 5, 2008, from http://www.childtrends.org/what_works/clarkwww/mentor/mentorrpt.pdf

Luecking, R. (2005). *In their own words: Employer perspectives on youth with disabilities in the workplace.* Minneapolis: University of Minnesota, National Center on Secondary Education and Transition.

Simonetti, J., Ariss, S., & Martinez, J. (1999). Through the top with mentoring. *Business Horizons, 42*, 56–62.

Sipe, C.L. (1999). Mentoring adolescents: What have we learned? In J. Grossman (Ed.), *Contemporary issues in mentoring.* Philadelphia: Public/Private Ventures.

Sword, C., & Hill, K. (2002). *Creating mentoring opportunities for youth with disabilities: Issues and suggested strategies.* Minneapolis: University of Minnesota, Institute on Community Integration, National Center on Secondary Education and Transition.

Timmons, J., Mack, M., Sims, A., Hare, R., & Wills, J. (2006). *Paving the way to work: A guide to career focused mentoring for youth with disabilities.* Washington, DC: National Collaborative on Workforce and Disability for Youth, Institute for Educational Leadership.

Unger, D. (2002). Employers' attitudes towards people with disabilities in the workforce: Myths or realities? *Focus on Autism and Other Developmental Disabilities, 17*(1), 2–10.

Appendix

- Quick Tips for Mentors Supporting Youth Workers

APPENDIX 9.1

Quick Tips for Mentors Supporting Youth Workers

- Model what you expect.

- Give clear, detailed, and repeated directions.

- Communicate your expectations for performance, behavior, and social interactions.

- Explain the consequences of inappropriate behavior.

- Discuss progress and improvements in performance—Don't stint the praise!

- Be alert to youth learning styles—ask youth how they best learn new tasks, for example, through oral directions, written directions, or just by demonstration.

- Keep an open door and open mind.

- Listen to and respond to concerns and questions.

- Share with youth "tricks of the trade" and what works for you.

- Stay in regular contact with school and youth agency staff for help, support, and information.

Note: Transition specialists and youth advocates are encouraged to offer an easy reference or brief handout that might guide the mentor in his or her relationship with youth in the workplace. The example above is a sample that can be reproduced or adapted.

10

• • •

Connecting with Professional and Agency Partners to Foster and Sustain Work Success

> This chapter provides the reader with
>
> - Basic information about common professional and agency partners in the work experience and transition process
> - A summary of the roles of these partners
> - Considerations for effectively collaborating with these partners
> - A Learning Lab on partners and their roles

"I was impressed and gratified at the way my son's teacher involved so many other necessary services to make my son's job happen."

Mother of an employed transitioning youth

During the middle of her work experience as a clerical aide in an insurance company, Sheryl had a major fight with her parents. The fight escalated to the point that they asked her to leave the house. Among other serious issues, this circumstance created an immediate dilemma related to her continuation in the work experience. Without a place to live, she could not continue in school or the work experience. More importantly, she was distraught about her relationship with her family. Without help addressing this situation, her emotional state would not be conducive to finishing school or the work experience. The transition specialist working with Sheryl connected her with an agency to find a temporary foster home and also helped her to get an immediate appointment with her counselor at the public mental health agency. The mental health counselor was instrumental in helping Sheryl cope with her family situation. In spite of missing a few days at school and at work during this crisis, Sheryl was able to return to work, finish the work experience, and finish the school year.

During his junior year individualized education program (IEP) meeting, David and his transition team set a goal for a paid work experience in his senior year. To participate in the work experience, David and his transition team identified the need for an adapted keyboard for whatever computer he might use at work, an accessible workstation to accommodate his wheelchair, and initial workplace support from the teacher. David and his teacher invited a counselor from the state vocational rehabilitation (VR) agency to David's IEP meeting. After the meeting, the VR counselor opened a case file on David. When it was time to begin his internship, VR helped David purchase the necessary equipment. With this equipment and the teacher's workplace support, David succeeded in the internship. In fact, the company hired him into a permanent position. He graduated with his career underway, thanks to the collaborative work between the school and VR.

Before his last year in school, Malcolm and his parents wanted to make sure that his work experiences throughout his secondary school years would culminate in a paid job targeted for long-term employment. They were therefore pleased when his school created a collaborative program designed to result in paid employment prior to school exit. This program featured job development by school personnel, shared job coaching by the school's instructional assistant and an adult service agency employment specialist, and the planned transfer of all necessary job coaching to the adult agency immediately upon school exit. Thus, Malcolm experienced a seamless transition in which the day after school exit looked the same as the day before he exited publicly supported education—he had the same job as a coffee shop attendant and the same agency staff supporting him in the job. This was made possible by collaborative planning between the school and the adult agency, as well as the planned funding support from VR and the state developmental disabilities agency, which paid for the postschool job coaching.

Work experiences for transitioning youth do not operate in a vacuum from the rest of their activities and circumstances. Similarly, a single transition specialist cannot be all things to all youth. Transition specialists will often need partners to collaborate in the effort to develop work experiences, support youth in the workplace, and address life circumstances that might affect the success of the work experience. Moreover, even if transition specialists do a great job in helping youth succeed in the workplace, the success cannot be sustained if the support to ensure comparable success after school exit is not available. Thus, additional support and solid partnerships with other professionals and other services may be integral to work experience success and a seamless transition to adult employment, as in David's and Malcolm's cases. Or, there may be a need to help youth and their families connect to social services and mental health support as in Sheryl's case. For these reasons, transition specialists will often need to identify and collaborate with agencies, professionals, and ancillary services to help youth achieve work experience and employment success.

Useful ancillary support for individual youth work experience success as well as for the youth's postschool employment success may include VR, community rehabilitation providers, mental health and/or developmental disabilities services, One-Stop Career Centers, Supplemental Security Income (SSI) and Social

Security Disability Insurance (SSDI) benefits counselors, social services, and an array of other generic community resources. This chapter identifies and discusses some of these partners, roles they might play, and considerations for organizing their participation in and support of specific work experience circumstances.

COMMON WORK EXPERIENCE AND TRANSITION PARTNERS

The work of transition specialists is often made much easier and more effective when there are targeted professional and agency partners who work collaboratively with them, as well as with youth and their families, as all plan for work experiences and sustained work success as the youth exit school. Although there are many more possible services and partners than presented here, this section will outline the roles of several of the most common partners in transition work activities.

Vocational Rehabilitation

A primary resource for transition employment support is the state VR agency. VR services are available in every community in the country through these state agencies. Each state has its own operational structure for VR services and the agency has slightly different names in different states (e.g., Department of Vocational Rehabilitation, Division of Rehabilitation Services, Rehabilitation Commission). However, federal government regulations under which state VR agencies operate provide considerable resources and direction to ensure a common set of procedures and practices that can facilitate and pay for such services as job coaching, assistive devices, and other accommodations needed for finding and keeping employment for eligible individuals. Federal regulations also favor the active participation of VR in planning for youth in transition, including participating in IEP planning meetings before school exit; being party to interagency cooperative transition agreements so that services are delivered as efficiently as possible; and collaborating in employment development plans before, during, and after school exit. Eligibility requirements for VR services are summarized in Table 10.1.

Many experts recommend referral of youth to services available through VR as early in their secondary school years as possible so that there is plenty of time

Table 10.1. Vocational rehabilitation (VR) program eligibility

To be eligible for VR services from the state VR agency, an individual must meet all of the following conditions:

- Have a physical or mental impairment, which results in a substantial impediment to employment
- Be able to benefit in terms of an employment outcome (a person with an impairment and impediment is *presumed* to be able to benefit; in the rare event that there are serious doubts about ability to benefit, the individual will be offered trial work experiences or a period of extended evaluation to further determine the ability to benefit)
- Require VR services to prepare for, secure, retain, or regain employment

Individuals who receive Supplemental Security Income or Social Security Disability Insurance are presumed to be eligible for VR services. Some states also specify that individuals eligible for long-term supports of the state's mental health and developmental disabilities agencies and who are pursuing competitive or supported employment are presumed eligible for VR services.

Table 10.2. Vocational rehabilitation (VR) program services

Assessment for determining eligibility and service needs

Vocational counseling, guidance, and referral services

Physical or mental restoration services

Vocational and other training, including on-the-job training

Maintenance for additional costs incurred while the individual is receiving certain VR services

Transportation related to other VR services

Interpreter services for individuals who are deaf

Reader services for individuals who are blind

Services to assist students with disabilities to make the transition from school to work

Personal assistance services while an individual is receiving VR services

Rehabilitation technology services and devices

Supported employment services

Job placement services

---

for services to be arranged prior to school exit (Steere, Rose, & Cavaiuolo, 2007; Wehman, 2006). Even better, early referral will often result in partnerships with VR and its vendors in joint efforts to assist youth in finding and keeping jobs—especially those jobs that are targeted for long-term employment after youth leave school. David's example at the beginning of this chapter is an illustration of how that type of collaboration can benefit youth. Of course, referral for VR services can also happen any time after school exit for those eligible youth who were not connected when still in school.

The range of services that VR can provide youth in transition is considerable and includes those listed in Table 10.2. It is important to understand that VR is not an entitlement service in the way that educational services are entitled to every youth with a disability. This means that not only do youth have to meet the eligibility requirements outlined in Table 10.1, but services are also contingent on available funding resources, which vary from state to state and are usually not sufficient to serve everyone who might be eligible. Because of finite resources, many state VR agencies now operate under an order of selection, which mandates that caseloads first include individuals whose disabilities are classified as "significant"—that is, those who are hardest to serve (e.g., Texas Rehabilitation Service Commission, 2006; Virginia Department of Rehabilitative Services, 2006). Nevertheless, because of the array of services that might be available through VR and because of the potentially important role VR can play in augmenting and supporting employment pursuits for people with disabilities, every transition specialist should be aware of this important resource and know how to link youth with the local VR agency.

State Mental Health/ Developmental Disabilities Agencies

Each state also has a structure for delivering mental health services and for delivering services to people with intellectual and developmental disabilities. These entities may operate from separate state agencies or from the same administrative structure. Sometimes they are managed by local community service boards, sometimes through a state administrative structure, and other times through distinct state regions. They also operate under a variety of names and maintain eligibility guidelines that differ from state to state. Confusing? In practice, it is less confusing than it sounds, as the applicable state mental health and developmental disability agencies will be well known in school districts and in the local transition service arena. In any case, these services are potentially important to the employment-related activities pursued by youth with disabilities.

For youth with emotional or mental health disabilities, mental health agencies will be potential sources for clinical services, counseling, medication management, and case management. As we saw in Sheryl's example at the beginning of this chapter, these services can be critical adjuncts to a youth's work experience. Often, mental health agencies can provide or fund intensive in-the-field case management whereby therapeutic support is made available as an integrated service as youth are pursuing employment while at the same time managing other concerns, such as relationships with families, judicial systems, substance abuse services, housing, and other life needs that may be affecting their ability to complete school and succeed in work experiences (Clark & Davis, 2000).

For youth with intellectual and developmental disabilities, developmental disability agencies offer case management, housing, and employment services and funding for eligible individuals. Job coaching and supported employment services are the most directly applicable employment-related services for eligible youth provided by developmental disability agencies. In some communities, the developmental disability agency provides this service, whereas in others it contracts for this service with community employment service providers, as described next. Malcolm benefited from the collaboration with the local developmental disability agency, which made sure that job coaching funding was in place immediately upon his exit from public education so that he could keep the job he started while still a student.

The services available from both mental health and developmental disabilities agencies are eligibility based. Not all youth are eligible for these services. Also, the services provided by mental health and developmental disabilities agencies are dictated by available public funds. Consequently, there are often waiting lists for these services, although some states have made transitioning youth a funding priority (Stancliffe & Lakin, 2005). Transition specialists will need to be aware of the circumstances in their local communities so that they can help youth identify and obtain these services accordingly.

Employment Service Providers

In every community, there are organizations and programs that are contracted by VR or other state agencies to offer job placement, supported employment, and other related services. These organizations are often referred to as community rehabilitation providers (CRPs) or adult employment service agencies. As with VR, when postschool work support will be necessary, it is useful to involve CRPs early in the transition process, such as including them in IEP meetings so that they can be involved in the planning for postschool employment support. For youth work experiences, CRP services are sometimes used for job development and job coaching for youth. In fact, many transition specialists are employed by CRPs for this purpose when schools need additional help with these activities.

Thus, there are two main roles of CRPs in relation to work experiences for youth. First, they are potential partners in planning for transition and for providing postschool employment services such as supported employment and job placement services. Second, they are potential partners during the development and support of work experiences and jobs while youth are still in school. They

---

The Baltimore Transition Connection

Many aspects of effective linkages between partners are illustrated in a transition program established in the Baltimore City School System called the Baltimore Transition Connection (BTC) (Grigal, Dwyre, & Davis, 2006). Students with intellectual and multiple disabilities enroll in the BTC to receive instruction in age-appropriate environments, including one of three college campuses and various worksites throughout the community. Before their last year in the program, students are referred to the state vocational rehabilitation agency and the state developmental disabilities agency so that eligibility can be established and funding arranged for postschool supported employment services.

Through a cooperative agreement between the school system and a local employment service provider, the employment service provider helps the students to find work experiences and job opportunities to supplement classroom instruction during the last year of school. The employment service provider also is available to provide ongoing job coaching if it is needed immediately upon school exit, ensuring a successful and seamless transition from school to a working adult life.

---

may have staff assigned to help youth obtain work and to provide worksite support such as job coaching. Both roles were assumed by a CRP in Malcolm's case.

One-Stop Career Centers

Every community has a designated location—most often called a One-Stop Career Center, One-Stop Center, or One-Stop—where anyone in that community, including youth with disabilities, can obtain job search and career information and where multiple services are available in one place. They may also offer such job search enhancements as résumé writing and interviewing skill classes, as well as job training and youth employment programs for eligible customers. Also among the resources of One-Stops are career development information and employer listings that may become contacts for work-based opportunities and jobs. Because state VR agencies and other employment service agencies often are also located there, it is useful for transition specialists to become familiar with how One-Stops operate, what services they may offer, and how these services can augment work experience and job development activities.

One-Stop Career Centers have an obligation by federal mandate to offer three levels of services to their community's job seekers:

1. *Core services,* which are available to anyone in the community who comes to the center to seek help exploring employment. Core services are not bound by any eligibility requirements but are limited in that they provide only basic job search assistance such as labor market information; job listings posted by community employers; resource rooms where there is computer, fax, telephone, and Internet access for résumé development or job search activities; and initial screening for additional employment service needs.

2. *Intensive services,* which are available only to certain categories of job seekers, such as individuals recently laid off from their jobs and those with low

income (which may include people with disabilities). Intensive services include comprehensive vocational assessments; individual job and career counseling; case management for individuals seeking specific vocational training; and short-term preemployment services such as interviewing, résumé writing, and professional conduct classes.

3. *Training services,* which are also available based on certain eligibility requirements. Eligible individuals may receive job readiness training, occupational skill training, on-the-job training, adult education and literacy activities, and company-based customized training conducted in accordance with an employer's commitment to hire the individual upon completion of the training.

For transition specialists and the youth they represent, One-Stops can enhance the development of work experiences in the following ways:

- They offer additional sources of career development information. Among the core services available through One-Stop Centers are labor market information, information on the area's economy and employers, Internet access to career development information, résumé development, and a host of other services that may provide useful adjuncts to youth, families, transition specialists, and others involved in planning for work experiences.

- They may offer opportunities to gain access to generic (i.e., not disability related) youth employment programs that can provide work experiences and jobs. Through youth programs and other services of the workforce development system often based in or operating in conjunction with One-Stop Centers, youth have the option of participating in a host of activities that are designed to give them exposure to work experiences, although there may be a need to assist One-Stop youth employment programs in making accommodations for youth with disabilities. Typically, youth programs operating out of or in conjunction with One-Stops are serving a percentage of youth with disabilities with IEPs without being aware of their status as special education recipients (Luecking, Crane, & Mooney, 2002). This is especially the case for youth with "hidden" disabilities, such as learning and emotional disabilities.

- They may offer access to generic career development and employment training services that are available to adults. With the advent of "disability program navigators" in many One-Stop Centers, many of the career development and training services offered to One-Stop customers have the potential of providing services previously unavailable to customers with disabilities due to the lack of accommodations, lack of expertise in disability, and/or excessive reliance on disability-specific services (U.S. Department of Labor, 2007).

- They provide indefinite, lifelong access to career development assistance. Core services of the One-Stop Centers are available to any individual older than 18 years of age at any time in his or her career. This opportunity allows youth to return for career and job search assistance without waiting for eligibility determination or designated program referrals.

Ancillary Social and Community Services Linkages

Nonwork life circumstances will often significantly influence how successful youth are in work experiences and jobs. Throughout the transition process, youth with disabilities will often require support to obtain and use resources essential to addressing life circumstances that may affect employment success. There are a host of such situations that occur in anyone's life, but youth with disabilities are especially vulnerable and often need targeted services that are unrelated to the work experience to properly address them. These situations may include access to or support in maintaining housing; dealing with financial challenges; securing mental health services; coping with health issues; and managing relationship, family, or marital issues—to name only a few.

For these reasons, transition specialists need to be aware of and help link students to supportive services that will help students to address these issues outside of school and work. In many cases, these services will be important partners in helping students and their families plan for the transition to adult life because these supports may be needed at the point of transition and intermittently throughout the students' adult lives. These services include but are not limited to agencies that link people with housing services, income support programs (e.g., Temporary Assistance to Needy Families, food stamps), counseling and mental health services and programs, and various social services agencies (e.g., disability advocacy organizations, family crisis centers, substance abuse intervention services, reproductive counseling services). Just as each student's employment and career path is unique, so too are other life circumstances. Thus, linking to any of these types of services will necessarily be individually determined. Table 10.3 lists common transition partners and their roles.

Public Income Benefits Supports

Many youth will be eligible for, or will already be receiving, services from a variety of government-sponsored programs designed to provide youth and their families with income support due to financial need. These include Temporary Assistance for Needy Families, which provides cash assistance to low-income families, food stamps, medical assistance, and others. Of particular relevance to transitioning youth with disabilities are two federal income support programs operated by the Social Security Administration (SSA): SSDI and SSI.

SSDI provides benefits, cash payments, and medical insurance called Medicare to individuals with disabilities or blind individuals who are insured by workers' contributions to the Social Security trust fund. To be eligible, a person with a disability must have worked and paid Social Security taxes for a specified amount of time or must be the child of such a worker. SSI makes cash assistance payments to individuals who are older, blind, or have disabilities (including children younger than the age of 18) who have limited income or resources. Beneficiaries also receive medical insurance called Medicaid.

Youth on SSDI or SSI and their families are often concerned about the potential effect of work earnings on their cash benefit and on the associated medical insurance. Because of work incentives offered by SSA, it is most often the case that youth will have more money if they work than if they do not. However, because concerns are common and because there are often complicated procedures for determining how and under what conditions benefits are affected by work, it is useful for students and their families to contact local resources called Work Incentives Program Assistance Organizations for advice and help. Benefits counseling is available from Certified Work Incentives

Table 10.3.   Common transition partners and their roles

Transition partner	Function	Potential activities[1]
State vocational rehabilitation agencies	Federally funded program to provide rehabilitation services to eligible individuals with disabilities, including assessment, planning, training, job placement, and other services leading to employment	Open cases on referred students well before school exit Participate in planning meetings for referred youth Facilitate and fund services that contribute to employment goals such as assistive devices, job development, and job coaching
Community rehabilitation providers and employment service agencies	Private or nonprofit agencies contracted by state agencies and/or school districts to provide job placement, supported employment, and related services	Accept early referrals prior to the end of secondary education Cooperatively develop work experiences and jobs with secondary education personnel Support youth in jobs and community life upon school exit as needed Attend planning meetings when invited and as appropriate Cooperate with other partners in service delivery Deliver services as needed to eligible youth
One-Stop Career Centers	Centralized location for career and job information, career assessment, career counseling, job training, and job placement services	Provide career development information and services Provide information on job listings Offer access to youth employment programs Facilitate access to services provided by co-located partners
State mental health and developmental disability agencies	Provide and/or fund case management services, clinical services, vocational services, and supported employment for eligible people with disabilities	Participate in planning for postsecondary support services Provide or fund supported employment and job coaching services Provide access to ancillary services such as clinical mental health services, housing, and case management
Ancillary health and social service programs	An array of community services to address the various social and medical needs of its citizens	Provide augmentative services for nonwork life needs such as medical services, income support, child care, and transportation
Public income benefits support	Cash support and medical insurance for financially needy or otherwise eligible individuals	Provide cash benefits and medical insurance for eligible youth Provide information about applicable work incentives Provide services to counsel beneficiaries on effects of earnings on benefits

[1]Potential activities to support work experiences and employment.

Coordinators associated with these organizations and has many advantages, including the following:

- Helping beneficiaries to navigate the often-complicated public and private benefits programs
- Allowing beneficiaries to take full advantage of the array of special work incentives available to them

- Providing counseling that helps beneficiaries plan their employment search so that they ultimately work and earn more
- Placing participants in a better position to manage the requirements to report their earnings to SSA so that they do not inadvertently cause a reduction in benefits

Transition specialists should become familiar with benefits counseling resources in their community in order to connect youth and their families to appropriate guidance on managing their benefits when they earn wages. Introductory resources on SSI and relevant work incentives can be obtained from several resources, including the local SSA office. SSA also offers comprehensive information about benefits and work incentive rules in what it calls *The Red Book* (see http://www. socialsecurity.gov/redbook/).

CONSIDERATIONS FOR EFFECTIVELY IDENTIFYING AND COLLABORATING WITH AGENCY PARTNERS AND ANCILLARY SERVICES

It is often tempting to make a referral to the most convenient, most available, or most familiar service when linking youth to agencies or professionals offering services that are potentially supportive to their efforts to succeed in work experiences and jobs. However, in keeping with what we know is important and effective for youth in transition—especially the concepts of individual self-determination and informed choice—the following considerations are offered for transition specialists when they are making efforts to accomplish these linkages.

• • • CONSIDERATION 1
Make service connections based on the individual youth's needs, not on what happens to be available.

The admonition here is to avoid the "one-size-fits-all" approach. It is common, but not always the best option, to steer youth to particular services or agencies based on a disability label.

Alvin, a youth with intellectual disabilities, was initially referred to a CRP specializing in serving people with intellectual disabilities to help him find a job during his last year in school. Although he wanted to work in an office, the CRP helped him to get a job at a cafeteria cleaning tables with several other individuals with intellectual disabilities. He hated it, and he failed to keep the job. Later, Alvin became involved in a program operated through the local One-Stop Career Center, which helped him to obtain a volunteer work experience as an office assistant in an investment firm. This eventually turned into a full-time paid job, in which Alvin has worked for several years.

• • • CONSIDERATION 2
Support youth in making their own decisions about services and programs.

As discussed in Chapter 3, individual choice and self-determination should guide planning for work experience. Similarly, it should guide linkages to agencies and services. Transition specialists should provide as much information as possible about potential services and potential service agencies so that they can make informed choices about them.

Kim was successful in her job as a part-time stock clerk at a large department store. However, she still needed occasional help from a job coach to make sure she could learn new tasks when they were assigned to her. As she prepared to leave the school system, there were four different CRPs funded by the state developmental disability agency that offered to provide job coaching to Kim after she was no longer a student. Her transition teacher arranged interviews with representatives from each of the CRPs and helped her to develop questions she could ask each CRP. Kim chose a CRP that answered her question about what they would do if she lost her job by saying, "We will help you find a new one that you like."

• • • CONSIDERATION 3
Help youth navigate supportive services.

Youth often are not aware of what services are available or where to get them. They will also often be understandably confused by the complexities of accessing many of them. Thus, transition specialists can be important facilitators in this regard.

Sheryl needed help to find a place to live due to a family emergency, as well as to make contact with her mental health counselor about the situation. Without help from a transition specialist, she may have foundered for a long time while trying to manage these situations on her own. Not only would she have been unable to eventually finish her work experience, but many more life problems may have resulted.

• • • CONSIDERATION 4
Help families help youth navigate supportive services.

As we discussed in Chapter 5, many families need help to assist their youth to obtain and manage the myriad resources and services that may support the pursuit of work experiences.

When Joe was about to start a paid job at a local hospital helping in the cardiology department, his mother was quite worried about how that might affect his SSI benefit. She was also not sure how to report his earnings to the local SSA office. Joe's transition specialist met with Joe's mother and explained that work incentives were available so that Joe could still keep some of his SSI benefits. The transition specialist also provided all of the contact information as well as accompanied her to the first appointment with the SSA representative. From that point on, Joe's mother was very supportive of his job and was conscientious about reporting the required earnings information to the SSA office.

• • • CONSIDERATION 5
Convene partners as necessary.

Because programs and services are often operated in isolation from one another because of different purposes or different sources of funding, they will not come together automatically when required for individual youth. Transition specialists will often need to act as an intermediary or a facilitator to get multiple partners to work together to support a youth's work experience. Pulling them together for meetings is often useful or necessary. At the very least, the transition specialist will need to maintain communication with these partners as well as help them communicate with each other.

Josie was nearing the end of her internship, in which she was helping to code security badges for a government security agency. With Josie's permission, her transition specialist called a meeting with her VR counselor, her mental health counselor, and her CRP employment specialist to talk about a plan to use her internship as a basis for looking for a permanent job. The plan would have to include VR funding for job coaching, incorporating regularly scheduled mental health counseling with her work schedule, and job development and coaching from the CRP based on her preferences and need for accommodation. The plan led to a successful job experience at a private security company.

SUMMARY

This chapter explored a selected list of supportive and ancillary services and programs that are often necessary and important to youth's success in work experiences, jobs, and later adult employment. Information was provided on state VR agencies, state mental health and developmental disabilities agencies, community rehabilitation providers, One-Stop Career Centers, ancillary social service programs, and services that address public income benefits. Any or all of these may come into play when youth are in work experiences and employment.

For many youth, the end of the secondary education—or postsecondary education, for that matter—will not mean the end of the need for support in the workplace. The youth may need periodic coaching to improve performance, maintain good work behavior, or learn new job tasks. The youth may also have nonwork life challenges that may periodically affect work attendance and performance if they are not attended to, such as housing needs, family crises, or personal finance management. They may also need ongoing help for managing public benefits, such as SSDI and SSI. For these reasons, it is important for transition specialists to be aware of the purpose and roles of supportive employment and social service partners and be prepared to help students link to those services and programs.

LEARNING LAB: *Scoping Out Potential Partners*

1. Make an appointment to meet with a state VR counselor. Find out the types of local activities and programs for youth in transition in which VR is a partner. Ask what services the local VR office typically makes available for youth in transition.

2. Make an appointment to visit the local One-Stop Career Center in your area to tour the facility.

   • During the visit, observe the services and staff in action. Identify the core, intensive, and training services that youth may obtain for employment preparation and development.

   • Find out what other agencies are located there, and determine which of them may offer services that potentially will benefit youth job seekers.

   • Find out where and in what format job listings are maintained. Look up several listings to find one that might be appropriate for a youth you know.

REFERENCES

Clark, H.B., & Davis, M. (Vol. Eds.). (2000). *Systems of care for children's mental health series: Transition to adulthood: A resource for assisting young people with emotional or behavioral difficulties.* Baltimore: Paul H. Brookes Publishing Co.

Grigal, M., Dwyre, A., & Davis, H. (2006). *Transition service for students aged 19–21 with intellectual disabilities in college and community settings: Models and implications for success.* Minneapolis: University of Minnesota, National Center on Secondary Educaion and Transition.

Luecking, R., Crane, K., & Mooney, M. (2002). *Addressing the transition needs of youth with disabilities through the WIA system.* Minneapolis: University of Minnesota, Institute on Community Integration, National Center on Secondary Education and Transition.

Stancliffe, R.J., & Lakin, C.K. (Eds.). (2005). *Costs and outcomes of community services for people with intellectual disabilities.* Baltimore: Paul H. Brookes Publishing Co.

Steere, D., Rose, E., & Cavaiuolo, D. (2007). *Growing up: Transition to adult life for students with disabilities.* Boston: Allyn & Bacon.

Texas Rehabilitation Services Commission. (2006). *State plan 2006.* Retrieved June 25, 2006, from http://www.dars.state.tx.us/drs/stateplan2006/Attachment412c2A.htm

U.S. Department of Labor. (2007). *Disability program navigator initiative.* Retrieved June 2008 from http://www.doleta.gov/disability/new_dpn_grants.cfm

Virginia Department of Rehabilitative Services. (2006). *Order of selection 2004.* Retrieved June 25, 2006, from http://www.vadrs.org/downloads/OOS_key_points.pdf

Wehman, P. (2006). *Life beyond the classroom: Transition strategies for young people with disabilities* (4th ed.). Baltimore: Paul H. Brookes Publishing Co.

11

• • •

The Pursuit of
Quality Work-Based Learning

This chapter provides the reader with

- A review of policy and practice issues that may challenge the pursuit of quality work experiences for youth in transition
- An exploration of promising practice developments that may enhance the pursuit of quality work experiences for youth in transition
- Pragmatic considerations for the future pursuit of quality work experiences

"Work is a central component of a quality adult life."

Rogan, Grossi, and Gajewski (2002, p. 104)

The value of work experience has been illustrated throughout this book. Along with an array of strategies to plan, negotiate, and support youth work experiences, there have been numerous case examples illustrating youth in the workplace—what it took to help them get there, what it took to help them get the most out of the experience, and what they may have learned from it. In other words, we know that work experiences are important educational adjuncts, and we know how to make them happen. However, practitioners and policy makers alike continue to be challenged to make it happen for more youth. The challenge exists across the board, regardless of whether youth have so-called low-incidence disabilities or high-incidence disabilities, whether they have one disability label or another, whether they have access to general education or not, or whether they will get a diploma or an alternate certificate of school completion.

"Learning by doing" is not new. The concept of infusing career development and work into education is as old as education itself. But in American education, its prominence has waxed and waned according to various legislative and policy reform initiatives. The emphasis on promoting work opportunities through youth-focused transition and employment programs has waxed and waned for the same reasons. The question now is, how do we organize these important features of transition so that they can become readily available for all youth? This final chapter presents considerations and issues that have potential impact on the more widespread adoption of work experiences and work as critical features of the career preparation for youth in transition.

CHALLENGES

There are several challenges that may impede the ability of transition professionals to help youth gain access to quality work experiences. These challenges are created by both policy and practice issues, and they are presented in the following sections.

Meeting Academic Standards

Unquestionably, higher educational achievement results in better earning power for youth (U.S. Census Bureau, 2008). Also, some form of standards-driven education is here to stay given the demand for educational accountability (Nelson, McGhee, Meno, & Slater, 2007). The Individuals with Disabilities Education Act (IDEA) of 1990 (PL-101-476) and its amendments, as well as past educational reform initiatives such as the School-to-Work Opportunities Act (PL 103-239), provided momentum for a focus on transition, and—by implication—on the value of pairing work with classroom learning. Many believe, however, that the standards-driven aspects of No Child Left Behind legislation (PL 107-110) have created an emphasis on academic outcomes to the detriment of postschool outcomes such as employment and careers, which are important features of adult life (Sitlington & Clark, 2006). Important questions arise as a result:

1. Can schools fit work experience into the daily schedule?
2. Will emphasis on high-stakes testing make work experience difficult to justify?
3. Will work experience activities for youth, particularly those who have access to general education and/or who are on a diploma track, be harder and harder to come by?

It appears that future opportunities to build work-based learning experiences into school curricula will be constricted for many youth. This means that summer and after-school jobs might be among the only available options for many youth to experience work. As will be discussed later, there are creative efforts to build work experiences into rigorous academic curricula, but it is far less than common. Thus, in spite of all the evidence that suggests that real work experiences are essential to building careers, there may be few opportunities to build these into secondary and postsecondary educational experiences without a concerted effort to do so. This will challenge educators and means that they will have to create alternative opportunities through project-based learning, youth employment programs, summer jobs programs, and other resources.

Scarce or Sporadic Preservice and In-Service Training for Professionals

The frontline practitioners who work directly with youth in facilitating work experiences are, for the most part, the largest intended audience for this book. The quest to do the best job in preparing transition specialists raises several questions:

1. Does initial professional and preservice training include how to help youth garner the types of work experience that will help them build careers?

2. Are future transition professionals taught how to help youth plan for work experiences and jobs, negotiate with employers, and support youth in the workplace?

3. Once on the job, do transition professionals receive appropriate training and support to do their jobs well?

Teacher training programs typically do not provide the types of courses or leaning opportunities that promote the skills and activities described in this book, which help youth to identify and gain access to workplaces (Morningstar & Clark, 2003). Teacher certification does not necessarily reflect practical skill in facilitating work experience and jobs for youth. In addition, across the various professional disciplines, there is little consistent or practical training content available for transition professionals (Sitlington & Clark, 2006). Much of the existing training is sporadically available, ill focused, or overly academically oriented (Asselin, Todd-Allen, & deFur, 1998). As well, many secondary special education curricula no longer include career development courses in favor of more generic preparation to teach academic subjects (Kleinhammer-Trammil, Geiger, & Morningstar, 2003). The fact is that few preservice and in-service training options provide practical training on how to help youth become employed. This means that transition specialists frequently are "baptized by fire," tasked with helping youth gain access to workplaces and work with little preparation to do so.

For those veteran practitioners already on the job, considerable time demands often make it difficult to break away for training. A number of factors contribute to this circumstance, including few convenient preservice and in-service learning offerings, difficulty in gaining release time for in-service, inadequate in-service budgets, and other factors out of the control of personnel who are directly responsible for helping youth participate in these critical contextual educational activities (Wehman, Barcus, & Wilson, 2002). These circumstances challenge transition specialists to implement strategies that sometimes are characterized more by trial and error than by proven techniques for promoting and supporting youth work experience.

Silo-ization of Transition Services

Youth often are eligible for and/or involved in a host of extraschool services, including mental health services, social and health services, youth employment programs, juvenile corrections services, and a host of other possible services that typically operate as disparate service systems. The task of linking these services for a singular, coordinated purpose is often difficult, resulting in disjointed and/or duplicated efforts on behalf of the same youth (Wills & Luecking, 2003). When these services are unknown to one another, there is often an adverse impact on the ability of youth to pursue work experiences and work, as discussed in the last chapter. The challenge is to integrate service provision in such a way as to support, rather than hinder, successful work experience.

For youth who will need ongoing postschool support, there is an additional challenge: how to seamlessly ensure the provision of support as youth move from the entitlement of special education services to the uncertain availability of adult disability employment and support services. For these youth exiting publicly supported special education services, one of three scenarios typically occur.

In the first scenario, youth may receive excellent preparation for post-school employment through rigorous curriculum and work experience. In the best of circumstances, this preparation is also likely to include individualized and student-driven transition planning and services with strong family involvement, as described in previous chapters. However, these students still may exit school on a waiting list for adult employment services, may experience a delay in receiving necessary postschool support, or may never be helped to make a connection to these postschool services. This is especially the case for youth with developmental disabilities (Certo et al., 2003). For those youth bound for postsecondary education, a related common scenario includes no connection to the support they may need to complete their coursework or to obtain campus disability services and career services. They are left to fend for themselves to make the necessary connections. Consequently, these youth flounder in their postsecondary education and/or employment life, unlikely to experience any sort of regular employment.

In another scenario, the school system provides a curriculum that is not bolstered by work experience. In such a case, even if youth eventually become connected to postschool services or adult system services when they leave school, adult employment services essentially begin from scratch to help these youth and their families identify job and career goals and to connect them to supportive services that might help achieve these goals. For these youth, regular employment remains an unlikely result.

In either of these two scenarios, the situation is particularly challenging for youth with serious emotional disabilities. They are more likely to either drop out of school early (Kaufman, Alt, & Chapman, 2000; Maag & Katsiyannis, 1998) or never opt for adult vocational and mental health services (Clark & Davis, 2000). They are consequently at higher risk for hospitalization, unemployment, incarceration, and substance abuse. For this group, early connections to mental health services and opportunities to experience purposeful paid work have been shown to contribute to school completion and successful adult employment (Karpur, Clark, Caproni, & Sterner, 2005; Tilson, Luecking, & Schmid, 2007). Without purposeful attention to transition services, these youth face dismal postschool outcomes.

These two scenarios challenge the educational and employment service systems to find efficient ways to seamlessly build a sequence of work experiences and work so that youth exit publicly supported education with employment and/or the means to continue pursuing it. Fortunately, there is a third scenario, in which school systems provide rigorous and appropriate educational services, individualized education programs (IEPs) are student driven and involve their families, work-based experiences and employment supplement the academic curricula, and connections with postsecondary support services such as developmental disabilities and mental health services and/or postsecondary education are made well in advance of projected school exit. It is this scenario that the research synthesis conducted by the National Alliance for Secondary Education and Transition (2005) and the National Collaborative on Workforce and Disability for Youth (2005) suggest as the optimal approach to ensure that youth transition seamlessly from publicly supported special education to successful employment or postsecondary education and adult life. More will be said about this later in the chapter.

Employer Recruitment

One of the most compelling arguments for work experiences—and one of the most important arguments for employer engagement in the process—is provided by Wehman:

> The strong focus on person-centered planning, business partnerships, and career development imparts a clear message: Unless business and industry are involved in more direct fashion, those training activities generated exclusively in the school environment are doomed to fail because they are largely ungeneralizable. (2006, p. xxvii)

At the same time, finding and keeping good workers are among the greatest challenges facing businesses in the 21st century (Society for Human Resource Management, 2005). Today more than ever, businesses need access to a skilled and diverse workforce. They cannot stay competitive and increase profitability without qualified personnel. These circumstances seem to offer great promise for both work experience during the formative years of career development as well as for future employment opportunities for youth in transition.

However, the matter of convincing employers to take a more active role in youth work experience programs in particular and transition programs in general has been a longstanding problem (Lynn & Wills, 1994). Regardless of job seeker category, studies consistently show that although employers' motivations for participating in transition work experience programs are fairly straightforward, employers' willingness to hire individuals represented by these programs is ultimately influenced by two factors: convenience of access to these job seekers and competent service from employment service programs and transition professionals (Luecking, 2004). Still, transition professionals and youth disability advocates occasionally suggest that employers are the ones who need to do more. As Katherine McCary, vice president of SunTrust Bank, who is at the forefront of the business leadership movement, has said, "I am surprised to keep hearing that employers need to step up to the plate and do their part [for youth transition]. It seems to me that people who say this do not understand business" (personal communication, June 3, 2008). In the absence of the strategies discussed in Chapters 6 and 7 of this book, effectively engaging employers so that they are willing and available partners in transition programs will continue to be a challenge.

Connecting Work Experience to Other Curricular Requirements

Even when class schedules and educational curricula allow for the type of flexibility that enables time for work experiences, there is the issue of making sure that students can maximize the experience by connecting it with curriculum requirements. Pairing work experience with academic content offers a potentially powerful means of preparing youth for successful careers, whether or not youth are receiving special education services (Cronin, Patton, & Wood, 2005; Hamilton & Hamilton, 1997). In fact, many educators have long advocated for making functional life skills—including those related to career development—a prominent component of the educational curriculum for all youth with disabilities (Clark, Field, Patton, Brolin, & Sitlington, 1994). The call for a functional life skills curriculum is based on the demands of adult life in all domains, including employment.

Several issues challenge this approach, however. First, as already mentioned, the realities of standards-driven education often allow little available time for work-based learning activities. Second, educators often receive little guidance on how to best pair knowledge acquisition and skill performance—that is, how to infuse classroom learning with work-based learning and vice versa (Morningstar & Clark, 2003). Third, an unfortunately pervasive attitude exists that teaching functional life skills—including work-based learning—is primarily for students with intellectual disabilities (Cronin et al., 2005). The fact is that everyone needs functional life skills, regardless of any disability label, whether they are going directly into the workforce from secondary school or whether they will be attending a prestigious university. Finally, school districts and their personnel have long struggled to integrate transition goals, especially career goals, with the IEP (Roessler, Brolin, & Johnson, 1992). The IEP often does not address work experience, but in fact it can be a vehicle for connecting curricular requirements and work experience (Wehman, 2006).

Given these various challenges, several questions arise:

1. Will standards-driven academic instruction impede work experiences?

2. Will transition specialists and educators have the administrative support to promote work experience as integral to classroom learning?

3. When work experiences are possible, will they blend with course content?

4. Are there creative ways to integrate work experiences into teaching strategies, such as through project-based teaching?

5. Can youth employment programs facilitate work experiences in lieu of or in conjunction with schools?

6. In the absence of appreciable secondary education work experiences, can postschool employment programs build on academic learning?

POSSIBILITIES

Evolving practice and policy offer many possibilities that will perhaps provide at least partial answers, as discussed in the following sections.

Improved Models of Linking
Work-Based Learning to Academic Instruction

Work experiences in isolation from academic instruction are still useful and important to youth career development, but in tandem with specific course of instruction, they can be powerful. Work-based learning is one way of "learning by doing" that reinforces course content. Work co-ops and work internships that are specific to a course of instruction are longstanding examples of this concept. In the absence of ready availability of these types of programs, alternative models of teaching and education exist, which offer enhanced connections between the classroom and the workplace. Career academies and project-based learning are two examples.

Career academies are "schools-within-schools" in high schools that offer structured, personalized learning through career-related classes that focus on technical skills for a chosen industry. For example, career academies might focus on industry sectors such as finance, engineering, information technology, or tourism and hospitality (National Academy Foundation, 2008). Students enrolled in career academies take regular academic courses that are augmented with career-related instruction. Mentorships and workplace internships associated with the industry focus of the academy are featured components of career academies. When students enrolled in career academies finish high school, they have both a diploma and considerable work-related experience in a specific industry sector. Career academies are potentially beneficial avenues for career preparation for diploma-bound students with IEPs. These academies are growing in popularity but are currently only in select school systems in the country. What they represent, however, is a way of infusing work experience with academic preparation that can be considered in many other educational contexts.

Another avenue for pairing work experience with academic content is through project-based teaching. Contextual learning is not a new educational approach, but a recent surge in interest in project-based learning has provided alternative ways of presenting academic subjects by supplementing existing courses with additional assignments to complete projects outside of the classroom (Contextual Learning Resources, 2001; Ravitz, 2008). Thus, real-world connections are made through the application and integration of content from different subject areas during a project assignment. For example, a teacher can assign students to visit businesses for informational interviews to learn about a company's processes as a project related to any number of academic courses. In this way, concerns about finding time for work experiences in the era of high-stakes testing are minimized, while the learning is augmented by real-world applications. Existing content courses can be augmented with complementary work-based assignments.

Advanced Training Options for Transition Professionals

Two areas of personnel training are emerging as popular and effective ways of advancing the skills of in-the-field transition professionals. First, there are a growing number of workshops and seminars that are available in almost any area of the country. They are often offered through university-sponsored continuing education programs and through independent or privately affiliated trainers (Kleinhammer-Trammil et al., 2003).

Training typically offered includes transition methodology, assessment strategies, work experience and job development, and workplace support strategies, along with a host of other related topics. These training programs often provide continuing education credits and/or university course credit. They fill an important need for in-the-field professionals who want and need to hone their skills, regardless of whether they are new to the field or seasoned professionals.

Although these workshops are often valuable ways for transition professionals to develop and enhance their skills, they are not always available when or where practitioners need them. Consequently, another burgeoning area of training is Internet based. Online training for special education and rehabilitation personnel is increasing in popularity due to its ease of access and scheduling (Jordan et al., 2004; University of North Carolina School of Education, 2007). The rising popularity of online courses generally, and the current use of them in the field of special education, has led to evaluation of their efficacy throughout the field. For example, McLinden et al. (2006) found that online training was an effective method of supplementing the training of specialist teachers of youth in special education. Chapman and Knapczyk (2003) showed the importance of distance learning for rural special educators who cannot easily travel to live training. Finally, Jordan et al. (2004) illustrated the viability of distance learning for delivering preservice and in-service education to teachers challenged by geography, time constraints, professional responsibilities, and other obstacles. As this technology continues to emerge, it is likely that there will be significant opportunities for transition professionals and youth service workers to have access to skill development workshops on demand and on a just-in-time basis, no matter where they live.

Employer-Led Transition Approaches

Chapters 6 and 7 discussed the many effective strategies for recruiting employers to host work experiences for youth. In addition, many employers are starting to take their own initiative to bring youth with disabilities into the workplace. From employers' perspectives, individuals with disabilities represent one of the largest groups seeking employment in today's market. Developing effective ways to bring them into the workforce is seen as imperative by some companies. Two examples of companies that are tackling this issue are Booz Allen Hamilton and Cincinnati Children's Hospital. Both of these entities have not only developed highly effective internal mechanisms to bring youth with disabilities into their workplaces, but they also have each taken strong leadership roles in promoting the idea to other businesses, both inside and outside of their respective industries.

In 2001, Booz Allen Hamilton (http://www.boozallen.com), a strategy and technology consulting firm, founded the Emerging Leaders Program (http://www.emerging-leaders.com/), which is designed to place college students with disabilities into internships within the company. Each year, interns are competitively selected from applicants around the country to spend the summer in the company's McLean, Virginia, headquarters. The program not only provides students with work experience in the private sector, but it also couples that experience with leadership development through an annual 2-day conference in collaboration with nonprofit organizations and federal agencies.

Led by the chairman and chief executive officer, Ralph Shrader, Booz Allen Hamilton transformed the Emerging Leaders Program into a new entity called the National Business and Disability Council, thus expanding the program to more students and companies. Today, the program not only assists corporations across the country in finding qualified young people to work for them, but it also helps them to consider diversity and inclusion in their hiring practices. According to Barbara Haight, one of the driving forces behind the Emerging Leaders Program, more than 30 companies participated in selecting interns from among more than 125 applicants during 2007 (personal communication, February 6, 2008).

Cincinnati Children's Hospital initiated a program called Project SEARCH in the mid-1990s. Under the energetic leadership of Erin Riehle, a former emergency room administrator who created the model, Project SEARCH has gained considerable attention as a progressive, employer-led model of transition preparation. Through partnerships with school systems, vocational rehabilitation, and developmental disabilities agencies, Project SEARCH offers a number of avenues for work experience and jobs for individuals with disabilities. One of these programs is called the High School Transition Program. This program offers a 1-year transition program for students with disabilities who are in their last year of school. The program is geared toward students whose main goal is employment and who are interested in career exploration in a health care setting.

During the school year, students rotate through three to four worksite experiences in the hospital. These site rotations allow participants to build various skills, including communication, problem solving, and specific job duties as they become ready for competitive work environments. During the second half of the school year, individualized job development and placement occur based on students' experiences, strengths, and skills. Students are given support with accommodations, adaptations, and on-the-job coaching by on-site staff. As the school year ends, linkages are made to appropriate community services to ensure a successful transition to work as well as retention and career advancement. Many participants become permanent employees of the hospital. Since its founding, Project SEARCH has expanded not only in the Cincinnati area, but throughout the country where hospitals, medical facilities, and even banks and financial institutions have adopted the Project SEARCH model.

The future of youth transition preparation and the future of work experience in particular may well prosper thanks to such forward-thinking companies. These are but two of many examples of businesses that have taken the initiative to offer internships and other work experience opportunities, primarily out of the need to prepare future workers for their industries. This action will not only lead to expanded work experience options for youth, but these employer-led approaches to transition work opportunities will also serve to teach the field better ways to engage business in the all-important effort to facilitate the connection of youth to workplaces. Much can be learned by watching these types of employer-led initiatives.

Collaborative Transition Models

More and more, school systems and postschool programs are collaborating in an effort to create seamless transition into adult employment. Chapter 1 presented information on several such programs. One program, the Transition Service Integration Model, ensures that—before school exit—youth with developmental disabilities have jobs in place and have identified agencies to continue to support them in those jobs (Certo & Luecking, 2006). As a result, the first day after school exit looks the same as the day before: same job, same supports. This transition occurs as the result of the collaboration of multiple service partners, including schools, vocational rehabilitation, and developmental disabilities agencies.

Chapter 1 also introduced a program with a similar intent for youth with emotional disabilities whereby case management, job development, and mental health services are coordinated with school services. A key feature of the program, called the Career Transition Program, is paid work as an adjunct to school and other services. This collaboration has created better graduation and employment outcomes for a group of youth who typically struggle to find a productive postschool and career path (Tilson, Luecking, & Schmid, 2007).

Similarly, postsecondary education dual-enrollment models offer additional examples of transition collaboration. The collaboration is mainly between school systems and postsecondary education programs, but the partnerships often include vocational rehabilitation and developmental disabilities agencies as additional collaborators. Grigal and Hart (in press) reported a range of models in which youth with intellectual disabilities are receiving public school special education services that are primarily based on the campuses of 2- and 4-year colleges. Although there is wide variation of how these models are configured, for the most part they feature a combination of classroom and community-based instruction of functional and life skills, paid and unpaid employment experiences, use of campus facilities (e.g., library, career center, fitness center), and participation in college courses as determined by individual interests, needs, and IEP goals. A critical benefit of this approach is the opportunity for students to interact and spend time with students without disabilities on the campus, thus learning social behaviors and establishing typical friendships. Just as critical is the time spent in community work environments, where youth learn job behaviors and skills that will benefit their career development. The primary objective of these programs is for students to exit mandated publicly supported education with a range of inclusive experiences, work experiences, and employment.

These programs represent scenarios in which school systems provide rigorous and appropriate educational services, IEPs are student driven and involve families, work-based experiences and employment supplement the academic curricula, and connections with postsecondary support services such as developmental disabilities and mental health services and/or postsecondary education are made well in advance of projected school exit. Research synthesis conducted by the National Alliance for Secondary Education and Transition (2005) and the National Collaborative on Workforce and Disability for Youth (2005) suggests that this is the optimal approach to ensure that youth transition seamlessly from publicly supported special education to successful employment or postsecondary education and adult life.

WHERE DO WE GO FROM HERE?

The National Transition Longitudinal Study 2 demonstrated that employment outcomes are improving for youth with disabilities as they make the transition into adulthood (Wagner, Newman, Cameto, & Levine, 2005). However, there is still a very long way to go before *all* youth making the transition from publicly supported education can reasonably expect that employment will be a central feature of their adult lives.

One of the many needed improvements in transition preparation remains the availability of work experience as an important educational adjunct. Even as the field waits for more favorable legislation that would allow—or better yet promote—work experience as a vital component of education, and even as professionals wrestle with many of the barriers discussed in this chapter, there is no reason not to charge ahead and create as many quality work experiences for as many youth as possible. Progressive contemporary initiatives illustrate what is possible. Barriers or not, there are pragmatic ways to make the most of what is now possible. In fact, the possibilities presented in the previous section point to a potential wave of creative improvements in both the availability of work experiences for youth and the effectiveness of these experiences in promoting meaningful career growth.

The good news is that the framework and the methodology exist to improve the work experience opportunities that are currently available. The availability of work experiences can be maximized through school curricula, through extraschool programs, and through the determination of youth and their families. Reiterating the concepts and strategies presented throughout this book, here are some final thoughts about elevating the prominence and effectiveness of work experiences and work for youth in transition.

Early and Often

Exposure to the idea of work and careers should begin as early as students begin school. At minimum, opportunities for career exploration activities such as job shadowing should be introduced in middle school. Project-based learning assignments are frequent additional opportunities to introduce aspects of work into the curriculum, which can be done throughout the secondary school years. Of course, work sampling, internships, and all other types of work experiences should be introduced whenever possible. Every opportunity to expose youth to the workplace and to working is valuable for their career development—the more the better! The stage is then set for multiple work experiences throughout high school and beyond, culminating in paid employment.

Paid Work Before School Exit

No matter the academic pressures, no matter if it is during school or a separate experience outside of school, every youth should have the opportunity to have at least one paid job prior to finishing secondary school. If youth go on to postsecondary education, they should also have a paid job experience during that experience as well. Ideally, the job should be related to the course of instruction, but any experience—connected or not—is valuable. One or more paid work experiences on a youth's résumé will significantly bolster later employment success.

Connections

Work experiences do not happen in a vacuum, nor do they happen without affecting or being affected by other aspects of youths' lives. When necessary, transition specialists should be aware of connecting youth to ancillary social and health services and be ready to collaborate with service partners. Most importantly, transition specialists will want to maintain and expand the network of employer partners to whose workplaces youth need connections.

Employers as Transition Program Customers

To connect youth with workplaces, it is essential to become more and more skilled at partnering with employers. One way to promote such partnership development is to regard employers as customers whose needs you strive to meet. After all, the success of linking youth to the workplace is as much about meeting employer needs as it is serving youth, as Chapters 6 and 7 illustrated.

Youth and Family Empowerment

Remember that nothing about youth should happen without their input. Not only does this create more youth buy-in to work experience planning, but it also is likely to contribute to a more successful work experience. As the youth empowerment movement gathers momentum, stakeholders in transition will be more and more reluctant to accept less than self-determined employment. Families are primary among the stakeholders. They can and should be engaged to the extent they are able and to the extent they choose. They know the youth best and can have important influence on the success of any work experience.

Assess for Success

Any information gathered for planning work experiences should be with an eye for positive youth attributes. Regardless of the accommodations or supports youth may require to plan for and obtain work experience, their interests and positive traits should guide the match to a workplace. The Positive Personal Profile introduced in Chapter 3 is a useful way to organize information gathered about youth in preparation for work experience. Transition specialists who can identify and promote the best features of youth will always be successful in helping youth succeed in the workplace.

Heightened Expectations

The premise of this book is that all youth who want to work can work. My experience at TransCen, as well as that of numerous skilled colleagues throughout the country, tells us that even those youth who do not know if they can or want to work will opt for it under encouraging circumstances. These circumstances include opportunities to see what the options are by being exposed to work experiences and by being shown how to use their best traits and interests as the basis for pursuing work. The presumption of employability should guide our work as transition specialists. Along with inclusive education and disability advocacy has come a welcomed push for higher expectations for youth employment.

Conclusion

It is my sincere hope that the strategies provided in this book make at least a modest contribution to expanding both the number and quality of available work experiences for youth. Work is a good thing! Let's all continue to do our very best to help youth experience it.

REFERENCES

Asselin, S., Todd-Allen, M., & deFur, S. (1998). Transition coordinators define yourselves. *Teaching Exceptional Children, 30,* 11–15.

Certo, N., & Luecking, R. (2006). Service integration and school to work transition: Customized employment as an outcome for youth with significant disabilities. *Journal of Applied Rehabilitation Counseling, 37,* 29–35.

Certo, N.J., Mautz, D., Pumpian, I., Sax, C., Smalley, K., Wade, H., et al. (2003). A review and discussion of a model for seamless transition to adulthood. *Education and Training in Mental Retardation and Developmental Disabilities, 21,* 33–42.

Chapman, C., & Knapczyk, D. (2003). Integrating web conferencing and field work for preparing rural special educators. *Proceedings of the Annual Conference of the American Council on Rural Special Education.* Bloomington: Indiana University.

Clark, G., Field, S., Patton, J., Brolin, D., & Sitlington, P. (1994). Life skills instruction: A necessary component of all students with disabilities. A position statement of the

Division of Career Development and Transition. *Career Development for Exceptional Individuals, 17,* 125–134.

Clark, H.B., & Davis, M. (Vol. Eds.). (2000). *Systems of care for children's mental health series: Transition to adulthood: A resource for assisting young people with emotional or behavioral difficulties.* Baltimore: Paul H. Brookes Publishing Co.

Contextual Learning Resources. (2001). *Project-based learning.* Retrieved June 25, 2008, from http://www.cord.org/project-based-learning/

Cronin, M., Patton, J., & Wood, S. (2005). *Life skills instruction for all students with special needs: A practical guide for integrating real-life content into the curriculum.* Austin, TX: PRO-ED.

Grigal, M.E., & Hart, D. (in press). *Postsecondary education options for youth with intellectual disabilities.* Baltimore: Paul H. Brookes Publishing Co.

Hamilton, M., & Hamilton, S. (1997). *Learning well at work: Choices for quality.* New York: Cornell University Press.

Individuals with Disabilities Education Act of 1990, PL 101-476, 20 U.S.C. §§ 1400 *et seq.*

Jordan, L., Smith, S., Dillon, A., Algozzine, B., Beattie, J., Spooner, F., et al. (2004). Improving content and technology skills in ADD/ADHD via a web enhanced course. *Teacher Education and Special Education, 27,* 231–239.

Karpur, A., Clark, H., Caproni, P., & Sterner, H. (2005). Transition to adult roles for students with emotional/behavioral disturbances. *Career Development for Exceptional Individuals, 28,* 36–46.

Kaufman, D., Alt, M.N., & Chapman, D. (2000). *Drop out rates in the United States: 2000.* Retrieved August 1, 2008, from http://nces.ed.gov/programs/quarterly/vol_3/3_4/q3-3.asp

Kleinhammer-Trammil, P.J., Geiger, W.L., & Morningstar, M. (2003). Policy contexts for transition personnel preparation: An analysis of transition-related credentials, standards, and course requirements in state certification and licensure policies. *Career Development for Exceptional Individuals, 26,* 185–206.

Luecking, R. (Ed.). (2004). *In their own words: Employer perspectives on youth with disabilities in the workplace.* Minneapolis: University of Minnesota, Institute on Community Integration, National Center on Secondary Education and Transition.

Lynn, I., & Wills, J. (1994). *School lessons, work lessons: Recruiting and sustaining employer involvement in school-to-work programs.* Washington, DC: Institute for Educational Leadership.

Maag, J., & Katsiyannis, A. (1998). Challenges facing successful transition for youths with EBD. *Behavior Disorders, 23,* 209–221.

McLinden, M., McCall, S., Hinton, D., Weston, A., & Douglas, G. (2006). Developing online problem based resources for the professional development of teachers of children with visual impairment. *Open Learning, 21,* 237–251.

Morningstar, M.E., & Clark, G.M. (2003). The status of personnel preparation for transition education and services: What is the critical content? How can it be offered? *Career Development for Exceptional Individuals, 26,* 227–237.

National Academy Foundation. (2008). *The academy internship experience.* Retrieved June 25, 2008, from http://www.naf.org/cps/rde/xchg

National Alliance for Secondary Education and Transition. (2005). *National standards and quality indicators: Transition toolkit for systems improvement.* Minneapolis: University of Minnesota, National Center on Secondary Education and Transition.

National Collaborative on Workforce and Disability for Youth. (2005). *Guideposts for success.* Washington, DC: Institute on Educational Leadership.

Nelson, S.W., McGhee, M.W., Meno, L.R., & Slater, C.L. (2007). Fulfilling the promise of the standards movement. *Phi Delta Kappan, 87,* 403.

No Child Left Behind Act of 2001, PL 107-110, 115 Stat. 1425, 20 U.S.C. §§ 6301 *et seq.*

Ravitz, J. (2008, April 27). *Project based learning as a catalyst in reforming high schools.* Paper presented at the Annual Meeting of the American Educational Research Association, New York.

Roessler, R., Brolin, D.E., & Johnson, J.A. (1992). Barriers to the implementation of career education for special education. *Journal of Career Development, 18,* 271.

Rogan, P., Grossi, T., & Gajewski, R. (2002). Vocational and career assessment. In C. Sax & C. Thoma, *Transition assessment: Wise practices for quality lives* (pp. 103–117). Baltimore: Paul H. Brookes Publishing Co.

School-to-Work Opportunities Act of 1994, PL 103-239, 20 U.S.C. §§ 6101 *et seq.*

Sitlington, P., & Clark, G. (2006). *Transition education and services for students with disabilities.* Boston: Pearson Education.

Society for Human Resource Management. (2005). *Future of the U.S. labor pool.* Washington, DC: Author

Tilson, G., Luecking, R., & Schmid, P. (2007). *Effective transition for youth with serious emotional disabilities: An evaluation of the career transition project.* Manuscript submitted for publication.

University of North Carolina School of Education. (2007). *The North Carolina Partnership Training System: Distance learning project final report.* Chapel Hill, NC: Author.

U.S. Census Bureau. (2008). *Mean earnings by highest degree earned: 2005.* Retrieved August 1, 2008, from http://www.census.gov/population/www/socdemo/educ-attn.html

Wagner, M., Newman, L., Cameto, R., & Levine, P. (2005). *Changes over time in the early post school outcomes of youth with disabilities.* Menlo Park, CA: SRI International.

Wehman, P. (2006). *Life beyond the classroom: Transition strategies for young people with disabilities* (4th ed.). Baltimore: Paul H. Brookes Publishing Co.

Wehman, P., Barcus, M., & Wilson, K. (2002). A survey of training and technical assistance needs of community-based rehabilitation providers. *Journal of Vocational Rehabilitation, 17,* 39–46.

Wills, J., & Luecking, R. (2003). *Making the connections: Growing and supporting new organizations—intermediaries.* Washington DC: National Collaborative on Workforce and Disability for Youth.

Index

Page numbers followed by *b* indicate boxes, numbers followed by *f* indicate figures, and those followed by *t* indicate tables.